D1586840

AS YOU LIKE IT

The RSC Shakespeare

Edited by Jonathan Bate and Eric Rasmussen
Chief Associate Editors: Héloïse Sénéchal and Jan Sewell
Associate Editors: Trey Jansen, Eleanor Lowe, Lucy Munro, Dee Anna Phares

AS YOU LIKE IT

Textual editing: Eric Rasmussen
Introduction and Shakespeare's Career in the Theatre: Jonathan Bate
Commentary: Takashi Kozuka and Héloïse Sénéchal
Scene-by-Scene Analysis: Esme Miskimmin
In Performance: Karin Brown (RSC stagings) and Jan Sewell (overview)
The Director's Cut (interviews by Jonathan Bate and Kevin Wright):
Dominic Cooke and Michael Boyd
Playing Rosalind: Naomi Frederick

Editorial Advisory Board

Gregory Doran, Chief Associate Director,
Royal Shakespeare Company
Jim Davis, Professor of Theatre Studies, University of Warwick, UK
Charles Edelman, Senior Lecturer, Edith Cowan University,
Western Australia
Lukas Erne, Professor of Modern English Literature,
Université de Genève, Switzerland
Akiko Kusunoki, Tokyo Woman's Christian University, Japan
Jacqui O'Hanlon, Director of Education, Royal Shakespeare Company
Ron Rosenbaum, author and journalist, New York, USA
James Shapiro, Professor of English and Comparative Literature,
Columbia University, USA
Tiffany Stern, Professor and Tutor in English, University of Oxford, UK

The RSC Shakespeare

WILLIAM SHAKESPEARE

AS YOU LIKE IT

Edited by
Jonathan Bate and Eric Rasmussen

Introduced by Jonathan Bate

Macmillan

© The Royal Shakespeare Company 2010

Published by arrangement with Modern Library, an imprint of The Random House Publishing Group, a division of Random House, Inc.

All rights reserved. No reproduction, copy or transmission of this publication may be made without written permission.

No portion of this publication may be reproduced, copied or transmitted save with written permission or in accordance with the provisions of the Copyright, Designs and Patents Act 1988, or under the terms of any licence permitting limited copying issued by the Copyright Licensing Agency, Saffron House, 6–10 Kirby Street, London EC1N 8TS.

Any person who does any unauthorised act in relation to this publication may be liable to criminal prosecution and civil claims for damages.

'Royal Shakespeare Company', 'RSC' and the RSC logo are trade marks or registered trade marks of The Royal Shakespeare Company.

The right of Jonathan Bate and Eric Rasmussen to be identified as the authors of the editorial apparatus to this work by William Shakespeare has been asserted by them in accordance with the Copyright, Designs and Patents Act 1988.

Published 2010 by
MACMILLAN PUBLISHERS LTD
registered in England, company number 785998, of Houndmills,
Basingstoke, Hampshire RG21 6XS.
Companies and representatives throughout the world

ISBN-13 978-0-230-24380-4 paperback

This book is printed on paper suitable for recycling and made from fully managed and sustained forest sources. Logging, pulping and manufacturing processes are expected to conform to the environmental regulations of the country of origin.

A catalogue record for this book is available from the British Library.

10   9   8   7   6   5   4   3   2   1
19 18 17 16 15 14 13 12 11 10

Printed in China

CONTENTS

INTRODUCTION

For centuries, trade and marriage have been the engines of social mobility in Britain. The story of the Lodge family in the age of the first Queen Elizabeth is typical. A boy called Thomas Lodge was born in Shropshire, deep in the countryside. His family sent him to the big city and he was apprenticed to a grocer. He made a good marriage and rose to become Lord Mayor of London. He was bankrupted when there was a business downturn, but he still managed to get his son Thomas educated as a 'poor scholar' at the Merchant Taylors' School. From there Thomas Lodge junior went to Oxford. Education was the route from trade to the professions: after graduating, Lodge enrolled at the Inns of Court to train as a lawyer.

But then he hit a barrier. Young Lodge had converted to Roman Catholicism. This immediately made him an outsider, a member of an oppressed minority. His father angrily excluded him from his will and it proved impossible to pursue a career in the law. So Lodge turned to writing and became a prolific author of plays, poems, pamphlets and short novels. The most successful of these – one of the bestselling literary works of the Elizabethan age – was *Rosalynd*, a story of exile from the court to the forest. Like a modern screenwriter turning a successful novel into a movie, Shakespeare dramatized the story for the London stage.

By rights, the play should have been named after its heroine. It is the Elizabethan equivalent of an 'adapted' as opposed to an 'original' screenplay. Shakespeare selects and compresses his material, but retains its essential spirit as a series of debates on the nature of love played out against a romantic woodland backdrop. The flavour of Lodge's story, its language studded with allusions to classical mythology, may be tasted from the climactic moment when Rosalynd reverts to her female identity: 'In went *Ganimede* and dressed herself in woman's attire, having on a gown of green, with kirtle of rich sandal, so quaint that she seemed *Diana* triumphing in the forest; upon her head she wore a chaplet of roses, which gave her such a grace that she looked like *Flora* perked in the pride of all her flowers.'

There are striking parallels between Shakespeare's background and Lodge's. Shakespeare's father, too, was upwardly mobile thanks to his success in trade. John Shakespeare's glove-making business secured him a position on the Stratford-upon-Avon town council. He eventually became town bailiff, the equivalent of mayor. But he, too, ran into financial trouble. It is also possible that the Shakespeares faced difficulties because of family associations with Catholicism. Like Thomas Lodge junior, Will Shakespeare sought his fortune in London. Not having a university degree, he could not enter a profession such as the law, so he drifted into the theatre.

The plot of *As You Like It* reflects aspects of the experience of both Lodge and Shakespeare. How can a young man improve himself if he is not given educational opportunities? In the first scene, we learn that whereas an older brother has gone off to college, young Orlando is forced to hang around at home. He sets off for the court and proves his mettle in the entertainment arena – not as a dramatist, but as a sportsman, the amateur upstart who bravely goes into the ring and unexpectedly defeats the professional court wrestler, Charles.

But he is then exiled from the centre of power. In a neat reversal of Shakespeare's own journey from the Forest of Arden in Warwickshire to the bustling world of London, with its commerce, its court and its theatres, Orlando goes into the forest and discovers his destiny there. Because the wicked Duke Frederick has taken power from his elder brother, the other major characters – the good duke and his courtiers, the disguised Rosalind and Celia, the wandering philosopher-gentleman Jaques – are also exiles in the forest.

Lodge's setting for his story was France, but he anglicized the name of the Ardennes forest to Arden. Perhaps this is what made the story so attractive to Shakespeare, who was born and raised close to the forest from which his mother Mary Arden took her family name. The play accordingly removes the action further from France: though some French names such as 'Le Beau' are retained, the location of the court is not specified. The deceased gentleman with three sons – the oldest who treats the youngest like a mere servant, the middle away at university and invisible until the closing twist – is Sir John of Bordeaux in Lodge, but the more symbolically named Sir Rowland de Bois in Shakespeare. De Bois means 'of the woods', and Sir Rowland is a name suggestive of a lost world of chivalry and romance, as in *The Song of Roland*. 'Orlando', the Italianized form of Rowland, is chosen by Shakespeare for his hero as a way of indicating that the youngest son has a special bond with his dead father, a duty to preserve his good name. To more educated members of the Elizabethan theatre audience, it would also have conjured up the eponymous hero of *Orlando Furioso*, an epic poem by Ariosto that was the sixteenth-century's great exemplar of chivalric romance. It is typical of Shakespeare's sceptical, ironic temperament that the Orlando who wanders round the forest defacing trees with second-rate love poems, and who needs to take lessons in courtship from a supposed teenage boy, does not quite live up to his heroic name – not, at least, until the play moves into the true mode of romance when he rescues his brother from a lion and a snake.

IN THE FOREST OF ARDEN

The first we hear of the exiled duke is that, 'like the old Robin Hood of England', he is in the forest with a group of 'merry men'. Ostensibly the qualifier 'of England' is an indication that the action is supposed to take place in France, but the deeper effect is to identify Arden with Sherwood. About a year before the play was written, rival acting company the Admiral's Men had played a two-part drama on the subject of Robin Hood called *Robert Earl of Huntingdon* – the first work in the long history of the legend to turn Robin into a disguised aristocrat as opposed to a genuinely subversive outlaw. The Arden scenes of *As You Like It* begin with the exiled duke contrasting the natural order of the forest to the flattery and envy of the court. As in the Robin Hood story, the wished-for conclusion is the restoration of the right ruler.

Yet the play ironizes as well as idealizes. The most prominent figure in the duke's forest circle is not a merry man but a melancholy man, the satirical Jaques. Often wrongly described as one of the duke's courtiers, he is a gentleman who has sold his lands in order to become a 'traveller', a wry, detached observer of manners and morals. The forest order is dependent on hunting, leading Jaques to sympathize with the wounded stag and suggest that the good duke usurps the place of the deer every bit as much as the bad duke has usurped power back at court. Jaques and Touchstone – the two key characters invented by Shakespeare without precedent in Lodge – spar with each other because the satire of the former and the witty foolery of the latter are rival modes of mocking courtly pretensions such as Orlando's highly romanticized language of love-service.

Arden is also compared to the mythological 'golden age' and the play duly has its complement of classically-named shepherds, signalling the influence of the ancient tradition of pastoral verse. The golden age was the imagined infancy of humankind, another Eden, a playground in which Nature offered up her fruits and the winter wind never blew. But Shakespeare complicates the picture. The duke's very first speech sees Arden as a place less to 'fleet the time carelessly as they did in the golden world' than to draw moral lessons from the natural world. This is no Arcadia of perpetual summer: the seasons do change, it is just that 'the penalty of Adam' – being forced to labour for subsistence – seems less harsh than the vicissitudes of the court. The myth of the golden age made Utopia into the state that society had fallen from rather than that which it aspired to: a place where everybody was happy and there was no such thing as property. The old shepherd Corin is a voice of happiness, but he has no illusions about the need for labour and his dependence on property that he does not own. He is shepherd to another man's flock and only keeps his job because Celia buys the farm.

'Under the greenwood tree / Who loves to lie with me', sings Amiens as the exiled lords come on dressed as foresters, and we are reminded of the rustic communities of Thomas Hardy, who used the opening line of that song as the title for one of his novels. The play has become central to the myth of 'deep England', the idea that English national identity is bound up with milkmaids dancing round the Maypole, tankards of nut-brown ale sipped in thatched taverns and lengthening shadows on the village green.

In 1987 the British West Indian artist Ingrid Pollard created a series of photographs called 'Pastoral Interlude' in which she explored the place of black people in the English countryside. 'It's as if the Black experience is only lived within an urban environment', Pollard wrote. 'I thought I liked the Lake District where I wandered lonely as a Black face in a sea of white.' For her, 'a visit to the countryside is always accompanied by a feeling of unease, dread'. A feeling, that is to say, that she does not belong in the world that, in shorthand, could be described as Arden. Yet the whole point of Shakespeare's Arden is that it is an adventure playground for exiles and outsiders. The world we encounter there does not have the homogeneity of an English village. Rather, it is a gloriously multicultural community. Shakespeare loves to mix and match the past and the present, the indigenous and the immigrant, down-to-earth observation from experience and wild fantasia from myth and folktale.

The denizens of the forest include not only Corin, the wise old agricultural labourer whose name is Greco-Roman yet whose nature is English, but also a country clergyman called Sir Oliver Martext who may well have been imagined as a dangerous Catholic, and a very English peasant of small brain power called William who in the original production may well have been acted by a very English countryman of great brain power called William Shakespeare. Among the exiles are the very French-sounding Amiens, with his musical gifts, and the quintessentially English stand-up comedian Touchstone. On the fringes of the forest, and of the play, is a mysterious 'magician', described but never seen, who converts the drama into a kind of fairytale (complete with a rather gentle lion) even as it remains grittily true to English environment and climate.

THE FESTIVE RESOLUTION

Shortly after the Second World War, the Canadian literary critic Northrop Frye published a short essay that inaugurated the modern understanding that Shakespeare's comedies, for all their lightness and play, are serious works of art, every bit as worthy of close attention as his tragedies. Entitled 'The Argument of Comedy', it proposed that the essential structure of Shakespearean comedy was ultimately derived from the 'new comedy' of ancient Greece, which was mediated to the Renaissance via its Roman exponents Plautus and Terence. The 'new comedy' pattern, described by Frye as 'a comic Oedipus situation', turned on 'the successful effort of a young man to outwit an opponent and possess the girl of his choice'. The girl's father, or some other authority figure of the older generation, resists the match, but is outflanked, often thanks to an ingenious scheme devised by a clever servant, perhaps involving disguise or flight (or both). Frye, writing during Hollywood's golden age, saw an unbroken line from the classics to Shakespeare to modern romantic comedy: 'The average movie of today is a rigidly conventionalized New Comedy proceeding toward an act which, like death in Greek tragedy, takes place offstage, and is symbolized by the final embrace.'

The union of the lovers brings 'a renewed sense of social integration', expressed by some kind of festival at the climax of the play – a marriage, a dance or a feast. The union often also involves social mobility: it certainly does here, as Orlando, the youngest son of a gentleman, finds himself bound to the daughter of a duke. All right-thinking people come over to the side of the lovers, but there are others 'who are in some kind of mental bondage, who are helplessly driven by ruling passions, neurotic compulsions, social rituals, and selfishness'. Malvolio in *Twelfth Night*, Don John in *Much Ado about Nothing*, Shylock in *The Merchant of Venice*: Shakespearean comedy frequently includes a party-pooper, a figure who refuses to be assimilated into the harmony. Jaques is of this company.

Frye's 'The Argument of Comedy' pinpoints a pervasive structure: 'the action of the comedy begins in a world represented as a normal world, moves into the green world, goes into a metamorphosis there in which the comic resolution is achieved, and returns to the normal world'. But for Shakespeare, the green world, the forest and its fairies, is no less real than the court. Frye, again, sums it up brilliantly:

> This world of fairies, dreams, disembodied souls, and pastoral lovers may not be a 'real' world, but, if not, there is something equally illusory in the stumbling and blinded follies of the 'normal' world, of Theseus' Athens with its idiotic marriage law, of Duke Frederick and his melancholy tyranny [in *As You Like It*], of Leontes and his mad jealousy [in *The Winter's Tale*], of the Court Party with their plots and intrigues. The famous speech of Prospero [in *The Tempest*] about the dream nature of reality applies equally to Milan and the enchanted island. We spend our lives partly in a waking world we call normal and partly in a dream world which we create out of our own desires. Shakespeare endows both worlds with equal imaginative power, brings them opposite one another, and makes each world seem unreal when seen by the light of the other.[*]

Many of Shakespeare's plays keep up a constant shuttle between symbolically opposed locations – Venice and Belmont, Rome and Egypt, Sicilian court and Bohemian country – but *As You Like It* moves all the major players to Arden as swiftly as possible. Once there, the scenes run together fluently. There is no clock ticking in the forest, no sense of time being marked by the scene breaks. Initially, however, there are two discernible imaginary locations: the farm and the cave, Corin's world of agricultural labour and the deep forest where the duke and his men play at being Robin Hood. Orlando and Jaques drift between the two, whereas Rosalind/Ganymede and Celia/Aliena are not allowed to penetrate too far into

* 'The Argument of Comedy' originally appeared in *English Institute Essays 1948*, ed. D. A. Robertson (1949), and has often been reprinted in critical anthologies. Frye himself adapted it for inclusion in his classic study, *Anatomy of Criticism* (1957).

the deep forest. Their reunion with the duke must be withheld for the climax.

ALIENA AND GANYMEDE

Crucially, this play belongs to the girls, who come to Arden because it is a place where they can try on new identities. Celia disguises herself as 'Aliena', suggesting the idea of the immigrant, the resident 'alien' who always feels like an outsider. And Rosalind switches gender to become 'Ganymede'. The more educated members of Shakespeare's original audience would have been acutely aware of the connotations of this assumed name. The original Ganymede was a young male abducted by Jove in classical mythology. In Shakespeare's time, the figure was synonymous with pederastic desire, as explained in a dictionary of the period: '*Ganymede:* the name of a Trojan boy, whom Jupiter so loved (say the poets) as he took him up to Heaven, and made him his Cup-bearer. Hence any boy that is loved for carnal abuse, or is hired to be used contrary to nature to commit the detestable sin of sodomy, is called a Ganymede; an Ingle.' The same dictionary's definition of 'ingle' is 'a youth kept or accompanied for sodomy'. The forest is the supremely *natural* place. By locating the playful wooing of Orlando and 'Ganymede' in this setting, Shakespeare asks his audience to imagine the possibility that same-sex desire may not, after all, be 'contrary to nature'.

The place of 'banishment' turns out to be the home of 'liberty' – free from the constraints of court hierarchy and customary deference, Arden is where you can play at being someone different and find out who you really are. It's where you learn to live alongside people who come from very different backgrounds to your own. And where, in the end, you all come together for a big party in celebration of multiple mixed marriages that cut across the traditional social order.

As You Like It is Shakespeare's most elegant play. At its climax Rosalind calls the cast into a circle, the figure of perfection, and resolves the plot with the assistance of Hymen, god of marriage. Whereas most of the other comedies are shadowed by death, this one offers four weddings and no funeral. The part of Rosalind is the longest and most joyous female role in the complete works. It would have been extraordinarily demanding for the boy-actor who first performed it, though made a little easier by the fact that Rosalind spends so much of the time dressed as a boy.

Shakespeare moves quickly from the multiple marriages to the closing dance. He introduces the magical 'conversion' of bad Frederick in place of the battle between the forces of good and evil that occurs at the end of Lodge's story, and he focuses on the realization of erotic desire rather than the questions of social advancement that preoccupied Lodge. The play omits the apportioning of rewards with which *Rosalynd* ended. In the novel, the figure who corresponds to Silvius becomes 'lord over all the forest of Arden', Corin is made master of the Celia-figure's flock, and loyal retainer Adam improbably becomes captain of the king's guard.

There is a curious stage direction when the women first arrive in Arden: '*Enter Rosalind for Ganymede, Celia for Aliena, and Clown alias Touchstone*' (Act 2 scene 4). Does *alias* mean that Touchstone has also taken on a disguised identity? It has been suggested that he would have begun the play in the long plain coat of the 'natural' (simpleton), then exchanged this for the 'motley' of the professional fool when he escapes from the court with the women. But there is no sense of his verbal style changing or of disguise being a means of self-discovery, as it is so profoundly for Rosalind when she plays the role of Ganymede; Touchstone appears always to have been a touchstone, a master of retort that reveals other people's foolishness. The question of Touchstone being recognized as the court fool, and thus blowing the disguise of Rosalind and Celia, is avoided by the device of keeping all three of them apart from the duke and his courtiers until the final scene. That is why Jaques cannot be a courtier: he must encounter Touchstone as a stranger and delight in him as a fellow outsider, albeit with a different linguistic style and a different end to his irony. Jaques offers 'invective' and formal discourses (most famously his anatomy of the 'seven ages' of human life) to Touchstone's one-line quips and riffs of extended word-mongering (most dazzlingly his explication of the seven stages of a quarrel).

Wherever the word 'natural' is found in the play, whether associated with Touchstone, Corin or the forest itself, it is possible to see happiness and a kind of innocence; the voice of Jaques is that of 'experience' bringing world-weary melancholy. Rosalind has no doubt which she prefers, observing to Jaques that 'your experience makes you sad: I had rather have a fool to make me merry than experience to make me sad'.

As in Lodge's *Rosalynd*, the plot of the play sometimes seems little more than a pretext for the setting up of debates and meditations. The heart of the play is to be found in the set-piece dialogues. Before their departure from court, Rosalind and Celia debate the relative importance of 'nature' and 'fortune'; in Arden, there are dialogues between the melancholy man and the fool, the cynic and the lover, the court fool and the 'natural' shepherd (who wins the debate by virtue of his recognition that social customs vary from place to place). With brilliant counterpoint, a prose wooing scene is played against a verse one. Reversing dramatic convention, it is the courtly characters who speak prose and the shepherds who court in verse.

Above all, there is the encounter between Orlando and Rosalind-as-Ganymede-as-Rosalind. With the added layer of the boy-actor for whom Shakespeare was writing – of which we are reminded by means of a joke in the epilogue – here a boy plays a girl playing a boy playing a girl. Whereas in the shepherd plot it is Phoebe who has romantic notions about love that make her natural partner Silvius a disappointment to her, in the main plot disguise enables the woman to offer the man down-to-earth 'counsel' as preparation for marriage. Through the illusions of cross-dressing and role-play, Rosalind exposes the illusions of romantic desire: 'the patterns of love' (Troilus, Leander) are not to be imitated, since the old stories about them are 'all lies'. '[M]en have died from time to time and worms have eaten them, but not for love.' So much for men.

As for women, the key to keeping them is not to restrain them. Rosalind-Ganymede's lesson is the opposite to that of *The Taming of the Shrew*: a desirable woman is not a tame one but a 'wayward' one, whose energies (verbal, emotional and sexual) are incorrigible.

'Make the doors upon a woman's wit and it will out at the casement. Shut that and 'twill out at the key-hole. Stop that, 'twill fly with the smoke out at the chimney.' In her poise and her playfulness, her knowledge of what makes people tick and her capacity for strong feeling, whether joyful, fearful or simply amazed ('O coz, coz, coz, my pretty little coz, that thou didst know how many fathom deep I am in love! But it cannot be sounded'), Rosalind is Shakespeare's most complete woman.

ABOUT THE TEXT

Shakespeare endures through history. He illuminates later times as well as his own. He helps us to understand the human condition. But he cannot do this without a good text of the plays. Without editions there would be no Shakespeare. That is why every twenty years or so throughout the last three centuries there has been a major new edition of his complete works. One aspect of editing is the process of keeping the texts up to date – modernizing the spelling, punctuation and typography (though not, of course, the actual words), providing explanatory notes in the light of changing educational practices (a generation ago, most of Shakespeare's classical and biblical allusions could be assumed to be generally understood, but now they can't).

Because Shakespeare did not personally oversee the publication of his plays, with some plays there are major editorial difficulties. Decisions have to be made as to the relative authority of the early printed editions, the pocket format 'quartos' published in Shakespeare's lifetime and the elaborately produced 'First Folio' text of 1623, the original 'Complete Works' prepared for the press after his death by Shakespeare's fellow-actors, the people who knew the plays better than anyone else. *As You Like It*, however, exists only in a Folio text that is exceptionally well printed, so there is little textual debate about this play.

The following notes highlight various aspects of the editorial process and indicate conventions used in the text of this edition:

Lists of Parts are supplied in the First Folio for only six plays, not including *As You Like It*, so the list here is editorially supplied. Capitals indicate that part of the name used for speech headings in the script (thus 'DUKE SENIOR, in exile').

Locations are provided by the Folio for only two plays, of which *As You Like It* is not one. Eighteenth-century editors, working in an age of elaborately realistic stage sets, were the first to provide detailed locations ('another part of the forest'). Given that Shakespeare wrote for a bare stage and often an imprecise sense of place, we have relegated locations to the explanatory notes at the foot of the page, where they are given at the beginning of each scene where the imaginary location is different from the one before. In the case of *As You Like It*, after the first act, almost all the action is set in the Forest of Arden.

Act and Scene Divisions were provided in the Folio in a much more thoroughgoing way than in the Quartos. Sometimes, however, they were erroneous or omitted; corrections and additions supplied by editorial tradition are indicated by square brackets. Five-act division is based on a classical model, and act breaks provided the opportunity to replace the candles in the indoor Blackfriars playhouse which the King's Men used after 1608, but Shakespeare did not necessarily think in terms of a five-part structure of dramatic composition. The Folio convention is that a scene ends when the stage is empty. Nowadays, partly under the influence of film, we tend to consider a scene to be a dramatic unit that ends with either a change of imaginary location or a significant passage of time within the narrative. Shakespeare's fluidity of composition accords well with this convention, so in addition to act and scene numbers we provide a *running scene* count in the right margin at the beginning of each new scene, in the typeface used for editorial directions. Where there is a scene break caused by a momentary bare stage, but the location does not change and extra time does not pass, we use the convention *running scene continues*. There is inevitably a degree of editorial judgement in making such calls, but the system is very valuable in suggesting the pace of the plays.

Speakers' Names are often inconsistent in Folio. We have regularized speech headings, but retained an element of deliberate inconsistency in entry directions, in order to give the flavour of Folio.

Thus TOUCHSTONE is always so-called in his speech headings, but 'Clown' in entry directions.

Verse is indicated by lines that do not run to the right margin and by capitalization of each line. The Folio printers sometimes set verse as prose, and vice versa (either out of misunderstanding or for reasons of space). We have silently corrected in such cases, although in some instances there is ambiguity, in which case we have leaned towards the preservation of Folio layout. Folio sometimes uses contraction ('turnd' rather than 'turned') to indicate whether or not the final '-ed' of a past participle is sounded, an area where there is variation for the sake of the five-beat iambic pentameter rhythm. We use the convention of a grave accent to indicate sounding (thus 'turnèd' would be two syllables), but would urge actors not to overstress. In cases where one speaker ends with a verse half-line and the next begins with the other half of the pentameter, editors since the late eighteenth century have indented the second line. We have abandoned this convention, since the Folio does not use it, and nor did actors' cues in the Shakespearean theatre. An exception is made when the second speaker actively interrupts or completes the first speaker's sentence.

Spelling is modernized, but older forms are very occasionally maintained where necessary for rhythm or aural effect.

Punctuation in Shakespeare's time was as much rhetorical as grammatical. 'Colon' was originally a term for a unit of thought in an argument. The semi-colon was a new unit of punctuation (some of the Quartos lack them altogether). We have modernized punctuation throughout, but have given more weight to Folio punctuation than many editors, since, though not Shakespearean, it reflects the usage of his period. In particular, we have used the colon far more than many editors: it is exceptionally useful as a way of indicating how many Shakespearean speeches unfold clause by clause in a developing argument that gives the illusion of enacting the process of thinking in the moment. We have also kept in mind the origin of punctuation in classical times as a way of assisting the actor and orator: the comma suggests the briefest of pauses for breath, the colon a middling one and a full stop or period a longer pause. Semi-colons, by contrast, belong to an era of punctuation that was only just coming in during Shakespeare's time and that is coming to an end now: we have accordingly only used them where they occur in our copy-texts (and not always then). Dashes are sometimes used for parenthetical interjections where the Folio has brackets. They are also used for interruptions and changes in train of thought. Where a change of addressee occurs within a speech, we have used a dash preceded by a full stop (or occasionally another form of punctuation). Often the identity of the respective addressees is obvious from the context. When it is not, this has been indicated in a marginal stage direction.

Entrances and Exits are fairly thorough in Folio, which has accordingly been followed as faithfully as possible. Where characters are omitted or corrections are necessary, this is indicated by square brackets (e.g. '[*and Attendants*]'). *Exit* is sometimes silently normalized to *Exeunt* and *Manet* anglicized to 'remains'. We trust Folio positioning of entrances and exits to a greater degree than most editors.

Editorial Stage Directions such as stage business, asides, indications of addressee and of characters' position on the gallery stage are only used sparingly in Folio. Other editions mingle directions of this kind with original Folio and Quarto directions, sometimes marking them by means of square brackets. We have sought to distinguish what could be described as *directorial* interventions of this kind from Folio-style directions (either original or supplied) by placing them in the right margin in a different typeface. There is a degree of subjectivity about which directions are of which kind, but the procedure is intended as a reminder to the reader and the actor that Shakespearean stage directions are often dependent upon editorial inference alone and are not set in stone. We also depart from editorial tradition in sometimes admitting uncertainty and thus printing permissive stage directions, such as an **Aside?** (often a line may be equally effective as an aside or a direct address – it is for each production or reading to make its own decision) or a *may exit* or a piece of business placed between arrows to indicate that it may occur at various different moments within a scene.

Line Numbers in the left margin are editorial, for reference and to key the explanatory and textual notes.

Explanatory Notes at the foot of each page explain allusions and gloss obsolete and difficult words, confusing phraseology, occasional major textual cruces, and so on. Particular attention is given to non-standard usage, bawdy innuendo and technical terms (e.g. legal and military language). Where more than one sense is given, commas indicate shades of related meaning, slashes alternative or double meanings.

Textual Notes at the end of the play indicate major departures from the Folio. They take the following form: the reading of our text is given in bold and its source given after an equals sign, with 'F2' indicating a correction that derives from the Second Folio of 1632, 'F3' a correction introduced in the Third Folio of 1664 and 'Ed' one that derives from the subsequent editorial tradition. The rejected Folio ('F') reading is then given. Thus, for example, '3.2.355 deifying = F2. F = defying' means that at Act 3 scene 2 line 355, the Folio compositor erroneously printed the word 'defying' and the Second Folio corrected it to 'deifying'.

KEY FACTS

MAJOR PARTS: (*with percentage of lines/number of speeches/scenes on stage*) Rosalind (25%/201/10), Orlando (11%/120/9), Celia (10%/108/7), Touchstone (10%/74/7), Jaques (8%/57/7), Oliver (6%/37/4), Duke Senior (4%/32/3), Silvius (3%/24/5), Phoebe (3%/23/3), Corin (3%/24/4), Frederick (3%/20/4), Le Beau (2%/14/1), Adam (2%10/4), Charles (2%/8/2), Amiens (1%/9/2), Hymen (1%/2/1), Audrey (1%/12/3).

LINGUISTIC MEDIUM: 55% prose, 45% verse. Several songs and interwoven (parodically bad) love-lyrics.

DATE: Not mentioned in Francis Meres' 1598 list of Shakespeare's plays, unless originally called *Love's Labour's Won* (mentioned by Meres, but now lost). Registered for publication in early summer 1600, but not printed at that time. Song 'It was a lover and his lass' printed in Thomas Morley's *First Book of Airs* (1600). Several literary allusions suggest composition in 1599 or early 1600.

SOURCES: Based closely on Thomas Lodge's prose romance *Rosalynde* (1590). Some names altered (e.g. Oliver and Orlando for Lodge's Saladyne and Rosader), others retained (e.g. Phoebe, 'Aliena', 'Ganymede'). Only major additions are characters of Jaques and Touchstone.

TEXT: First printed in the 1623 Folio. Very high quality printing, perhaps from the theatrical 'book'.

AS YOU LIKE IT

DUKE SENIOR in exile

ROSALIND, his daughter

DUKE FREDERICK, his usurping brother

CELIA, Frederick's daughter

TOUCHSTONE, the court jester

AMIENS, a lord attending on Duke Senior

LE BEAU, a courtier attending on Frederick

CHARLES, wrestler to Frederick

OLIVER ⎫
JAQUES ⎬ the three sons of Sir Rowland de Bois
ORLANDO ⎭

ADAM, an old servant of Sir Rowland, now in service to Oliver

DENNIS, servant to Oliver

JAQUES, a melancholy traveller

CORIN, an old shepherd

SILVIUS, a young shepherd, in love with Phoebe

PHOEBE, a shepherdess

WILLIAM, a countryman, in love with Audrey

AUDREY, a goatherd

SIR OLIVER MARTEXT, a country clergyman

HYMEN, god of marriage, perhaps played by Amiens or another courtier

Lords, Pages, Attendants

Act 1 Scene 1

Enter Orlando and Adam

ORLANDO As I remember, Adam, it was upon this fashion bequeathed me by will but poor a thousand crowns, and, as thou sayest, charged my brother on his blessing to breed me well: and there begins my
5   sadness. My brother Jaques he keeps at school, and report speaks goldenly of his profit. For my part, he keeps me rustically at home, or, to speak more properly, stays me here at home unkept, for call you that keeping for a gentleman of my birth, that differs
10   not from the stalling of an ox? His horses are bred better, for, besides that they are fair with their feeding, they are taught their manage, and to that end riders dearly hired: but I, his brother, gain nothing under him but growth, for the which his
15   animals on his dunghills are as much bound to him as I. Besides this nothing that he so plentifully gives me, the something that nature gave me his countenance seems to take from me: he lets me feed with his hinds, bars me the place of a brother,
20   and, as much as in him lies, mines my gentility with my education. This is it, Adam, that grieves me. And the spirit of my father, which I think is within me, begins to mutiny against this servitude. I will no longer endure it, though yet I know no wise remedy
25   how to avoid it.

Enter Oliver

ADAM Yonder comes my master, your brother.

ORLANDO Go apart, Adam, and thou shalt hear how he will shake me up.   *Adam stands*
                                                                                                              aside

OLIVER Now, sir, what make you here?

30   **ORLANDO** Nothing: I am not taught to make anything.

OLIVER What mar you then, sir?

1.1 *Location: the whereabouts of Oliver's household is unspecified* **1 Adam** name evocative of the biblical first man   **2 poor** only   **3 crowns** gold coins   **charged** order was given to   **4 breed** bring up   **5 keeps at school** maintains at university   **8 stays** detains   **unkept** poorly maintained   **10 stalling** stall accommodation   **11 fair** in fine condition   **12 manage** trained movements   **13 riders** horse trainers **dearly** at great cost   **15 bound** indebted   **18 countenance** behaviour/attitude to me/support   **19 hinds** servants/farm-workers   **20 as … lies** to the best of his ability   **mines my gentility** undermines my status as a gentleman   **21 grieves** vexes   **25 avoid** put an end to   **27 Go apart** stand aside   **28 shake me up** abuse/scold me   **29 make** do (Orlando picks up on the sense of 'create')   **31 mar** ruin

ORLANDO Marry, sir, I am helping you to mar that which God made, a poor unworthy brother of yours, with idleness.

35 **OLIVER** Marry, sir, be better employed, and be naught awhile.

ORLANDO Shall I keep your hogs and eat husks with them? What prodigal portion have I spent that I should come to such penury?

40 **OLIVER** Know you where you are, sir?

ORLANDO O, sir, very well: here in your orchard.

OLIVER Know you before whom, sir?

ORLANDO Ay, better than him I am before knows me. I know you are my eldest brother, and, in the gentle
45 condition of blood, you should so know me. The courtesy of nations allows you my better, in that you are the first-born, but the same tradition takes not away my blood, were there twenty brothers betwixt us: I have as much of my father in me as you, albeit I
50 confess your coming before me is nearer to his reverence.

OLIVER What, boy!   *Raises his hand or hits him*

ORLANDO Come, come, elder brother, you are too young   *Grabs him*
in this.

55 **OLIVER** Wilt thou lay hands on me, villain?

ORLANDO I am no villain: I am the youngest son of Sir Rowland de Bois, he was my father, and he is thrice a villain that says such a father begot villains. Wert thou not my brother, I would not take this hand from
60 thy throat till this other had pulled out thy tongue for saying so. Thou hast railed on thyself.

ADAM Sweet masters, be patient: for your father's remembrance, be at accord.

OLIVER Let me go, I say.

65 **ORLANDO** I will not, till I please: you shall hear me. My father charged you in his will to give me good education: you have trained me like a peasant,

---

32 Marry by the Virgin Mary (perhaps plays on **mar**)   **35 be naught awhile** i.e. be gone   **38 prodigal portion** biblical allusion to the prodigal (wastefully lavish) son, who, having spent all his money, had to look after pigs and eat their scraps   **41 orchard** garden   **43 knows** is aware of/acknowledges the claims of   **44 in ... blood** because of our noble breeding   **46 courtesy of nations** established custom of civilized society (i.e. rights of inheritance)   **47 tradition** custom/surrender (of privilege)   **48 blood** nobility/kinship/ anger   **50 is ... reverence** accords you more of the respect that was due to him   **53 young** immature/ inexperienced   **55 villain** scoundrel (Orlando plays up the sense of 'low-born person')   **57 de Bois** 'of the woods' (French, though probably anglicized to pronunciation 'boys')   **58 begot** conceived   **61 railed on** insulted   **62 father's remembrance** the sake of your father's memory

obscuring and hiding from me all gentleman-like
qualities. The spirit of my father grows strong in me,
70 and I will no longer endure it: therefore allow me
such exercises as may become a gentleman, or give
me the poor allottery my father left me by testament,
with that I will go buy my fortunes.   *Lets him go*

OLIVER And what wilt thou do? Beg when that is spent?
75 Well, sir, get you in. I will not long be troubled with
you. You shall have some part of your will. I pray
you leave me.

ORLANDO I will no further offend you than becomes me
for my good.

80 **OLIVER** Get you with him, you old dog.   *To Adam*

ADAM Is 'old dog' my reward? Most true, I have lost my
teeth in your service. God be with my old master, he
would not have spoke such a word.
                              Exeunt Orlando [and] Adam

OLIVER Is it even so? Begin you to grow upon me? I will
85 physic your rankness, and yet give no thousand
crowns neither. Holla, Dennis!
Enter Dennis

DENNIS Calls your worship?

OLIVER Was not Charles, the duke's wrestler, here to
speak with me?

90 **DENNIS** So please you, he is here at the door and
importunes access to you.

OLIVER Call him in.   *[Exit Dennis]*
'Twill be a good way, and tomorrow the wrestling is.
Enter Charles

CHARLES Good morrow to your worship.

95 **OLIVER** Good Monsieur Charles, what's the new news at
the new court?

CHARLES There's no news at the court, sir, but the old
news: that is, the old duke is banished by his younger
brother the new duke, and three or four loving lords
100 have put themselves into voluntary exile with him,
whose lands and revenues enrich the new duke,
therefore he gives them good leave to wander.

---

69 qualities accomplishments   **71 exercises** activities/skills   **become** suit   **72 allottery** share,
allocation   **testament** will   **76 will** (father's) bequest/(your)wish   **78 offend** vex/assail   **84 grow upon**
trouble/take liberties with   **85 physic** cure   **rankness** insolence/overgrowth/disease   **86 neither** either
Holla a shout to catch attention   **90 So** if it   **91 importunes** asks insistently for   **94 morrow** morning
99 loving i.e. loyal   **102 good leave** full permission

OLIVER Can you tell if Rosalind, the duke's daughter, be
    banished with her father?

105 **CHARLES** O, no; for the duke's daughter, her cousin, so
    loves her, being ever from their cradles bred together,
    that she would have followed her exile, or have died
    to stay behind her; she is at the court, and no less
    beloved of her uncle than his own daughter, and
110   never two ladies loved as they do.

OLIVER Where will the old duke live?

CHARLES They say he is already in the Forest of Arden,
    and a many merry men with him; and there they live
    like the old Robin Hood of England: they say many
115   young gentlemen flock to him every day, and fleet
    the time carelessly as they did in the golden world.

OLIVER What, you wrestle tomorrow before the new
    duke?

CHARLES Marry do I, sir, and I came to acquaint you
120   with a matter. I am given, sir, secretly to understand
    that your younger brother Orlando hath a disposition
    to come in disguised against me to try a fall.
    Tomorrow, sir, I wrestle for my credit, and he that
    escapes me without some broken limb shall acquit
125   him well. Your brother is but young and tender, and
    for your love I would be loath to foil him, as I must
    for my own honour if he come in: therefore, out of
    my love to you, I came hither to acquaint you withal,
    that either you might stay him from his intendment,
130   or brook such disgrace well as he shall run into, in
    that it is a thing of his own search and altogether
    against my will.

OLIVER Charles, I thank thee for thy love to me, which
    thou shalt find I will most kindly requite. I had myself
135   notice of my brother's purpose herein and have by
    underhand means laboured to dissuade him from it;
    but he is resolute. I'll tell thee, Charles, it is the
    stubbornest young fellow of France, full of ambition,
    an envious emulator of every man's good parts, a

---

106 ever constantly **108 to stay** by staying **110 loved** i.e. one other **112 Forest of Arden** the Forêt des Ardennes in France; Shakespeare would have also known the Forest of Arden near Stratford-upon-Avon **114 Robin Hood** popular English outlaw who lived in a forest and robbed the rich to feed the poor **115 fleet** pass **116 carelessly** in a carefree way **golden world** in classical mythology, the earliest of ages, when life was idyllic **122 fall** (wrestling) bout **123 credit** reputation **125 tender** inexperienced **126 foil** defeat **128 withal** with this **129 stay ... intendment** keep him from carrying out his intention **130 brook** endure **131 search** seeking **134 kindly requite** fittingly/graciously reward **136 underhand** secret **139 envious emulator** malicious disparager **parts** qualities

140   secret and villainous contriver against me his natural
      brother: therefore use thy discretion. I had as lief
      thou didst break his neck as his finger. And thou wert
      best look to't; for if thou dost him any slight disgrace,
      or if he do not mightily grace himself on thee, he will
145   practise against thee by poison, entrap thee by some
      treacherous device and never leave thee till he hath
      ta'en thy life by some indirect means or other, for I
      assure thee, and almost with tears I speak it, there is
      not one so young and so villainous this day living. I
150   speak but brotherly of him, but should I anatomize
      him to thee as he is, I must blush and weep and thou
      must look pale and wonder.

      CHARLES I am heartily glad I came hither to you. If he
      come tomorrow, I'll give him his payment. If ever he
155   go alone again, I'll never wrestle for prize more. And
      so God keep your worship!   *Exit*

      OLIVER Farewell, good Charles. Now will I stir this
      gamester: I hope I shall see an end of him; for my
      soul, yet I know not why, hates nothing more than
160   he. Yet he's gentle, never schooled and yet learnèd,
      full of noble device, of all sorts enchantingly beloved,
      and indeed so much in the heart of the world, and
      especially of my own people, who best know him,
      that I am altogether misprised. But it shall not be so
165   long: this wrestler shall clear all. Nothing remains
      but that I kindle the boy thither, which now I'll go
      about.   *Exit*

Act 1 Scene 2   *running scene 2*

Enter Rosalind and Celia

CELIA I pray thee Rosalind, sweet my coz, be merry.
ROSALIND Dear Celia, I show more mirth than I am
      mistress of, and would you yet I were merrier? Unless
      you could teach me to forget a banished father, you

---

141 **lief** willingly   143 **look to't** beware   144 **grace … thee** gain honour at your expense   145 **practise**
scheme   146 **device** stratagem   150 **anatomize** dissect, reveal   154 **payment** punishment   155 **go
alone** walk unaided   158 **gamester** sportsman   160 **gentle** well-born/honourable/kind   161 **device**
ingenuity/intention/witty expression/conversation   **sorts** social classes/types of people   164 **misprised**
despised/undervalued   165 **clear** settle   166 **kindle … thither** encourage Orlando to go to the wrestling
match   **1.2** *Location: the whereabouts of the court is unspecified*   1 **coz** short for 'cousin'
3 **would** wish

5   must not learn me how to remember any
extraordinary pleasure.

CELIA Herein I see thou lovest me not with the full
weight that I love thee. If my uncle, thy banished
father, had banished thy uncle, the duke my father,
10   so thou hadst been still with me, I could have taught
my love to take thy father for mine; so wouldst thou,
if the truth of thy love to me were so righteously
tempered as mine is to thee.

ROSALIND Well, I will forget the condition of my estate,
15   to rejoice in yours.

CELIA You know my father hath no child but I, nor none
is like to have; and truly, when he dies, thou shalt be
his heir; for what he hath taken away from thy father
perforce, I will render thee again in affection. By
20   mine honour, I will, and when I break that oath, let
me turn monster: therefore, my sweet Rose, my dear
Rose, be merry.

ROSALIND From henceforth I will, coz, and devise sports.
Let me see, what think you of falling in love?

25   CELIA Marry, I prithee do, to make sport withal: but love
no man in good earnest, nor no further in sport
neither than with safety of a pure blush thou mayst
in honour come off again.

ROSALIND What shall be our sport, then?

30   CELIA Let us sit and mock the good housewife Fortune
from her wheel, that her gifts may henceforth be
bestowed equally.

ROSALIND I would we could do so, for her benefits are
mightily misplaced, and the bountiful blind woman
35   doth most mistake in her gifts to women.

CELIA 'Tis true, for those that she makes fair she scarce
makes honest, and those that she makes honest she
makes very ill-favouredly.

ROSALIND Nay, now thou goest from Fortune's office to
40   Nature's: Fortune reigns in gifts of the world, not in
the lineaments of Nature.

5 learn teach   10 so provided that   12 righteously tempered correctly constituted/properly tuned
14 estate fortune   17 like likely   19 perforce of necessity   23 sports pastimes   25 make sport have
fun (plays on the sense of 'have sex')   withal with (perhaps with play on 'with all')   27 neither ... again
without being able to escape virtuously with no more than an innocent blush (come off plays on the sense of
'have an orgasm')   30 housewife mistress of the household/hussy   34 bountiful blind woman i.e.
Fortune, traditionally depicted as a blind woman turning a wheel   36 fair beautiful   37 honest chaste/
virtuous   38 ill-favouredly ugly   39 office role   41 lineaments features

Enter Clown [*Touchstone*]

CELIA No? When Nature hath made a fair creature, may
she not by Fortune fall into the fire? Though Nature
hath given us wit to flout at Fortune, hath not
45   Fortune sent in this fool to cut off the argument?

ROSALIND Indeed, there is Fortune too hard for Nature,
when Fortune makes Nature's natural the cutter-off
of Nature's wit.

CELIA Peradventure this is not Fortune's work neither,
50   but Nature's, who perceiveth our natural wits too
dull to reason of such goddesses, hath sent this
natural for our whetstone, for always the dullness of
the fool is the whetstone of the wits.— How now,
wit? Whither wander you?

55   **TOUCHSTONE** Mistress, you must come away to your
father.

CELIA Were you made the messenger?

TOUCHSTONE No, by mine honour, but I was bid to come
for you.

60   **ROSALIND** Where learned you that oath, fool?

TOUCHSTONE Of a certain knight that swore by his
honour they were good pancakes, and swore by his
honour the mustard was naught: now I'll stand to it,
the pancakes were naught, and the mustard was
65   good, and yet was not the knight forsworn.

CELIA How prove you that in the great heap of your
knowledge?

ROSALIND Ay, marry, now unmuzzle your wisdom.

TOUCHSTONE Stand you both forth now: stroke your
70   chins, and swear by your beards that I am a knave.

CELIA By our beards, if we had them, thou art.

TOUCHSTONE By my knavery, if I had it, then I were, but
if you swear by that that is not, you are not forsworn.
No more was this knight swearing by his honour, for
75   he never had any; or if he had, he had sworn it away
before ever he saw those pancakes or that mustard.

CELIA Prithee, who is't that thou meanest?

TOUCHSTONE One that old Frederick, your father, loves.

Touchstone stone used to test the quality or genuineness of gold and silver alloys?   **43 fall** ... **fire** i.e. come
to disaster (by being burned and disfigured, by losing her virginity, or by contracting venereal disease)
44 wit intelligence   **flout at** mock   **45 fool** i.e. Touchstone   **47 natural** idiot   **49 Peradventure**
perhaps   **52 whetstone** stone used for sharpening tools   **54 wit** ... **you** 'Wit, whither wilt thou?' (i.e.
proverbial; refers to one with 'wandering' wits)   **57 messenger** bearer of news/official employed to
apprehend state prisoners   **62 pancakes** these could also have savoury fillings   **63 naught** worthless
stand to maintain, insist upon   **65 forsworn** perjured

{o}

CELIA My father's love is enough to honour him enough;
80 speak no more of him, you'll be whipped for taxation
    one of these days.   hot water

TOUCHSTONE The more pity that fools may not speak
    wisely what wise men do foolishly.

CELIA By my troth, thou sayest true, for since the little
85 wit that fools have was silenced, the little foolery that
    wise men have makes a great show. Here comes
    Monsieur the Beau.

Enter Le Beau

ROSALIND With his mouth full of news.

CELIA Which he will put on us, as pigeons feed their
90 young.

ROSALIND Then shall we be news-crammed.

CELIA All the better: we shall be the more marketable.—
    Bonjour, Monsieur Le Beau, what's the news?

LE BEAU Fair princess, you have lost much good sport.

95 **CELIA** Sport? Of what colour?

LE BEAU What colour, madam? How shall I answer you?

ROSALIND As wit and fortune will.

TOUCHSTONE Or as the destinies decrees.   *Imitates Le Beau*

CELIA Well said, that was laid on with a trowel.

100 **TOUCHSTONE** Nay, if I keep not my rank—

ROSALIND Thou losest thy old smell.

LE BEAU You amaze me, ladies. I would have told you of
    good wrestling, which you have lost the sight of.

ROSALIND Yet tell us the manner of the wrestling.

105 **LE BEAU** I will tell you the beginning, and if it please
    your ladyships, you may see the end, for the best is
    yet to do: and here, where you are, they are coming
    to perform it.

CELIA Well, the beginning that is dead and buried.

110 **LE BEAU** There comes an old man and his three sons—

CELIA I could match this beginning with an old tale.

LE BEAU Three proper young men, of excellent growth
    and presence.

ROSALIND With bills on their necks, 'Be it known unto
115 all men by these presents.'

---

80 taxation slander   **84 troth** faith   *Le Beau* 'the handsome' (French)   **89 put** force   **92 marketable**
i.e. like **pigeons** fattened for sale   **94 lost** missed   **95 colour** kind   **99 laid … trowel** expressed
excessively/bluntly   **100 rank** standing as a wit (Rosalind plays on the sense of 'foul-smelling' for a joke
about farting)   **101 losest** lose/let loose, release   **old** ripe/stale/customary   **102 amaze** bewilder
107 do come   **111 tale** puns on 'tail' (as opposed to **beginning**)   **112 proper** handsome/fine   **114 bills**
advertisements/legal documents   **115 presents** legal documents; plays on **presence**

LE BEAU The eldest of the three wrestled with Charles,
the duke's wrestler, which Charles in a moment
threw him and broke three of his ribs, that there is
little hope of life in him. So he served the second, and
120 so the third. Yonder they lie, the poor old man, their
father, making such pitiful dole over them that all the
beholders take his part with weeping.

ROSALIND Alas!

TOUCHSTONE But what is the sport, monsieur, that the
125 ladies have lost?

LE BEAU   Why, this that I speak of.

TOUCHSTONE Thus men may grow wiser every day. It is
the first time that ever I heard breaking of ribs was
sport for ladies.

130 **CELIA** Or I, I promise thee.

ROSALIND But is there any else longs to see this broken
music in his sides? Is there yet another dotes upon
rib-breaking? Shall we see this wrestling, cousin?

LE BEAU You must if you stay here, for here is the place
135 appointed for the wrestling, and they are ready to
perform it.

CELIA Yonder, sure they are coming. Let us now stay
and see it.

*Flourish. Enter Duke [Frederick], Lords, Orlando, Charles
and Attendants*

DUKE FREDERICK   Come on. Since the youth will not be
140 entreated, his own peril on his forwardness.

ROSALIND Is yonder the man?   *To Le Beau*

LE BEAU Even he, madam.

CELIA Alas, he is too young, yet he looks successfully.

DUKE FREDERICK How now, daughter and cousin!
145 Are you crept hither to see the wrestling?

ROSALIND Ay, my liege, so please you give us leave.

DUKE FREDERICK You will take little delight in it, I can
tell you, there is such odds in the man. In pity of the
challenger's youth, I would fain dissuade him, but he
150 will not be entreated. Speak to him, ladies, see if you
can move him.

---

118 that so that   **119 So** in the same way   **121 dole** lamentation   **131 any** anyone   **broken** discordant/ with parts arranged for different instruments (plays on the idea of broken **ribs**)   *Flourish* trumpet fanfare, usually accompanying a person in authority   **140 his … forwardness** whatever danger results is due to his reckless confidence   **143 looks successfully** seems likely to succeed   **144 cousin** term used for any relative beyond the immediate family   **146 leave** permission   **148 odds** advantage   **man** i.e. Charles   **149 fain** gladly

CELIA Call him hither, good Monsieur Le Beau.

DUKE FREDERICK Do so. I'll not be by.   *He stands aside*

LE BEAU Monsieur the challenger, the princess calls for   *To Orlando*
155   you.

ORLANDO I attend them with all respect and duty.

ROSALIND Young man, have you challenged Charles the
    wrestler?

ORLANDO No, fair princess, he is the general challenger: I
160   come but in, as others do, to try with him the
    strength of my youth.

CELIA Young gentleman, your spirits are too bold for
    your years. You have seen cruel proof of this man's
    strength: if you saw yourself with your eyes or knew
165   yourself with your judgement, the fear of your
    adventure would counsel you to a more equal
    enterprise. We pray you for your own sake to
    embrace your own safety and give over this attempt.

ROSALIND Do, young sir: your reputation shall not
170   therefore be misprized. We will make it our suit to
    the duke that the wrestling might not go forward.

ORLANDO I beseech you, punish me not with your hard
    thoughts, wherein I confess me much guilty, to deny
    so fair and excellent ladies anything. But let your fair
175   eyes and gentle wishes go with me to my trial;
    wherein if I be foiled, there is but one shamed that
    was never gracious, if killed, but one dead that is
    willing to be so. I shall do my friends no wrong, for I
    have none to lament me, the world no injury, for in it
180   I have nothing. Only in the world I fill up a place,
    which may be better supplied when I have made it
    empty.

ROSALIND The little strength that I have, I would it were
    with you.

185   **CELIA** And mine, to eke out hers.

ROSALIND Fare you well: pray heaven I be deceived in you!

CELIA Your heart's desires be with you!

CHARLES Come, where is this young gallant that is so
    desirous to lie with his mother earth?

---

160 come but in merely enter the field   **try** test   **166 adventure** venture   **equal** evenly matched
170 misprized undervalued/scorned   **suit** request, petition   **176 foiled** thrown/defeated   **177 gracious**
favoured   **178 friends** relatives/supporters   **185 eke out** supplement   **186 deceived** mistaken
189 lie ... earth be thrown on the ground/have sex with **his mother earth**/die and be buried (may
anticipate the implied reference to Antaeus, son of Earth who renewed his strength by lying on the ground
and whom **Hercules** defeated in wrestling)

190 ORLANDO Ready, sir, but his will hath in it a more
modest working.

DUKE FREDERICK You shall try but one fall.

CHARLES No, I warrant your grace you shall not entreat
him to a second, that have so mightily persuaded him
195 from a first.

ORLANDO You mean to mock me after, you should not
have mocked me before. But come your ways.

ROSALIND Now Hercules be thy speed, young man!

CELIA I would I were invisible, to catch the strong fellow
200 by the leg.   *Wrestle*

ROSALIND O excellent young man!

CELIA If I had a thunderbolt in mine eye, I can tell who   *Charles is thrown*
should down.   *Shout*

DUKE FREDERICK No more, no more.

205 ORLANDO Yes, I beseech your grace:
I am not yet well breathed.

DUKE FREDERICK How dost thou, Charles?

LE BEAU He cannot speak, my lord.

DUKE FREDERICK Bear him away.— What is thy name,   *Charles is*
210 young man?   *carried out/To Orlando*

ORLANDO Orlando, my liege, the youngest son of Sir
Rowland de Bois.

DUKE FREDERICK I would thou hadst been son to some
man else:

The world esteemed thy father honourable,
215 But I did find him still mine enemy.

Thou shouldst have better pleased me with this deed
Hadst thou descended from another house.
But fare thee well, thou art a gallant youth.
I would thou hadst told me of another father.

          Exit Duke [with others; Celia, Orlando and
                              Rosalind remain]

220 CELIA Were I my father, coz, would I do this?   *To Rosalind*

ORLANDO I am more proud to be Sir Rowland's son,   *Aside?*
His youngest son, and would not change that calling
To be adopted heir to Frederick.

ROSALIND My father loved Sir Rowland as his soul,   *To Celia*
225 And all the world was of my father's mind:
Had I before known this young man his son,

---

190 will wish/lust/penis   **191 working** aim/sexual activity   **192 fall** conclusive throw   **193 warrant**
assure   **197 come your ways** come on   **198 Hercules** demigod who wrestled with and defeated the
mighty giant Antaeus   **speed** protector   **203 down** fall   **206 breathed** exercised/out of breath   **215 still**
always   **222 calling** name/position in life

I should have given him tears unto entreaties,
Ere he should thus have ventured.

CELIA Gentle cousin,

230   Let us go thank him and encourage him.   *To Rosalind*
My father's rough and envious disposition
Sticks me at heart.— Sir, you have well deserved,   *To Orlando*
If you do keep your promises in love
But justly, as you have exceeded all promise,

235   Your mistress shall be happy.

ROSALIND Gentleman,   *Gives him a chain from her neck*
Wear this for me, one out of suits with fortune,
That could give more, but that her hand lacks means.
Shall we go, coz?   *To Celia*

240   CELIA Ay.— Fare you well, fair gentleman.

ORLANDO Can I not say, I thank you? My better parts
Are all thrown down, and that which here stands up
Is but a quintain, a mere lifeless block.

ROSALIND He calls us back. My pride fell with my
fortunes.

245   I'll ask him what he would.— Did you call, sir?   *To Orlando*
Sir, you have wrestled well and overthrown
More than your enemies.

CELIA Will you go, coz?

ROSALIND Have with you. Fare you well.
                    Exeunt [Rosalind and Celia]

250   ORLANDO What passion hangs these weights upon my
tongue?
I cannot speak to her, yet she urged conference.
Enter Le Beau
O poor Orlando, thou art overthrown!
Or Charles or something weaker masters thee.

LE BEAU Good sir, I do in friendship counsel you

255   To leave this place. Albeit you have deserved
High commendation, true applause and love,
Yet such is now the duke's condition
That he misconstrues all that you have done.
The duke is humorous: what he is indeed

260   More suits you to conceive than I to speak of.

---

227 **unto** in addition to   228 **Ere** before   231 **envious** malicious   232 **Sticks** pierces   234 **justly** exactly   **promise** expectation   235 **mistress** sweetheart   237 **suits** favour   241 **parts** qualities/ spirits   243 **quintain** post used as a target when practising jousting or darts   245 **would** wants   249 **Have with you** I'm coming   251 **conference** conversation   253 **Or** either   257 **condition** disposition   259 **humorous** temperamental   **indeed** in reality   260 **conceive** understand/imagine

ORLANDO I thank you, sir; and pray you tell me this:
    Which of the two was daughter of the duke
    That here was at the wrestling?
LE BEAU Neither his daughter, if we judge by manners,
265   But yet indeed the taller is his daughter,
    The other is daughter to the banished duke,
    And here detained by her usurping uncle
    To keep his daughter company, whose loves
    Are dearer than the natural bond of sisters.
270   But I can tell you that of late this duke
    Hath ta'en displeasure 'gainst his gentle niece,
    Grounded upon no other argument
    But that the people praise her for her virtues
    And pity her for her good father's sake;
275   And, on my life, his malice 'gainst the lady
    Will suddenly break forth. Sir, fare you well.
    Hereafter, in a better world than this,
    I shall desire more love and knowledge of you.
ORLANDO I rest much bounden to you. Fare you well.
                          [Exit Le Beau]
280   Thus must I from the smoke into the smother,
    From tyrant duke unto a tyrant brother.
    But heavenly Rosalind!   *Exit*

Act 1 Scene 3

running scene 2 continues

Enter Celia and Rosalind

CELIA Why, cousin? Why, Rosalind? Cupid have mercy,
    not a word?
ROSALIND Not one to throw at a dog.
CELIA No, thy words are too precious to be cast away
5   upon curs, throw some of them at me; come, lame
    me with reasons.
ROSALIND Then there were two cousins laid up, when
    the one should be lamed with reasons and the other
    mad without any.
10   **CELIA** But is all this for your father?

---

265 **taller** more elegant/more attractive (some editors assume a reference to height and emend to 'smaller' or 'shorter', since Celia is less tall than Rosalind)   271 **gentle** well-born/kind   272 **argument** reason
276 **suddenly** at any time   278 **knowledge** acquaintance   279 **rest** remain   **bounden** indebted
280 **from … smother** i.e. from bad to worse   **smother** dense, suffocating smoke/smouldering fire
1.3   1 **Cupid** god of love   5 **curs** dogs/worthless fellows   6 **reasons** remarks/explanations   7 **Then there were** if I did, then there would be

ROSALIND No, some of it is for my child's father. O, how
full of briars is this working-day world!

CELIA They are but burs, cousin, thrown upon thee in
holiday foolery: if we walk not in the trodden paths

15   our very petticoats will catch them.

ROSALIND I could shake them off my coat: these burs are
in my heart.

CELIA Hem them away.

ROSALIND I would try, if I could cry 'hem' and have him.

20 **CELIA** Come, come, wrestle with thy affections.

ROSALIND O, they take the part of a better wrestler than
myself!

CELIA O, a good wish upon you! You will try in time, in
despite of a fall. But turning these jests out of service,

25   let us talk in good earnest: is it possible, on such a
sudden, you should fall into so strong a liking with
old Sir Rowland's youngest son?

ROSALIND The duke my father loved his father dearly.

CELIA Doth it therefore ensue that you should love his

30   son dearly? By this kind of chase, I should hate him,
for my father hated his father dearly; yet I hate not
Orlando.

ROSALIND No, faith, hate him not, for my sake.

CELIA Why should I not? Doth he not deserve well?

Enter Duke with Lords

35 **ROSALIND** Let me love him for that, and do you love him
because I do. Look, here comes the duke.

CELIA With his eyes full of anger.

DUKE FREDERICK Mistress, dispatch you with your   *To Rosalind*
safest haste
And get you from our court.

40 **ROSALIND** Me, uncle?

DUKE FREDERICK You, cousin
Within these ten days if that thou be'st found

---

11 **child's father** i.e. one who might become the father of my children (Orlando)   12 **briars** i.e.
obstacles   **working-day** ordinary, everyday   13 **burs** prickly seed-heads that stick easily to clothing
15 **petticoats** skirts   16 **coat** petticoat/skirt   18 **Hem** cough (as if to dislodge something stuck in the
throat or to clear the chest; pun on 'sew a hem')   19 **'hem'** puns on 'him'   **have** win, possess (plays on the
sense of 'have sex with')   20 **wrestle** plays on the sense of 'grapple sexually'   21 **take** … **of** support (**part**
plays on the sense of 'penis')   23 **a** … **you** bless you/good luck to you (**upon** may play on the sense of
'mount sexually')   **try** fight/have sex   24 **fall** throw in wrestling/bout of sex/moral lapse   **turning** …
service to finish with this joking (**turning, jests** and **service** all play on the sense of 'copulation')
30 **dearly** deeply (possible pun on 'deer' is generated by **chase**)   **chase** pursuit/hunt   34 **Why** … **not?**
i.e. Why should I hate him?   38 **your safest haste** sufficient haste to ensure your safety

So near our public court as twenty miles,
Thou diest for it.

45   ROSALIND I do beseech your grace,
Let me the knowledge of my fault bear with me:
If with myself I hold intelligence
Or have acquaintance with mine own desires,
If that I do not dream or be not frantic —
50   As I do trust I am not — then, dear uncle,
Never so much as in a thought unborn
Did I offend your highness.

DUKE FREDERICK Thus do all traitors.
If their purgation did consist in words,
55   They are as innocent as grace itself;
Let it suffice thee that I trust thee not.

ROSALIND Yet your mistrust cannot make me a traitor;
Tell me whereon the likelihood depends.

DUKE FREDERICK Thou art thy father's daughter,
there's enough.

60   ROSALIND So was I when your highness took his
dukedom,
So was I when your highness banished him;
Treason is not inherited, my lord,
Or if we did derive it from our friends,
What's that to me? My father was no traitor.
65   Then, good my liege, mistake me not so much
To think my poverty is treacherous.

CELIA Dear sovereign, hear me speak.

DUKE FREDERICK Ay, Celia, we stayed her for your sake,
Else had she with her father ranged along.

70   CELIA I did not then entreat to have her stay,
It was your pleasure and your own remorse.
I was too young that time to value her,
But now I know her: if she be a traitor,
Why so am I. We still have slept together,
75   Rose at an instant, learned, played, eat together,
And wheresoe'er we went, like Juno's swans,
Still we went coupled and inseparable.

DUKE FREDERICK She is too subtle for thee, and her
smoothness,

47 **intelligence** communication   49 **frantic** mad   50 **dear** noble   54 **purgation** acquittal   55 **grace** salvation, divine grace   58 **whereon** on what   63 **friends** relatives   68 **stayed** kept   69 **Else** otherwise   **ranged** wandered   71 **pleasure** will   **remorse** compassion   72 **young** immature   74 **still** always   75 **an instant** the same time   **eat** eaten   76 **like Juno's swans** i.e. yoked together to pull the chariot of the Roman queen of the gods   78 **subtle** crafty   **smoothness** plausibility/friendliness

Her very silence and her patience
80   Speak to the people, and they pity her.
Thou art a fool: she robs thee of thy name,
And thou wilt show more bright and seem more
    virtuous
When she is gone. Then open not thy lips.
Firm and irrevocable is my doom
85   Which I have passed upon her: she is banished.
CELIA Pronounce that sentence then on me, my liege:
I cannot live out of her company.
DUKE FREDERICK You are a fool. You, niece, provide
    yourself:
If you outstay the time, upon mine honour,
90   And in the greatness of my word, you die.
                              Exeunt Duke and others
CELIA O my poor Rosalind, whither wilt thou go?
Wilt thou change fathers? I will give thee mine.
I charge thee be not thou more grieved than I am.
ROSALIND I have more cause.
95   CELIA Thou hast not, cousin.
Prithee be cheerful; know'st thou not the duke
Hath banished me, his daughter?
ROSALIND That he hath not.
CELIA No, hath not? Rosalind lacks then the love
100   Which teacheth thee that thou and I am one.
Shall we be sundered? Shall we part, sweet girl?
No, let my father seek another heir:
Therefore devise with me how we may fly,
Whither to go and what to bear with us.
105   And do not seek to take your change upon you,
To bear your griefs yourself and leave me out,
For, by this heaven, now at our sorrows pale,
Say what thou canst, I'll go along with thee.
ROSALIND Why, whither shall we go?
110   CELIA To seek my uncle in the Forest of Arden.
ROSALIND Alas, what danger will it be to us,
Maids as we are, to travel forth so far!
Beauty provoketh thieves sooner than gold.

---

81 name reputation   **84 doom** judgement   **88 provide** prepare   **90 greatness** authority   **92 change** exchange   **101 sundered** separated   **105 change** i.e. of circumstances   **107 at … pale** depending on whether **pale** is an adjective or a noun, either 'the sky is pale in shock and grief', or 'our **sorrows** have reached their utmost limit'

CELIA I'll put myself in poor and mean attire
115   And with a kind of umber smirch my face.
           The like do you. So shall we pass along
           And never stir assailants.
ROSALIND Were it not better,
           Because that I am more than common tall,
120   That I did suit me all points like a man?
           A gallant curtle-axe upon my thigh,
           A boar-spear in my hand, and — in my heart
           Lie there what hidden woman's fear there will —
           We'll have a swashing and a martial outside,
125   As many other mannish cowards have
           That do outface it with their semblances.
CELIA What shall I call thee when thou art a man?
ROSALIND I'll have no worse a name than Jove's own page,
           And therefore look you call me Ganymede.
130   But what will you be called?
CELIA Something that hath a reference to my state:
           No longer Celia, but Aliena.
ROSALIND But, cousin, what if we assayed to steal
           The clownish fool out of your father's court?
135   Would he not be a comfort to our travel?
CELIA He'll go along o'er the wide world with me.
           Leave me alone to woo him. Let's away,
           And get our jewels and our wealth together,
           Devise the fittest time and safest way
140   To hide us from pursuit that will be made
           After my flight. Now go in we content
           To liberty and not to banishment.   *Exeunt*

Act 2 Scene 1   *running scene 3*

Enter Duke Senior, Amiens and two or three Lords, like
foresters
DUKE SENIOR   Now, my co-mates and brothers in exile,
           Hath not old custom made this life more sweet

---

114 **mean** lowly   115 **umber** brown pigment (to conceal aristocratically pale complexions)   120 **suit ...**
points dress myself in every respect   121 **gallant curtle-axe** fine cutlass   122 **boar-spear** weapon used
for boar hunting   124 **swashing** swaggering/dashing   126 **outface ... semblances** brazen it out with
appearances   128 **Jove** in Roman mythology, king of the gods   129 **Ganymede** a beautiful youth, carried
off by Jove to be his cupbearer; the name was also used by Elizabethans to refer to a youth who was the
subject of an older man's homosexual desire   131 **state** status   132 **Aliena** from the Latin for 'stranger'
133 **assayed** attempted   135 **travel** journey/hardship   137 **Leave me alone** leave it to me   **woo**
persuade   141 **content** contentment   2.1   *Location: the Forest of Arden   Amiens* name of a northern
French town; may suggest 'friendliness' (from the Latin)   *foresters* forest dwellers   2 **old custom**
established practice/experience

Than that of painted pomp? Are not these woods
More free from peril than the envious court?
5   Here feel we not the penalty of Adam,
The seasons' difference, as the icy fang
And churlish chiding of the winter's wind,
Which, when it bites and blows upon my body,
Even till I shrink with cold, I smile and say
10 'This is no flattery: these are counsellors
That feelingly persuade me what I am.'
Sweet are the uses of adversity,
Which, like the toad, ugly and venomous,
Wears yet a precious jewel in his head.
15 And this our life exempt from public haunt
Finds tongues in trees, books in the running brooks,
Sermons in stones and good in everything.

AMIENS I would not change it. Happy is your grace
That can translate the stubbornness of fortune
20 Into so quiet and so sweet a style.

DUKE SENIOR Come, shall we go and kill us venison?
And yet it irks me the poor dappled fools,
Being native burghers of this desert city,
Should in their own confines with forkèd heads
25 Have their round haunches gored.

FIRST LORD Indeed, my lord,
The melancholy Jaques grieves at that,
And in that kind swears you do more usurp
Than doth your brother that hath banished you.
30 Today my Lord of Amiens and myself
Did steal behind him as he lay along
Under an oak whose antique root peeps out
Upon the brook that brawls along this wood,
To the which place a poor sequestered stag
35 That from the hunter's aim had ta'en a hurt,
Did come to languish; and indeed, my lord,
The wretched animal heaved forth such groans
That their discharge did stretch his leathern coat

---

3 painted pomp artificial show   **4 envious** malicious   **5 penalty of Adam** i.e. the harsher seasons and greater toil that followed loss of Eden   **6 difference** change   **as** such as   **7 churlish chiding** harsh brawling/rebuking   **11 feelingly** tangibly/intensely   **12 uses** benefits   **13 toad ... head** supposedly, venomous toads had precious stones in their heads that were antidotes to poisons   **15 exempt ... haunt** not visited by people   **16 tongues** speech   **18 change** alter/exchange   **19 translate** transform/re-express (one thing in terms of another)   **20 style** mode of expression/way of life   **22 fools** poor creatures   **23 burghers** citizens   **desert** lonely, uninhabited   **24 confines** territories   **forkèd heads** i.e. barbed arrow-heads   **28 kind** manner   **31 along** stretched out   **32 antique** ancient/antic (i.e. grotesquely gnarled)   **33 brawls** rushes noisily   **34 sequestered** separated (from his herd)

Almost to bursting, and the big round tears
40   Coursed one another down his innocent nose
In piteous chase: and thus the hairy fool
Much markèd of the melancholy Jaques,
Stood on th'extremest verge of the swift brook,
Augmenting it with tears.
45 DUKE SENIOR But what said Jaques?
Did he not moralize this spectacle?
FIRST LORD O, yes, into a thousand similes.
First, for his weeping into the needless stream;
'Poor deer,' quoth he, 'thou mak'st a testament
50   As worldlings do, giving thy sum of more
To that which had too much.' Then, being there
      alone,
Left and abandoned of his velvet friend,
''Tis right,' quoth he, 'thus misery doth part
The flux of company.' Anon a careless herd,
55   Full of the pasture, jumps along by him
And never stays to greet him. 'Ay,' quoth Jaques,
'Sweep on, you fat and greasy citizens,
'Tis just the fashion; wherefore do you look
Upon that poor and broken bankrupt there?'
60   Thus most invectively he pierceth through
The body of country, city, court,
Yea, and of this our life, swearing that we
Are mere usurpers, tyrants, and what's worse,
To fright the animals and to kill them up
65   In their assigned and native dwelling-place.
DUKE SENIOR And did you leave him in this
      contemplation?
SECOND LORD We did, my lord, weeping and
      commenting
Upon the sobbing deer.
DUKE SENIOR Show me the place.
70   I love to cope him in these sullen fits,
For then he's full of matter.
FIRST LORD I'll bring you to him straight.   *Exeunt*

40 Coursed flowed/chased (plays on the sense of 'hunted')   42 markèd of noticed by   43 extremest verge very edge   46 moralize draw a moral from, interpret   48 needless having no need (for more water)   49 testament will   50 worldlings materially minded mortals   sum of more store/additional amount   52 velvet friend deer with smooth coat/richly clothed person/syphilitic lover   53 part depart from/separate   54 flux continuous stream   Anon instantly/soon   careless carefree   56 stays stops   57 greasy plump and fit for killing/wealthy   58 wherefore why   60 invectively in violent terms   63 mere absolute   64 up off   67 commenting pondering   70 cope encounter   71 matter ideas/material for discussion   72 straight straight away

Act 2 Scene 2   *running scene 4*

Enter Duke [Frederick], with Lords

DUKE FREDERICK Can it be possible that no man saw
          them?
      It cannot be: some villains of my court
      Are of consent and sufferance in this.
FIRST LORD I cannot hear of any that did see her.
5   The ladies, her attendants of her chamber,
      Saw her abed, and in the morning early
      They found the bed untreasured of their mistress.
SECOND LORD My lord, the roynish clown, at whom so oft
      Your grace was wont to laugh, is also missing.
10   Hisperia, the princess' gentlewoman,
      Confesses that she secretly o'erheard
      Your daughter and her cousin much commend
      The parts and graces of the wrestler
      That did but lately foil the sinewy Charles,
15   And she believes, wherever they are gone,
      That youth is surely in their company.
DUKE FREDERICK Send to his brother, fetch that
          gallant hither.
      If he be absent, bring his brother to me.
      I'll make him find him. Do this suddenly,
20   And let not search and inquisition quail
      To bring again these foolish runaways.   *Exeunt*

Act 2 Scene 3   *running scene 5*

Enter Orlando and Adam, [meeting]

ORLANDO Who's there?
ADAM What, my young master? O, my gentle master!
      O my sweet master! O you memory
      Of old Sir Rowland! Why, what make you here?
5   Why are you virtuous? Why do people love you?
      And wherefore are you gentle, strong and valiant?
      Why would you be so fond to overcome
      The bonny priser of the humorous duke?
      Your praise is come too swiftly home before you.

2.2 *Location: the court*   2 **villains** servants/wrongdoers   3 **sufferance** acquiescence   7 **untreasured**
robbed/emptied of a treasure   8 **roynish** coarse   9 **wont** accustomed   13 **parts** qualities   17 **gallant** fine
fellow/daring young man/ladies' man (i.e. Orlando)   19 **suddenly** immediately   20 **quail** fail   21 **again**
back   2.3   *Location: Oliver's household*   3 **memory** reminder   4 **make you** are you doing   7 **fond**
foolish   8 **bonny priser** robust prize-fighter   **humorous** temperamental

10   Know you not, master, to some kind of men
        Their graces serve them but as enemies?
        No more do yours: your virtues, gentle master,
        Are sanctified and holy traitors to you.
        O, what a world is this, when what is comely
15   Envenoms him that bears it!
ORLANDO Why, what's the matter?
ADAM O, unhappy youth,
        Come not within these doors! Within this roof
        The enemy of all your graces lives:
20   Your brother — no, no brother, yet the son —
        Yet not the son, I will not call him son —
        Of him I was about to call his father —
        Hath heard your praises, and this night he means
        To burn the lodging where you use to lie
25   And you within it. If he fail of that,
        He will have other means to cut you off;
        I overheard him and his practices.
        This is no place, this house is but a butchery;
        Abhor it, fear it, do not enter it.
30 **ORLANDO** Why, whither, Adam, wouldst thou have
        me go?
ADAM No matter whither, so you come not here.
ORLANDO What, wouldst thou have me go and beg
        my food?
        Or with a base and boist'rous sword enforce
        A thievish living on the common road?
35   This I must do, or know not what to do:
        Yet this I will not do, do how I can.
        I rather will subject me to the malice
        Of a diverted blood and bloody brother.
ADAM But do not so. I have five hundred crowns,
40   The thrifty hire I saved under your father,
        Which I did store to be my foster-nurse
        When service should in my old limbs lie lame
        And unregarded age in corners thrown.

---

12 more better   **13 sanctified** sanctimonious, hypocritical   **14 comely** fair   **15 Envenoms** poisons
23 your praises people's praises of you   **24 use** are accustomed   **25 of** to do   **26 cut you off** kill
you   **27 practices** schemes   **28 place** i.e. safe place   **butchery** slaughterhouse   **31 so** so long as
33 boist'rous massive/savage   **enforce** gain by force   **34 common** public   **38 diverted blood**
kinship drawn away from its natural course   **40 thrifty hire** wages thriftily saved   **41 foster-nurse** nurse
who brings up another's child as her own   **42 service … lame** i.e. when I am too weak to work
43 unregarded uncared for, ignored

Take that, and he that doth the ravens feed,
45 Yea, providently caters for the sparrow,
Be comfort to my age. Here is the gold,   *Gives gold*
All this I give you. Let me be your servant.
Though I look old, yet I am strong and lusty;
For in my youth I never did apply
50 Hot and rebellious liquors in my blood,
Nor did not with unbashful forehead woo
The means of weakness and debility:
Therefore my age is as a lusty winter,
Frosty, but kindly. Let me go with you.
55 I'll do the service of a younger man
In all your business and necessities.

ORLANDO O good old man, how well in thee appears
The constant service of the antique world,
When service sweat for duty, not for meed!
60 Thou art not for the fashion of these times,
Where none will sweat but for promotion,
And having that, do choke their service up
Even with the having: it is not so with thee.
But, poor old man, thou prun'st a rotten tree,
65 That cannot so much as a blossom yield
In lieu of all thy pains and husbandry.
But come thy ways, we'll go along together,
And ere we have thy youthful wages spent,
We'll light upon some settled low content.

70 ADAM Master, go on, and I will follow thee
To the last gasp with truth and loyalty.
From seventeen years till now almost fourscore
Here livèd I, but now live here no more.
At seventeen years many their fortunes seek,
75 But at fourscore it is too late a week.
Yet fortune cannot recompense me better
Than to die well and not my master's debtor.

Exeunt

---

48 lusty vigorous   **51 unbashful forehead** shameless audacity   **54 Frosty** i.e. white-haired   **kindly** pleasant/thriving   **58 constant** faithful   **59 sweat** i.e. worked   **meed** reward   **62 choke** ... **having** i.e. stop working once they have gained their reward/promotion   **66 In lieu of** in return for   **husbandry** cultivation/domestic management   **67 come thy ways** come on   **69 low content** humble contentment   **72 fourscore** eighty (four times twenty)   **75 too** ... **week** i.e. far too late

Act 2 Scene 4

running scene 6

*Enter Rosalind for Ganymede, Celia for Aliena, and Clown
alias Touchstone*

ROSALIND O Jupiter, how merry are my spirits!

TOUCHSTONE I care not for my spirits, if my legs were
        not weary.

ROSALIND I could find in my heart to disgrace my man's   *Aside?*

5   apparel and to cry like a woman, but I must comfort
        the weaker vessel, as doublet and hose ought to show
        itself courageous to petticoat: therefore courage, good
        Aliena!

CELIA I pray you bear with me. I cannot go no further.

10   **TOUCHSTONE** For my part, I had rather bear with you
        than bear you: yet I should bear no cross if I did bear
        you, for I think you have no money in your purse.

ROSALIND Well, this is the Forest of Arden.

TOUCHSTONE Ay, now am I in Arden, the more fool I.

15   When I was at home, I was in a better place, but
        travellers must be content.

Enter Corin and Silvius

ROSALIND   Ay, be so, good Touchstone. Look you, who
        comes here: a young man and an old in solemn talk. *They stand aside*

CORIN That is the way to make her scorn you still.

20   **SILVIUS** O Corin, that thou knew'st how I do love her!

CORIN I partly guess, for I have loved ere now.

SILVIUS No, Corin, being old, thou canst not guess,
        Though in thy youth thou wast as true a lover
        As ever sighed upon a midnight pillow:

25   But if thy love were ever like to mine —
        As sure I think did never man love so —
        How many actions most ridiculous
        Hast thou been drawn to by thy fantasy?

CORIN Into a thousand that I have forgotten.

30   **SILVIUS** O, thou didst then never love so heartily!
        If thou rememb'rest not the slightest folly
        That ever love did make thee run into,
        Thou hast not loved.

2.4 *Location: the Forest of Arden; except for one brief scene (Act 3 scene 1) the remainder of the
action takes place in various parts of the forest* **for** i.e. disguised as   **alias** may indicate a change of
costume (see Introduction)   **1 Jupiter** Roman king of the gods (Jove)   **6 weaker vessel** i.e. woman
doublet and hose man's close-fitting jacket and breeches   **11 cross** burden/coin (with cross stamped
on it)   *Silvius* from Latin for 'woods'   **18 solemn** serious   **28 fantasy** amorous imaginings/desire
30 heartily sincerely, from the heart   **31 folly** foolishness/lewdness

Or if thou hast not sat as I do now,
35   Wearing thy hearer in thy mistress' praise,
Thou hast not loved.
Or if thou hast not broke from company
Abruptly, as my passion now makes me,
Thou hast not loved.
40   O Phoebe, Phoebe, Phoebe!   *Exit*

ROSALIND Alas, poor shepherd! Searching of thy wound,
I have by hard adventure found mine own.

TOUCHSTONE And I mine. I remember when I was in
love, I broke my sword upon a stone and bid him take
45   that for coming a-night to Jane Smile. And I
remember the kissing of her batler and the cow's
dugs that her pretty chopt hands had milked; and I
remember the wooing of a peascod instead of her,
from whom I took two cods and, giving her them
50   again, said with weeping tears, 'Wear these for my
sake.' We that are true lovers run into strange
capers; but as all is mortal in nature, so is all nature
in love mortal in folly.

ROSALIND Thou speakest wiser than thou art ware of.

55   TOUCHSTONE Nay, I shall ne'er be ware of mine own wit
till I break my shins against it.

ROSALIND Jove, Jove! This shepherd's passion
Is much upon my fashion.

TOUCHSTONE And mine, but it grows something stale
60   with me.

CELIA I pray you one of you question yond man
If he for gold will give us any food.
I faint almost to death.

TOUCHSTONE Holla, you clown!   *To Corin*

65   ROSALIND Peace, fool, he's not thy kinsman.

CORIN Who calls?

TOUCHSTONE Your betters, sir.

CORIN Else are they very wretched.

---

35 Wearing wearing out, wearying   **37 broke from** escaped   **40 Phoebe** a name for Diana/Artemis,
goddess of the moon, chastity and hunting   **41 Searching of** probing   **wound** Touchstone will shift the
sense to 'vagina'   **42 adventure** fortune   **44 sword** weapon/penis   **him** the **stone**/his **sword**
45 coming visiting/ejaculating   **a-night** at night   **46 batler** wooden club (for beating wet laundry)
47 dugs teats   **chopt** chapped   **milked** plays on the sense of 'caused to ejaculate'   **48 peascod** pea-pod
(with genital connotations; a reversal of 'codpiece')   **49 cods** pods/testicles   **50 Wear** plays on the sense of
'have sex with, exhaust'   **52 capers** frolicsome leaps/fornications   **mortal** subject to decay (sense then
shifts to 'only human')   **54 ware** aware (puns on **wear**; Touchstone shifts the sense to 'wary')   **55 wit**
possible play on 'penis'   **58 upon my fashion** like mine   **59 something** somewhat   **stale** may play on the
sense of 'prostitute'   **61 yond** yonder, that   **64 clown** rustic (Rosalind picks up on the sense of 'jester')

ROSALIND Peace, I say. Good even to you, friend.

70   **CORIN** And to you, gentle sir, and to you all.

ROSALIND I prithee, shepherd, if that love or gold
　　Can in this desert place buy entertainment,
　　Bring us where we may rest ourselves and feed:
　　Here's a young maid with travel much oppressed

75   　　And faints for succour.

CORIN Fair sir, I pity her
　　And wish, for her sake more than for mine own,
　　My fortunes were more able to relieve her.
　　But I am shepherd to another man

80   　　And do not shear the fleeces that I graze:
　　My master is of churlish disposition
　　And little recks to find the way to heaven
　　By doing deeds of hospitality.
　　Besides, his cote, his flocks and bounds of feed

85   　　Are now on sale, and at our sheepcote now,
　　By reason of his absence, there is nothing
　　That you will feed on. But what is, come see,
　　And in my voice most welcome shall you be.

ROSALIND What is he that shall buy his flock and
　　pasture?

90   **CORIN** That young swain that you saw here but
　　erewhile,
　　That little cares for buying anything.

ROSALIND I pray thee if it stand with honesty,
　　Buy thou the cottage, pasture and the flock,
　　And thou shalt have to pay for it of us.

95   **CELIA** And we will mend thy wages. I like this place
　　And willingly could waste my time in it.

CORIN Assuredly the thing is to be sold.
　　Go with me: if you like upon report
　　The soil, the profit and this kind of life,

100   I will your very faithful feeder be
　　And buy it with your gold right suddenly.   *Exeunt*

---

69 even evening (i.e. afternoon)   **72 desert** deserted   **entertainment** hospitality, provisions   **75 succour**
help   **80 shear … graze** i.e. make any profit from the sheep I tend   **82 recks** cares   **84 cote**
cottage   **bounds of feed** range of pasture land   **85 sheepcote** building sheltering sheep (perhaps here a
shepherd's cottage)   **88 in my voice** as far as I am concerned   **90 swain** low-ranking man/rustic   **but
erewhile** only a while ago   **92 stand** is consistent   **94 to pay** i.e. money   **95 mend** improve   **96 waste**
spend   **100 feeder** servant   **101 suddenly** at once

Act 2 Scene 5

Enter Amiens, Jaques and others

AMIENS   *Song*
            Under the greenwood tree
            Who loves to lie with me,
            And turn his merry note
            Unto the sweet bird's throat,
5   Come hither, come hither, come hither:
            Here shall he see no enemy
            But winter and rough weather.

JAQUES More, more, I prithee more.

AMIENS It will make you melancholy, Monsieur Jaques.

10 **JAQUES** I thank it. More, I prithee more.
            I can suck melancholy out of a song,
            As a weasel sucks eggs. More, I prithee more.

AMIENS My voice is ragged. I know I cannot please you.

JAQUES I do not desire you to please me,
15   I do desire you to sing.
            Come, more: another stanzo — call you 'em stanzos?

AMIENS What you will, Monsieur Jaques.

JAQUES Nay, I care not for their names. They owe me
            nothing. Will you sing?

20 **AMIENS** More at your request than to please myself.

JAQUES Well then, if ever I thank any man, I'll thank
            you. But that they call compliment is like
            th'encounter of two dog-apes, and when a man
            thanks me heartily, methinks I have given him a
25   penny and he renders me the beggarly thanks. Come,
            sing; and you that will not, hold your tongues.

AMIENS Well, I'll end the song. Sirs, cover the while. The
            duke will drink under this tree. He hath been all this
            day to look you.   *A table with food and*

30 **JAQUES**   And I have been all this day to avoid him.   *drink is set out*
            He is too disputable for my company:
            I think of as many matters as he, but I give
            Heaven thanks and make no boast of them.
            Come, warble, come.

2.5 **1 greenwood** leafy **2 Who** anyone who **3 turn** adapt, tune **note** melody **4 throat** voice
13 ragged hoarse/harsh **16 stanzo** stanza, verse **18 I … nothing** Jaques refers to the **names** on a loan
document of those who **owe** money **22 that** that which **compliment** etiquette **23 th'encounter** the
meeting/sexual encounter **dog-apes** dog-faced baboons **25 beggarly** i.e. effusive **27 end** complete
cover the while in the meantime lay the cloth for a meal **29 look** look for **31 disputable**
argumentative **32 matters** topics

Song. All together here
35   Who doth ambition shun
            And loves to live i'th'sun,
            Seeking the food he eats
            And pleased with what he gets,
            Come hither, come hither, come hither:
40   Here shall he see etc.
JAQUES I'll give you a verse to this note
            That I made yesterday in despite of my invention.   *Hands Amiens*
AMIENS And I'll sing it. Thus it goes: *a paper*
            If it do come to pass   *Sings*
45   That any man turn ass,
            Leaving his wealth and ease,
            A stubborn will to please,
            Ducdame, ducdame, ducdame:
            Here shall he see gross fools as he,
50   An if he will come to me.
            What's that 'ducdame'?
JAQUES 'Tis a Greek invocation, to call fools into a circle.
            I'll go sleep, if I can. If I cannot, I'll rail against all the
            first-born of Egypt.
55 AMIENS And I'll go seek the duke. His banquet is
            prepared.   *Exeunt [separately]*

Act 2 Scene 6   *running scene 7 continues*

Enter Orlando and Adam

ADAM Dear master, I can go no further.
        O, I die for food! Here lie I down,   *Lies down*
        And measure out my grave. Farewell, kind master.
ORLANDO Why, how now, Adam? No greater heart in
5   thee? Live a little, comfort a little, cheer thyself a
        little. If this uncouth forest yield anything savage, I
        will either be food for it or bring it for food to thee.
        Thy conceit is nearer death than thy powers. For my
        sake be comfortable, hold death awhile at the arm's
10   end. I will here be with thee presently, and if I bring

36 i'th'sun i.e. free from care   40 etc. indicates repeat of 'no enemy / But winter and rough weather'
42 in … invention in spite of my poor imagination   48 Ducdame meaning unclear: probably a nonsense
word   49 gross great/dull/coarse   50 An if if   52 Greek i.e. gibberish   circle magic circle/circle of
gaping idiots (i.e. the others, gathered round Amiens)   53 rail rant   all … Egypt in punishment for
Pharaoh's ill-treatment of the Jews, God slaughtered all first-born children and animals in Egypt, which
resulted in a great lament being raised in the night   55 banquet light meal/course of fruit, sweetmeats and
wine   2.6   5 comfort take comfort   6 uncouth unknown   8 conceit imagination   9 comfortable
cheerful   10 presently immediately/soon

thee not something to eat, I will give thee leave to
die. But if thou diest before I come, thou art a mocker
of my labour. Well said! Thou look'st cheerly, and I'll
be with thee quickly. Yet thou liest in the bleak air.
15 Come, I will bear thee to some shelter, and thou shalt
not die for lack of a dinner, if there live anything in
this desert. Cheerly, good Adam!   *Exeunt*

Act 2 Scene 7   *running scene 7 continues*

Enter Duke Senior and Lord[s], like outlaws

DUKE SENIOR I think he be transformed into a beast,
For I can nowhere find him like a man.

FIRST LORD My lord, he is but even now gone hence:
Here was he merry, hearing of a song.

5 **DUKE SENIOR** If he, compact of jars, grow musical,
We shall have shortly discord in the spheres.
Go, seek him: tell him I would speak with him.

Enter Jaques

FIRST LORD He saves my labour by his own approach.

DUKE SENIOR Why, how now, monsieur! What a life is
this,

10 That your poor friends must woo your company?
What, you look merrily.

JAQUES A fool, a fool! I met a fool i'th'forest,
A motley fool — a miserable world.
As I do live by food, I met a fool

15 Who laid him down and basked him in the sun,
And railed on Lady Fortune in good terms,
In good set terms, and yet a motley fool.
'Good morrow, fool', quoth I. 'No, sir,' quoth he,
'Call me not fool till heaven hath sent me fortune.'

20 And then he drew a dial from his poke,
And looking on it with lack-lustre eye,
Says very wisely, 'It is ten o'clock,
Thus we may see', quoth he, 'how the world wags.
'Tis but an hour ago since it was nine,

25 And after one hour more 'twill be eleven,
And so, from hour to hour, we ripe and ripe,

---

13 said done **cheerly** cheerful **2.7 5 compact of jars** made up of discords **6 spheres** stars and planets were thought to be contained by crystalline spheres, which produced beautiful music as they rotated **13 motley** in a professional fool's multicoloured clothing **17 set terms** roundly/in an articulate manner **19 Call … fortune** 'Fortune favours fools' (proverbial) **20 dial** watch **poke** pocket **23 wags** goes (may pun on the sense of 'moves sexually') **24 hour** may pun on 'whore' **nine … eleven** possibly suggestive of growing erection **26 ripe** mature/grow erect/search

And then, from hour to hour, we rot and rot,
And thereby hangs a tale.' When I did hear
The motley fool thus moral on the time,
30   My lungs began to crow like chanticleer,
That fools should be so deep contemplative,
And I did laugh sans intermission
An hour by his dial. O noble fool!
A worthy fool! Motley's the only wear.
35   **DUKE SENIOR** What fool is this?
JAQUES O worthy fool! One that hath been a courtier,
And says, if ladies be but young and fair,
They have the gift to know it. And in his brain,
Which is as dry as the remainder biscuit
40   After a voyage, he hath strange places crammed
With observation, the which he vents
In mangled forms. O, that I were a fool!
I am ambitious for a motley coat.
DUKE SENIOR Thou shalt have one.
45   **JAQUES** It is my only suit,
Provided that you weed your better judgements
Of all opinion that grows rank in them
That I am wise. I must have liberty
Withal, as large a charter as the wind,
50   To blow on whom I please, for so fools have.
And they that are most gallèd with my folly,
They most must laugh. And why, sir, must they so?
The 'why' is plain as way to parish church:
He that a fool doth very wisely hit
55   Doth very foolishly, although he smart,
Seem senseless of the bob. If not,
The wise man's folly is anatomized
Even by the squandering glances of the fool.
Invest me in my motley, give me leave
60   To speak my mind, and I will through and through

27 **rot** decay/detumesce/become infected with venereal disease (possibly puns on 'rut')   28 **tale** puns on 'tail' (i.e. 'penis')   29 **moral** moralize   30 **chanticleer** a cockerel   31 **deep contemplative** thoughtful/familiar with sexual matters   32 **sans** without   34 **wear** thing worth wearing   39 **dry** according to Elizabethan physiology, one with a dry brain was slow to grasp matters but sure to remember them **remainder** remaining   40 **places** nooks and corners/topics   41 **vents** expresses   45 **suit** request/outfit   46 **weed** puns on the sense of 'clothing'   47 **rank** luxuriantly, wild   49 **Withal** as well   **charter** privilege   51 **gallèd** vexed, irritated   53 **way** puns on why   **church** attendance was required by law   54 **that … hit** who is the target of a fool's taunts   55 **smart** feels pain   56 **senseless … bob** insensible to the jest; the line is a foot short, suggesting that words may have been omitted, so some editors emend (e.g. 'Not to seem senseless' or 'If he seem senseless')   57 **anatomized** dissected   58 **squandering glances** random jibes   59 **Invest** clothe

Cleanse the foul body of th'infected world,
If they will patiently receive my medicine.

DUKE SENIOR Fie on thee! I can tell what thou wouldst
  do.

JAQUES What, for a counter, would I do but good?

65 **DUKE SENIOR** Most mischievous foul sin, in chiding sin.
For thou thyself hast been a libertine,
As sensual as the brutish sting itself;
And all th'embossèd sores and headed evils
That thou with licence of free foot hast caught

70 Wouldst thou disgorge into the general world.

JAQUES Why, who cries out on pride,
That can therein tax any private party?
Doth it not flow as hugely as the sea,
Till that the weary very means do ebb?

75 What woman in the city do I name,
When that I say the city woman bears
The cost of princes on unworthy shoulders?
Who can come in and say that I mean her,
When such a one as she, such is her neighbour?

80 Or what is he of basest function
That says his bravery is not on my cost,
Thinking that I mean him, but therein suits
His folly to the mettle of my speech?
There then, how then, what then? Let me see
  wherein

85 My tongue hath wronged him: if it do him right,
Then he hath wronged himself. If he be free,
Why then my taxing like a wild-goose flies,
Unclaimed of any man. But who comes here?

Enter Orlando

ORLANDO Forbear, and eat no more.   *Draws his sword*

90 **JAQUES** Why, I have eat none yet.

ORLANDO Nor shalt not, till necessity be served.

JAQUES Of what kind should this cock come of?

DUKE SENIOR Art thou thus boldened, man, by thy
  distress,

---

61 Cleanse purge medically **64 counter** worthless token used to represent a coin **66 libertine** wild,
lecherous, dissolute person **67 brutish sting** animal urging of lust **68 th'embossèd ... evils** swellings
and sores caused by venereal disease **70 disgorge** vomit **71 pride** sexual desire/arrogance **72 tax ...
party** censure any particular individual **74 weary ... ebb** the very stuff it feeds on is exhausted and used
up **77 cost of princes** i.e. excessively costly garments **78 come in** come forward in the law court/
intervene **80 function** occupation **81 bravery** fine clothes **not ... cost** none of my business as I did
not pay for it **82 suits** fits/dresses **83 mettle** spirit/substance **85 do him right** speak truly of him
86 free innocent **89 Forbear** stop **92 Of ... of?** Where has this young cockerel sprung from?

Or else a rude despiser of good manners,
95   That in civility thou seem'st so empty?
ORLANDO You touched my vein at first. The thorny point
        Of bare distress hath ta'en from me the show
        Of smooth civility: yet am I inland bred
        And know some nurture. But forbear, I say:
100   He dies that touches any of this fruit
        Till I and my affairs are answerèd.
JAQUES An you will not be answered with reason, I
        must die.
DUKE SENIOR What would you have? Your gentleness
        shall force
        More than your force move us to gentleness.
105 ORLANDO I almost die for food, and let me have it.
DUKE SENIOR Sit down and feed, and welcome to our
        table.
ORLANDO Speak you so gently? Pardon me, I pray you.
        I thought that all things had been savage here,
        And therefore put I on the countenance
110   Of stern commandment. But whate'er you are
        That in this desert inaccessible,
        Under the shade of melancholy boughs,
        Lose and neglect the creeping hours of time,
        If ever you have looked on better days,
115   If ever been where bells have knolled to church,
        If ever sat at any good man's feast,
        If ever from your eyelids wiped a tear
        And know what 'tis to pity and be pitied,
        Let gentleness my strong enforcement be:
120   In the which hope I blush, and hide my sword.   *Sheathes his sword*
DUKE SENIOR True is it that we have seen better days,
        And have with holy bell been knolled to church,
        And sat at good men's feasts, and wiped our eyes
        Of drops that sacred pity hath engendered:
125   And therefore sit you down in gentleness,
        And take upon command what help we have
        That to your wanting may be ministered.
ORLANDO Then but forbear your food a little while,
        Whiles, like a doe, I go to find my fawn

---

94 **rude** uncivilized   96 **touched … first** hit it with your first suggestion   98 **inland bred** civilized
99 **nurture** education, good upbringing   101 **answerèd** satisfied   102 **reason** may pun on 'raisin' (grape),
possibly part of the fruit at the meal   103 **gentleness** nobility/civilized conduct   109 **countenance**
appearance/expression   112 **melancholy** dark, gloomy   115 **knolled** rung (to summon people)
119 **enforcement** constraint   126 **upon command** at will   127 **wanting** needs

130 And give it food. There is an old poor man,
Who after me hath many a weary step
Limped in pure love: till he be first sufficed,
Oppressed with two weak evils, age and hunger,
I will not touch a bit.

135 **DUKE SENIOR** Go find him out.
And we will nothing waste till you return.

ORLANDO I thank ye, and be blest for your good comfort!

[*Exit*]

DUKE SENIOR Thou see'st we are not all alone unhappy:
This wide and universal theatre

140 Presents more woeful pageants than the scene
Wherein we play in.

JAQUES All the world's a stage,
And all the men and women merely players;
They have their exits and their entrances,

145 And one man in his time plays many parts,
His acts being seven ages. At first the infant,
Mewling and puking in the nurse's arms.
Then the whining schoolboy, with his satchel
And shining morning face, creeping like snail

150 Unwillingly to school. And then the lover,
Sighing like furnace, with a woeful ballad
Made to his mistress' eyebrow. Then a soldier,
Full of strange oaths and bearded like the pard,
Jealous in honour, sudden and quick in quarrel,

155 Seeking the bubble reputation
Even in the cannon's mouth. And then the justice,
In fair round belly with good capon lined,
With eyes severe and beard of formal cut,
Full of wise saws and modern instances.

160 And so he plays his part. The sixth age shifts
Into the lean and slippered pantaloon,
With spectacles on nose and pouch on side,
His youthful hose, well saved, a world too wide
For his shrunk shank, and his big manly voice,

165 Turning again toward childish treble, pipes
And whistles in his sound. Last scene of all,

133 weak causing weakness   **136 waste** consume   **138 unhappy** ill-fated   **146 acts** actions/divisions of a play   **147 Mewling** whimpering, mewing   **153 strange** foreign   **bearded … pard** with a bristling beard like a leopard's whiskers   **Jealous in** quick to defend his   **157 capon** chicken (technically a castrated cockerel)   **159 saws** sayings   **modern instances** everyday examples   **161 pantaloon** in Italian comedy, the foolish elderly man who wore spectacles, pantaloons (type of trousers) and slippers   **163 hose** breeches   **164 shank** leg   **166 his** its

That ends this strange eventful history,
Is second childishness and mere oblivion,
Sans teeth, sans eyes, sans taste, sans everything.

Enter Orlando, with Adam

170 **DUKE SENIOR** Welcome. Set down your venerable burden,
And let him feed.

ORLANDO I thank you most for him.   *Sets down Adam*

ADAM So had you need.
I scarce can speak to thank you for myself.

175 **DUKE SENIOR** Welcome, fall to. I will not trouble you
As yet, to question you about your fortunes.—
Give us some music, and, good cousin, sing.

            Song
            Blow, blow, thou winter wind,
            Thou art not so unkind
180   As man's ingratitude.
            Thy tooth is not so keen,
            Because thou art not seen,
            Although thy breath be rude.
            Heigh-ho, sing heigh-ho, unto the green holly.
185   Most friendship is feigning, most loving mere
                folly:
            The hey-ho, the holly.
            This life is most jolly.

            Freeze, freeze, thou bitter sky
            That dost not bite so nigh
190   As benefits forgot:
            Though thou the waters warp,
            Thy sting is not so sharp
            As friend remembered not.
            Hey-ho, sing, etc.

195 **DUKE SENIOR** If that you were the good Sir Rowland's   *To Orlando*
        son,
As you have whispered faithfully you were,
And as mine eye doth his effigies witness
Most truly limned and living in your face,
Be truly welcome hither: I am the duke
200 That loved your father. The residue of your fortune,

---

167 history history play/narrative   **168 mere** complete   **169 Sans** without   **eyes** eyesight   **175 fall to
eat**   *Song* often sung by Amiens, assuming he is among the lords on stage for this scene   **179 unkind**
cruel/unnatural   **181 keen** sharp   **183 rude** rough   **189 nigh** close   **191 warp** wrinkle/become
corrugated by turning to ice   **196 faithfully** convincingly/truly   **197 effigies** likeness   **198 limned**
portrayed

Go to my cave and tell me. Good old man,
Thou art right welcome as thy master is.
Support him by the arm. Give me your hand,
And let me all your fortunes understand.   *Exeunt*

Act 3 Scene 1

Enter Duke [Frederick], Lords and Oliver

DUKE FREDERICK Not see him since? Sir, sir, that cannot
          be:
          But were I not the better part made mercy,
          I should not seek an absent argument
          Of my revenge, thou present. But look to it:
5   Find out thy brother, wheresoe'er he is.
          Seek him with candle. Bring him dead or living
          Within this twelvemonth, or turn thou no more
          To seek a living in our territory.
          Thy lands and all things that thou dost call thine
10   Worth seizure do we seize into our hands,
          Till thou canst quit thee by thy brother's mouth
          Of what we think against thee.

OLIVER O, that your highness knew my heart in this!
          I never loved my brother in my life.

15   **DUKE FREDERICK** More villain thou. Well, push him
          out of doors,
          And let my officers of such a nature
          Make an extent upon his house and lands.
          Do this expediently and turn him going.   *Exeunt*

Act 3 Scene 2

Enter Orlando   *With a paper*

ORLANDO   Hang there, my verse, in witness of my love:
          And thou, thrice-crownèd queen of night, survey
          With thy chaste eye, from thy pale sphere above,
          Thy huntress' name that my full life doth sway.

204 fortunes adventures   **3.1** *Location: the court*   **1 him** i.e. Orlando   **2 better** greater   **made** made
of   **3 argument** subject   **4 present** being present (i.e. I would vent my wrath on you instead)   **7 turn**
return   **10 seizure** taking legal possession of   **11 quit ... mouth** acquit yourself by means of your
brother's own testimony   **16 of ... nature** whose responsibility it is   **17 Make ... upon** seize
18 expediently promptly   **turn him going** send him packing   **3.2** *Location: the forest (where all
remaining scenes are set)*   **2 thrice-crownèd ... night** the goddess of the moon, hunting and chastity,
known as Luna/Cynthia/Phoebe in the heavens, Diana/Artemis on earth and Proserpina/Hecate/Lucina in
the underworld   **4 Thy huntress** i.e. Rosalind   **sway** rule

5   O Rosalind! These trees shall be my books,
         And in their barks my thoughts I'll character,
         That every eye which in this forest looks
         Shall see thy virtue witnessed everywhere.
         Run, run, Orlando, carve on every tree
10   The fair, the chaste and unexpressive she.   *Exit*
Enter Corin and Clown [Touchstone]
CORIN And how like you this shepherd's life, Master
         Touchstone?
TOUCHSTONE Truly, shepherd, in respect of itself, it is a
         good life; but in respect that it is a shepherd's life, it is
15   naught. In respect that it is solitary, I like it very well;
         but in respect that it is private, it is a very vile life.
         Now in respect it is in the fields, it pleaseth me well;
         but in respect it is not in the court, it is tedious. As it
         is a spare life, look you, it fits my humour well; but as
20   there is no more plenty in it, it goes much against my
         stomach. Hast any philosophy in thee, shepherd?
CORIN No more but that I know the more one sickens
         the worse at ease he is: and that he that wants
         money, means and content is without three good
25   friends: that the property of rain is to wet and fire to
         burn: that good pasture makes fat sheep: and that a
         great cause of the night is lack of the sun: that he
         that hath learned no wit by nature nor art may
         complain of good breeding or comes of a very dull
30   kindred.
TOUCHSTONE Such a one is a natural philosopher. Wast
         ever in court, shepherd?
CORIN No, truly.
TOUCHSTONE Then thou art damned.
35 CORIN Nay, I hope.
TOUCHSTONE Truly thou art damned, like an ill-roasted
         egg: all on one side.
CORIN For not being at court? Your reason.
TOUCHSTONE Why, if thou never wast at court, thou
40   never saw'st good manners. If thou never saw'st
         good manners, then thy manners must be wicked,

---

6 character write   10 unexpressive inexpressible   16 private lonely   19 spare frugal   humour
temperament   20 plenty abundance/comforts of life/food   21 stomach inclination/appetite   23 wants
lacks   28 art education   29 complain of lament the lack of/complain about   31 natural instinctive/
foolish/rustic   35 hope i.e. hope not   36 ill-roasted ... side eggs were roasted in the hot ashes of the fire
and required turning for even cooking   40 manners proper behaviour/morals

and wickedness is sin, and sin is damnation. Thou art in a parlous state, shepherd.

CORIN Not a whit, Touchstone. Those that are good
45 manners at the court are as ridiculous in the country as the behaviour of the country is most mockable at the court. You told me you salute not at the court, but you kiss your hands; that courtesy would be uncleanly, if courtiers were shepherds.

50 **TOUCHSTONE** Instance, briefly. Come, instance.

CORIN Why, we are still handling our ewes, and their fells, you know are greasy.

TOUCHSTONE Why, do not your courtier's hands sweat? And is not the grease of a mutton as wholesome as
55 the sweat of a man? Shallow, shallow. A better instance, I say, come.

CORIN Besides, our hands are hard.

TOUCHSTONE Your lips will feel them the sooner. Shallow again. A more sounder instance, come.

60 **CORIN** And they are often tarred over with the surgery of our sheep, and would you have us kiss tar? The courtier's hands are perfumed with civet.

TOUCHSTONE Most shallow man! Thou worms-meat in respect of a good piece of flesh indeed. Learn of the
65 wise, and perpend: civet is of a baser birth than tar, the very uncleanly flux of a cat. Mend the instance, shepherd.

CORIN You have too courtly a wit for me. I'll rest.

TOUCHSTONE Wilt thou rest damned? God help thee,
70 shallow man. God make incision in thee. Thou art raw.

CORIN Sir, I am a true labourer: I earn that I eat, get that I wear, owe no man hate, envy no man's happiness, glad of other men's good, content with my harm, and
75 the greatest of my pride is to see my ewes graze and my lambs suck.

---

43 parlous perilous   **48 but you kiss** without kissing   **50 Instance** evidence/give an example   **51 still** always   **52 fells** fleeces   **54 grease** sweat   **60 tarred … sheep** tar, having antiseptic properties, was applied to injured sheep   **62 civet** musky substance used in perfume and obtained from the anal glands of the civet cat   **63 worms-meat** i.e. rotten flesh   **64 respect of** comparison with   **65 perpend** consider **66 flux** flow   **Mend** improve   **68 rest** cease (Touchstone shifts sense to 'remain')   **70 make incision** cut, as **raw** meat is scored and salted for cooking/cut, for the medical purpose of letting blood (and curing folly)/ graft on (wisdom), as a plant is cultivated   **71 raw** inexperienced/ignorant/uncooked   **72 that** what   **get** earn   **74 content … harm** patient in my own afflictions

TOUCHSTONE That is another simple sin in you: to bring
the ewes and the rams together and to offer to get
your living by the copulation of cattle, to be bawd to
80   a bell-wether, and to betray a she-lamb of a
twelvemonth to a crooked-pated, old, cuckoldly
ram, out of all reasonable match. If thou be'st not
damned for this, the devil himself will have no
shepherds. I cannot see else how thou shouldst scape.

85   CORIN Here comes young Master Ganymede, my new
mistress' brother.

Enter Rosalind   *With a paper*

ROSALIND 'From the east to western Ind,   *Reads*
   No jewel is like Rosalind.
   Her worth, being mounted on the wind,
90   Through all the world bears Rosalind.
   All the pictures fairest lined
   Are but black to Rosalind.
   Let no face be kept in mind
   But the fair of Rosalind.'

95   TOUCHSTONE I'll rhyme you so eight years together,
dinners and suppers and sleeping-hours excepted. It
is the right butter-women's rank to market.

ROSALIND Out, fool!

TOUCHSTONE For a taste:
100   If a hart do lack a hind,
   Let him seek out Rosalind.
   If the cat will after kind,
   So be sure will Rosalind.
   Wintered garments must be lined,
105   So must slender Rosalind.
   They that reap must sheaf and bind,
   Then to cart with Rosalind.
   Sweetest nut hath sourest rind,

77 **simple** foolish   78 **offer** presume/venture   79 **cattle** animals/whores   **bawd** pimp   80 **bell-wether** leading male sheep of a flock (with a bell around its neck)   81 **crooked-pated** with crooked/curled horns   **cuckoldly** a cuckold (man with an unfaithful wife) was traditionally said to grow horns   82 **out of** beyond the limits of   87 **Ind** Indies   91 **lined** drawn   92 **black to** dark-complexioned, foul compared to   94 **fair** beauty/light complexion   95 **together** continuously   96 **It . . . market** i.e. the predictable verse resembles either the jogging to market of country women in a cart or the eager lust of a whore to put herself to sale   97 **butter-women** butter-sellers/lecherous women/whores   **rank** movement in line/lustful   100 **hart** male deer   **hind** female deer   102 **after kind** act according to its nature (proverbial: plays on the sense of 'have sex')   104 **Wintered** worn in winter/old   **lined** plays on notion of sex between dogs, giving bawdy connotations to the next line (i.e. Rosalind will lose her slenderness to pregnancy)   106 **reap** perhaps with slang sense of 'have sex'   **sheaf and bind** tie the crop into bundles (perhaps with suggestion of pregnancy)   107 **cart** transport the crop in a cart/punish a prostitute by publicly carrying her in or whipping her behind a cart   108 **nut** plays on the sense of 'vagina'

                Such a nut is Rosalind.
110   He that sweetest rose will find
                Must find love's prick and Rosalind.
          This is the very false gallop of verses. Why do you
          infect yourself with them?
     ROSALIND Peace, you dull fool! I found them on a tree.
115 TOUCHSTONE Truly the tree yields bad fruit.
     ROSALIND I'll graff it with you, and then I shall graff it
          with a medlar. Then it will be the earliest fruit
          i'th'country, for you'll be rotten ere you be half ripe,
          and that's the right virtue of the medlar.
120 TOUCHSTONE You have said, but whether wisely or no,
          let the forest judge.
     Enter Celia, with a writing
     ROSALIND Peace! Here comes my sister, reading. Stand
          aside.   *They stand aside*
     CELIA 'Why should this a desert be?   *Reads*
125   For it is unpeopled? No.
                Tongues I'll hang on every tree
                That shall civil sayings show.
                Some, how brief the life of man
                Runs his erring pilgrimage,
130   That the stretching of a span
                Buckles in his sum of age.
                Some, of violated vows
                'Twixt the souls of friend and friend:
                But upon the fairest boughs,
135   Or at every sentence end,
                Will I Rosalinda write,
                Teaching all that read to know
                The quintessence of every sprite
                Heaven would in little show.
140   Therefore heaven Nature charged
                That one body should be filled
                With all graces wide-enlarged.

---

110 **rose** plays on the sense of 'vagina' 111 **prick** thorn/penis 112 **false gallop** canter 115 **fruit** plays on sense of 'genitals' 116 **graff** graft – i.e. make one plant grow onto another (plays on the sense of 'have sex') 117 **medlar** tree bearing apple-like fruits/medlar fruit (resembles the vagina)/pun on 'meddler' (prostitute) 118 **rotten** infected with venereal disease 119 **right virtue** true character 125 **For** because 127 **civil sayings** civilized reflections 129 **his erring** its wandering 130 **span** distance from thumb to little finger 131 **Buckles in** encompasses 138 **quintessence** purest essence/extract **sprite** spirit 139 **in little** in miniature (i.e. in the form of Rosaline) 140 **Nature charged** ordered Nature 142 **wide-enlarged** (that had been) widely dispersed

Nature presently distilled
Helen's cheek, but not her heart,
145   Cleopatra's majesty,
Atalanta's better part,
Sad Lucretia's modesty.
Thus Rosalind of many parts
By heavenly synod was devised,
150   Of many faces, eyes and hearts,
To have the touches dearest prized.
Heaven would that she these gifts should have,
And I to live and die her slave.'

ROSALIND O most gentle Jupiter! What tedious homily of   *Steps forward*
155   love have you wearied your parishioners withal, and
never cried 'Have patience, good people!'

CELIA How now? Back, friends. Shepherd, go off a
little.— Go with him, sirrah.   *To Touchstone*

TOUCHSTONE Come, shepherd, let us make an
160   honourable retreat, though not with bag and
baggage, yet with scrip and scrippage.
Exeunt [Corin and Touchstone]

CELIA Didst thou hear these verses?

ROSALIND O, yes, I heard them all, and more too, for
some of them had in them more feet than the verses
165   would bear.

CELIA That's no matter: the feet might bear the verses.

ROSALIND Ay, but the feet were lame and could not bear
themselves without the verse, and therefore stood
lamely in the verse.

170   **CELIA** But didst thou hear without wondering how thy
name should be hanged and carved upon these trees?

ROSALIND I was seven of the nine days out of the wonder
before you came, for look here what I found on a
palm-tree. I was never so berhymed since

143 **presently** immediately   144 **Helen's ... heart** i.e. Helen of Troy's beauty but not her deceitful heart; when Paris carried Helen off to Troy war broke out between the Grecians and the Trojans   145 **Cleopatra** famous Egyptian queen   146 **Atalanta's better part** presumably her beauty or perhaps athletic skill; Atalanta declared that she would only marry the man who could defeat her in a race, whilst losing suitors would be killed   147 **Lucretia's modesty** raped by Tarquin, Lucretia was so ashamed she committed suicide   149 **synod** assembly/conjunction of planets   151 **touches** features   152 **would** willed   153 **I to** that I should   154 **Jupiter**, king of the gods who carried off the beautiful youth Ganymede   157 **Back** (to Corin and Touchstone) move back   158 **sirrah** sir (used to an inferior)   160 **bag and baggage** collective property of an army   161 **scrip and scrippage** nonce phrase referring to a shepherd's pouch (scrip) and its contents   164 **feet** i.e. metrical feet   172 **seven ... wonder** from the phrase 'a nine days' wonder' (so Rosalind has been wondering about the verses for quite a while)

175   Pythagoras' time that I was an Irish rat, which I can
       hardly remember.

CELIA Trow you who hath done this?

ROSALIND Is it a man?

CELIA And a chain, that you once wore, about his neck.
180   Change you colour?

ROSALIND I prithee who?

CELIA O lord, lord! It is a hard matter for friends to meet;
       but mountains may be removed with earthquakes
       and so encounter.

185   **ROSALIND** Nay, but who is it?

CELIA Is it possible?

ROSALIND Nay, I prithee now with most petitionary
       vehemence, tell me who it is.

CELIA O wonderful, wonderful, and most wonderful
190   wonderful! And yet again wonderful, and after that,
       out of all whooping!

ROSALIND Good my complexion! Dost thou think,
       though I am caparisoned like a man, I have a
       doublet and hose in my disposition? One inch of delay
195   more is a South Sea of discovery. I prithee tell me
       who is it quickly, and speak apace. I would thou
       couldst stammer, that thou mightst pour this
       concealed man out of thy mouth, as wine comes
       out of a narrow-mouthed bottle, either too much
200   at once, or none at all. I prithee take the cork out of
       thy mouth that I may drink thy tidings.

CELIA So you may put a man in your belly.

ROSALIND Is he of God's making? What manner of man?
       Is his head worth a hat? Or his chin worth a beard?
205   **CELIA** Nay, he hath but a little beard.

ROSALIND Why, God will send more, if the man will be
       thankful: let me stay the growth of his beard, if thou
       delay me not the knowledge of his chin.

---

175 Pythagoras Greek philosopher who believed in the transmigration of souls from humans to animals
that when   **Irish rat** supposedly the Irish could kill rats with rhyming incantations   **177 Trow** know
179 And a chain i.e. yes, it is, and one with a chain   **180 Change you colour?** Are you blushing?
182 friends ... encounter inversion of the proverb 'friends may meet, but mountains never
greet'   **friends** plays on the sense of 'lovers'   **encounter** plays on the sense of 'sexual union'
186 possible i.e. that you do not know   **187 I ... vehemence** I earnestly beg you   **189 wonderful**
incredible   **191 out ... whooping** beyond what all shouts of astonishment can express   **192 Good my**
complexion! Oh (have mercy on) my temperament/curiosity!   **193 caparisoned** dressed   **195 South ...**
discovery i.e. as lengthy as an exploratory voyage over the South Seas   **196 apace** swiftly   **202 belly**
stomach/womb (playing on **drink** in its slang sense of 'have sex')   **203 of God's making** i.e. a real
man   **207 stay** wait for

CELIA It is young Orlando that tripped up the wrestler's
210   heels and your heart both in an instant.

ROSALIND Nay, but the devil take mocking: speak, sad
brow and true maid.

CELIA I'faith, coz, 'tis he.

ROSALIND Orlando?

215   **CELIA** Orlando.

ROSALIND Alas the day! What shall I do with my doublet
and hose? What did he when thou saw'st him? What
said he? How looked he? Wherein went he? What
makes he here? Did he ask for me? Where remains
220   he? How parted he with thee? And when shalt thou
see him again? Answer me in one word.

CELIA You must borrow me Gargantua's mouth first: 'tis
a word too great for any mouth of this age's size. To
say ay and no to these particulars is more than to
225   answer in a catechism.

ROSALIND But doth he know that I am in this forest and
in man's apparel? Looks he as freshly as he did the
day he wrestled?

CELIA It is as easy to count atomies as to resolve the
230   propositions of a lover, but take a taste of my finding
him, and relish it with good observance. I found him
under a tree, like a dropped acorn.

ROSALIND It may well be called Jove's tree, when it drops
forth such fruit.   *Aside?*

235   **CELIA** Give me audience, good madam.

ROSALIND Proceed.

CELIA There lay he, stretched along, like a wounded
knight.

ROSALIND Though it be pity to see such a sight, it well
240   becomes the ground.

CELIA Cry 'holla' to the tongue, I prithee. It curvets
unseasonably. He was furnished like a hunter.

ROSALIND O, ominous! He comes to kill my heart.

CELIA I would sing my song without a burden. Thou
245   bringest me out of tune.

---

211 sad … maid i.e. seriously and truly   218 **Wherein went he?** What was he wearing?   219 **makes**
he is he doing   222 **Gargantua** the giant in FranÔois Rabelais' book *Gargantua* (1534)   224 **particulars**
details   225 **catechism** series of set questions and answers used as a form of instruction by the Church
229 **atomies** motes, atoms   **resolve the propositions** answer the questions   231 **relish** flavour   **good**
observance close attention   233 **Jove's tree** oak trees were associated with Jove   235 **Give me**
audience listen to me   237 **along** out   241 **'holla'** stop (used to a horse)   **curvets** leaps about
242 **furnished** dressed   243 **heart** puns on 'hart' (male deer)   244 **burden** chorus

ROSALIND Do you not know I am a woman? When I
   think, I must speak. Sweet, say on.

Enter Orlando and Jaques

CELIA You bring me out. Soft! Comes he not here?

ROSALIND 'Tis he. Slink by, and note him.   *They stand aside*

250 **JAQUES** I thank you for your company, but, good faith, I   *To Orlando*
   had as lief have been myself alone.

ORLANDO And so had I, but yet, for fashion sake,
   I thank you too for your society.

JAQUES God buy you. Let's meet as little as we can.

255 **ORLANDO** I do desire we may be better strangers.

JAQUES I pray you mar no more trees with writing love-
   songs in their barks.

ORLANDO I pray you mar no more of my verses with
   reading them ill-favouredly.

260 **JAQUES** Rosalind is your love's name?

ORLANDO Yes, just.

JAQUES I do not like her name.

ORLANDO There was no thought of pleasing you when
   she was christened.

265 **JAQUES** What stature is she of?

ORLANDO Just as high as my heart.

JAQUES You are full of pretty answers. Have you not
   been acquainted with goldsmiths' wives, and conned
   them out of rings?

270 **ORLANDO** Not so, but I answer you right painted cloth,
   from whence you have studied your questions.

JAQUES You have a nimble wit; I think 'twas made of
   Atalanta's heels. Will you sit down with me? And we
   two will rail against our mistress the world and all

275   our misery.

ORLANDO I will chide no breather in the world but
   myself, against whom I know most faults.

JAQUES The worst fault you have is to be in love.

ORLANDO 'Tis a fault I will not change for your best

280   virtue. I am weary of you.

JAQUES By my troth, I was seeking for a fool when I
   found you.

---

248 bring me out make me forget what I was saying   **Soft!** Wait a moment!   **251 lief** willingly
253 society company   **259 ill-favouredly** poorly   **261 just** exactly   **267 pretty** clever   **268 acquainted**
plays on the sense of 'sexually familiar'   **conned** learned by heart   **269 rings** which had verses engraved
on them (also slang for 'vaginas')   **270 right painted cloth** in the manner of a cheap hanging depicting
commonplace mythological scenes   **271 questions** topics   **273 Atalanta** famed for her swiftness
276 breather i.e. living being   **279 change** exchange   **281 troth** faith

ORLANDO He is drowned in the brook. Look but in, and you shall see him.

285 **JAQUES** There I shall see mine own figure.

ORLANDO Which I take to be either a fool or a cipher.

JAQUES I'll tarry no longer with you. Farewell, good Signior Love.

ORLANDO I am glad of your departure. Adieu, good
290   Monsieur Melancholy.   [*Exit Jaques*]

ROSALIND I will speak to him like a saucy lackey, and   *Aside to Celia*
under that habit play the knave with him.— Do you
hear, forester?

ORLANDO Very well. What would you?

295 **ROSALIND** I pray you, what is't o'clock?

ORLANDO You should ask me what time o'day: there's no clock in the forest.

ROSALIND Then there is no true lover in the forest, else sighing every minute and groaning every hour would
300   detect the lazy foot of time as well as a clock.

ORLANDO And why not the swift foot of time? Had not that been as proper?

ROSALIND By no means, sir; time travels in divers paces with divers persons. I'll tell you who time ambles
305   withal, who time trots withal, who time gallops withal and who he stands still withal.

ORLANDO I prithee, who doth he trot withal?

ROSALIND Marry, he trots hard with a young maid between the contract of her marriage and the day it
310   is solemnized. If the interim be but a se'nnight, time's pace is so hard that it seems the length of seven year.

ORLANDO Who ambles time withal?

ROSALIND With a priest that lacks Latin and a rich man that hath not the gout, for the one sleeps easily
315   because he cannot study, and the other lives merrily because he feels no pain: the one lacking the burden of lean and wasteful learning, the other knowing no burden of heavy tedious penury. These time ambles withal.

320 **ORLANDO** Who doth he gallop withal?

---

285 **figure** image (Orlando plays on the sense of 'number')   286 **cipher** zero   291 **saucy lackey** insolent
minion   292 **habit** appearance   **play the knave** play a boy/trick him   300 **detect** reveal   303 **divers**
various   308 **hard** with an uneasy pace, with difficulty   309 **contract** ... **marriage** formal betrothal
310 **se'nnight** week (seven nights)   317 **lean** unrewarding/thin   **wasteful** time-wasting/causing one to
waste away   318 **tedious** troublesome/painful

ROSALIND With a thief to the gallows, for though he go
as softly as foot can fall, he thinks himself too soon
there.

ORLANDO Who stays it still withal?

325 **ROSALIND** With lawyers in the vacation, for they sleep
between term and term, and then they perceive not
how time moves.

ORLANDO Where dwell you, pretty youth?

ROSALIND With this shepherdess, my sister, here in the
330 skirts of the forest, like fringe upon a petticoat.

ORLANDO Are you native of this place?

ROSALIND As the cony that you see dwell where she is
kindled.

ORLANDO Your accent is something finer than you could
335 purchase in so removed a dwelling.

ROSALIND I have been told so of many: but indeed an old
religious uncle of mine taught me to speak, who was
in his youth an inland man, one that knew courtship
too well, for there he fell in love. I have heard him
340 read many lectures against it, and I thank God I am
not a woman, to be touched with so many giddy
offences as he hath generally taxed their whole sex
withal.

ORLANDO Can you remember any of the principal evils
345 that he laid to the charge of women?

ROSALIND There were none principal. They were all like
one another as half-pence are, every one fault
seeming monstrous till his fellow fault came to
match it.

350 **ORLANDO** I prithee recount some of them.

ROSALIND No, I will not cast away my physic but on
those that are sick. There is a man haunts the forest
that abuses our young plants with carving 'Rosalind'
on their barks; hangs odes upon hawthorns and
355 elegies on brambles; all, forsooth, deifying the name
of Rosalind. If I could meet that fancy-monger, I
would give him some good counsel, for he seems to
have the quotidian of love upon him.

322 **softly** slowly   325 **vacation** period during which the law courts are suspended   326 **term** period
appointed for the sitting of courts of law   330 **skirts** outskirts   332 **cony** rabbit   333 **kindled** born
335 **purchase** acquire   **removed** remote   337 **religious** pious/monastic/scrupulous   338 **inland** of
civilized society   **courtship** court life/wooing   341 **touched** tainted   342 **generally** without exception
348 **his** its   351 **physic** medicine   352 **haunts** who hangs around   356 **fancy-monger** dealer in love
358 **quotidian** daily recurring fever

ORLANDO I am he that is so love-shaked. I pray you tell
360   me your remedy.
ROSALIND There is none of my uncle's marks upon you:
    he taught me how to know a man in love, in which
    cage of rushes I am sure you are not prisoner.
ORLANDO What were his marks?
365 ROSALIND A lean cheek, which you have not: a blue eye
    and sunken, which you have not: an unquestionable
    spirit, which you have not: a beard neglected, which
    you have not — but I pardon you for that, for simply
    your having in beard is a younger brother's revenue.
370   Then your hose should be ungartered, your bonnet
    unbanded, your sleeve unbuttoned, your shoe untied
    and everything about you demonstrating a careless
    desolation: but you are no such man: you are rather
    point-device in your accoutrements, as loving
375   yourself than seeming the lover of any other.
ORLANDO Fair youth, I would I could make thee believe I
    love.
ROSALIND Me believe it? You may as soon make her that
    you love believe it, which I warrant she is apter to do
380   than to confess she does: that is one of the points in
    the which women still give the lie to their
    consciences. But, in good sooth, are you he that
    hangs the verses on the trees, wherein Rosalind is so
    admired?
385 ORLANDO I swear to thee, youth, by the white hand of
    Rosalind, I am that he, that unfortunate he.
ROSALIND But are you so much in love as your rhymes
    speak?
ORLANDO Neither rhyme nor reason can express how
390   much.
ROSALIND Love is merely a madness, and, I tell you,
    deserves as well a dark house and a whip as madmen
    do: and the reason why they are not so punished and
    cured is that the lunacy is so ordinary that the
395   whippers are in love too. Yet I profess curing it by
    counsel.

---

361 **marks** signs, symptoms   363 **cage of rushes** i.e. flimsy prison   365 **blue** i.e. with dark circles
366 **unquestionable** unwilling to be questioned   369 **your … revenue** your beard is like a younger
brother's income (i.e. small)   370 **ungartered** not tied up   371 **unbanded** without a coloured hat-band
374 **point-device** immaculate   **accoutrements** clothes   **as** as if   379 **apter** more likely   381 **still**
always   382 **sooth** truth   391 **merely** entirely   392 **dark … do** imprisonment in the dark and whipping
were 'treatments' for the insane   395 **profess** practise, have knowledge in

ORLANDO Did you ever cure any so?

ROSALIND Yes, one, and in this manner. He was to imagine me his love, his mistress, and I set him every

400 day to woo me. At which time would I, being but a moonish youth, grieve, be effeminate, changeable, longing and liking, proud, fantastical, apish, shallow, inconstant, full of tears, full of smiles, for every passion something and for no passion truly anything,

405 as boys and women are for the most part cattle of this colour: would now like him, now loathe him: then entertain him, then forswear him: now weep for him, then spit at him; that I drave my suitor from his mad humour of love to a living humour of madness,

410 which was, to forswear the full stream of the world, and to live in a nook merely monastic. And thus I cured him, and this way will I take upon me to wash your liver as clean as a sound sheep's heart, that there shall not be one spot of love in't.

415 **ORLANDO** I would not be cured, youth.

ROSALIND I would cure you, if you would but call me Rosalind and come every day to my cote and woo me.

ORLANDO Now, by the faith of my love, I will. Tell me

420 where it is.

ROSALIND Go with me to it and I'll show it you, and by the way you shall tell me where in the forest you live. Will you go?

ORLANDO With all my heart, good youth.

425 **ROSALIND** Nay, you must call me Rosalind.— Come, sister, will you go?   *Exeunt*

Act 3 Scene 3   *running scene 9 continues*

Enter Clown [Touchstone], Audrey and Jaques [behind]

TOUCHSTONE   Come apace, good Audrey. I will fetch up your goats, Audrey. And how, Audrey, am I the man yet? Doth my simple feature content you?

AUDREY Your features? Lord warrant us! What features?

---

401 **moonish** changeable   402 **fantastical** fanciful, impulsive   **apish** foolish   405 **cattle** ... **colour** beasts of this kind   407 **entertain** welcome, treat well   **forswear** deny, reject   408 **that** so that   **drave** drove   409 **living** genuine   411 **merely** utterly   413 **liver** thought to be the seat of the passions   **sound** healthy   417 **cote** cottage   421 **by** on   3.3   1 **apace** quickly   2 **how** what   3 **simple feature** plain appearance (Audrey may understand 'specific part/penis')   4 **warrant** protect

5 **TOUCHSTONE** I am here with thee and thy goats, as the most capricious poet, honest Ovid, was among the Goths.

JAQUES O, knowledge ill-inhabited, worse than Jove in a thatched house.   *Aside*

10 **TOUCHSTONE** When a man's verses cannot be understood, nor a man's good wit seconded with the forward child, understanding, it strikes a man more dead than a great reckoning in a little room. Truly, I would the gods had made thee poetical.

15 **AUDREY** I do not know what 'poetical' is. Is it honest in deed and word? Is it a true thing?

TOUCHSTONE No, truly, for the truest poetry is the most feigning, and lovers are given to poetry, and what they swear in poetry may be said as lovers, they do

20 feign.

AUDREY Do you wish then that the gods had made me poetical?

TOUCHSTONE I do truly, for thou swear'st to me thou art honest. Now if thou wert a poet, I might have some

25 hope thou didst feign.

AUDREY Would you not have me honest?

TOUCHSTONE No, truly, unless thou wert hard-favoured, for honesty coupled to beauty is to have honey a sauce to sugar.

30 **JAQUES** A material fool!   *Aside*

AUDREY Well, I am not fair, and therefore I pray the gods make me honest.

TOUCHSTONE Truly, and to cast away honesty upon a foul slut were to put good meat into an unclean dish.

35 **AUDREY** I am not a slut, though I thank the gods I am foul.

TOUCHSTONE Well, praised be the gods for thy foulness; sluttishness may come hereafter. But be it as it may

---

6 capricious lascivious, fickle (from the Latin *caper* meaning 'goat'; the word play is reinforced by **goats/ Goths** having similar pronunciations)   **Ovid … Goths** Roman poet **Ovid**, author of *The Art of Love*, was banished to live among the **Goths**; he complained that they did not understand his **verses**   **8 ill-inhabited** poorly lodged   **Jove … house** having been turned away by others, the disguised **Jove** and his son Mercury were welcomed into the humble dwelling of Philemon and Baucis   **11 seconded** backed, supported **12 forward** precocious   **13 great … room** large bill for insubstantial accommodation; some critics see a reference to the 1593 tavern murder of playwright Christopher Marlowe, supposedly the result of a dispute about the bill   **15 honest** respectable/genuine   **18 feigning** imaginative/deceitful   **24 honest** truthful/ chaste   **27 hard-favoured** ugly   **30 material** meaningful, full of matter/concerned with earthly things **34 foul** loathsome/filthy/ugly   **slut** woman of slovenly habits/kitchen maid/whore   **meat** food (plays on the sense of 'penis')   **dish** plays on the sense of 'vagina'

be, I will marry thee, and to that end I have been
40   with Sir Oliver Martext, the vicar of the next village,
who hath promised to meet me in this place of the
forest and to couple us.

JAQUES I would fain see this meeting.   *Aside*

AUDREY Well, the gods give us joy!

45 TOUCHSTONE Amen. A man may, if he were of a fearful
heart, stagger in this attempt, for here we have no
temple but the wood, no assembly but horn-beasts.
But what though? Courage! As horns are odious,
they are necessary. It is said, 'many a man knows no
50   end of his goods'. Right. Many a man has good horns,
and knows no end of them. Well, that is the dowry of
his wife: 'tis none of his own getting. Horns? Even so.
Poor men alone? No, no: the noblest deer hath them
as huge as the rascal. Is the single man therefore
55   blessed? No: as a walled town is more worthier than
a village, so is the forehead of a married man more
honourable than the bare brow of a bachelor. And by
how much defence is better than no skill, by so much
is a horn more precious than to want.

Enter Sir Oliver Martext

60   Here comes Sir Oliver.— Sir Oliver Martext, you are
well met. Will you dispatch us here under this tree,
or shall we go with you to your chapel?

SIR OLIVER Is there none here to give the woman?

TOUCHSTONE I will not take her on gift of any man.

65 SIR OLIVER Truly, she must be given, or the marriage is
not lawful.

JAQUES Proceed, proceed I'll give her.   *Steps forward*

TOUCHSTONE Good even, good Master What-ye-call't.
How do you, sir? You are very well met. God 'ild you
70   for your last company, I am very glad to see you.
Even a toy in hand here, sir. Nay, pray be covered.

JAQUES Will you be married, motley?

---

40 Sir Oliver Martext 'Sir' was sometimes used for priests who were not university graduates; **Martext** (mar-text) suggests an uneducated priest who could not expound upon the Scriptures **next** nearest
42 couple marry (plays on the sense of 'get us to have sex') **43 fain** willingly **meeting** encounter/sexual union **46 stagger** falter **47 assembly** congregation **horn-beasts** suggestive of cuckolds **48 what though** what of it **49 necessary** inevitable **knows … goods** i.e. is very well off **53 deer** plays on the sense of 'dear' **54 rascal** young or inferior deer in a herd/ordinary husband **55 walled** i.e. fortified
58 defence possibly plays on type of fortification known as 'hornwork' **59 to want** be lacking
61 dispatch us settle (i.e. marry) **64 on** as the **68 What-ye-call't** probably a joking reluctance to say 'Jaques' (i.e. 'jakes' meaning 'lavatory') **69 'ild** yield (i.e. reward) **70 last** most recent (i.e. present)
71 toy in hand trifle to attend to **covered** i.e. put on your (respectfully removed) hat

TOUCHSTONE As the ox hath his bow, sir, the horse his
  curb and the falcon her bells, so man hath his desires,
75 and as pigeons bill, so wedlock would be nibbling.
JAQUES And will you, being a man of your breeding, be
  married under a bush like a beggar? Get you to
  church, and have a good priest that can tell you
  what marriage is: this fellow will but join you
80 together as they join wainscot, then one of you will
  prove a shrunk panel and, like green timber, warp,
  warp.
TOUCHSTONE I am not in the mind but I were better to   *Aside*
  be married of him than of another, for he is not
85 like to marry me well, and not being well married, it
  will be a good excuse for me hereafter to leave my
  wife.
JAQUES Go thou with me, and let me counsel thee.
TOUCHSTONE Come, sweet Audrey:
90 We must be married, or we must live in bawdry.
  Farewell, good Master Oliver. Not —
    'O sweet Oliver, O brave Oliver,
    Leave me not behind thee'
  but —
95   'Wind away,
    Begone, I say,
    I will not to wedding with thee.'
SIR OLIVER 'Tis no matter; ne'er a fantastical knave of
  them all shall flout me out of my calling.
              Exeunt [separately]

Act 3 Scene 4   *running scene 9 continues*

Enter Rosalind and Celia

ROSALIND Never talk to me. I will weep.
CELIA Do, I prithee, but yet have the grace to consider
  that tears do not become a man.
ROSALIND But have I not cause to weep?
5 **CELIA** As good cause as one would desire: therefore weep.
ROSALIND His very hair is of the dissembling colour.

73 **bow** yoke 74 **curb** restraining strap attached to the bit **bells** attached to the falcon's leg 75 **bill**
stroke beak with beak **nibbling** having sex/seizing 80 **wainscot** wooden panelling 81 **green** not dried
thoroughly/unseasoned **warp** shrink/go wrong 83 **I … but** I am inclined to think that 84 **of** by
85 **like** likely **well** properly 90 **bawdry** lewdness 92 **'O … thee'** lines from a lost Elizabethan ballad,
originally paired with a reply; Touchstone rejects the lines of the abandoned woman, in favour of the
dismissive answer **brave** fine worthy 95 **Wind** wend, go 98 **fantastical** capricious, mad 99 **flout**
mock/jeer 3.4 6 **dissembling … Judas** i.e. reddish, traditionally the hair colour of **Judas**, the disciple
who betrayed Christ with a kiss **dissembling** deceitful

CELIA Something browner than Judas'. Marry, his kisses
are Judas' own children.

ROSALIND I'faith, his hair is of a good colour.

10 **CELIA** An excellent colour, your chestnut was ever the
only colour.

ROSALIND And his kissing is as full of sanctity as the
touch of holy bread.

CELIA He hath bought a pair of cast lips of Diana. A nun

15 of winter's sisterhood kisses not more religiously, the
very ice of chastity is in them.

ROSALIND But why did he swear he would come this
morning, and comes not?

CELIA Nay, certainly, there is no truth in him.

20 **ROSALIND** Do you think so?

CELIA Yes, I think he is not a pick-purse nor a horse-
stealer, but for his verity in love, I do think him as
concave as a covered goblet or a worm-eaten nut.

ROSALIND Not true in love?

25 **CELIA** Yes, when he is in, but I think he is not in.

ROSALIND You have heard him swear downright he was.

CELIA 'Was' is not 'is'. Besides, the oath of a lover is no
stronger than the word of a tapster: they are both the
confirmer of false reckonings. He attends here in the

30 forest on the duke your father.

ROSALIND I met the duke yesterday and had much
question with him: he asked me of what parentage I
was; I told him, of as good as he, so he laughed and
let me go. But what talk we of fathers, when there is

35 such a man as Orlando?

CELIA O, that's a brave man! He writes brave verses,
speaks brave words, swears brave oaths and breaks
them bravely, quite traverse, athwart the heart of his
lover, as a puny tilter, that spurs his horse but on one

40 side, breaks his staff like a noble goose; but all's brave
that youth mounts and folly guides. Who comes
here?

---

7 his ... children refers to the kiss with which Judas betrayed Christ   **10 your** this   **11 only** i.e. most
desirable   **13 holy bread** bread blessed and distributed to those who had not taken Communion; after the
Reformation, bread provided for the Eucharist   **14 cast** sculpted/cast-off/chaste   **Diana** goddess of
chastity   **15 of winter's sisterhood** i.e. sworn to coldness   **22 verity** sincerity   **23 concave** hollow
covered goblet empty drinking vessel (covered when not in use)   **28 tapster** barman, tavern keeper
29 reckonings personal esteem/bills   **32 question** conversation   **38 traverse** crosswise/poorly aimed and
broken across (jousting term)   **39 puny tilter** insignificant, petty jouster   **40 goose** fool

Enter Corin

CORIN Mistress and master, you have oft inquired
After the shepherd that complained of love,
45   Who you saw sitting by me on the turf,
Praising the proud disdainful shepherdess
That was his mistress.

CELIA Well, and what of him?

CORIN If you will see a pageant truly played,
50   Between the pale complexion of true love
And the red glow of scorn and proud disdain,
Go hence a little and I shall conduct you,
If you will mark it.

ROSALIND O, come, let us remove:
55   The sight of lovers feedeth those in love.
Bring us to this sight, and you shall say
I'll prove a busy actor in their play.   *Exeunt*

Act 3 Scene 5

running scene 9 continues

Enter Silvius and Phoebe

SILVIUS Sweet Phoebe, do not scorn me, do not, Phoebe.
Say that you love me not, but say not so
In bitterness. The common executioner,
Whose heart th'accustomed sight of death makes hard,
5   Falls not the axe upon the humbled neck
But first begs pardon: will you sterner be
Than he that dies and lives by bloody drops?

Enter Rosalind, Celia and Corin   *They stand aside*

PHOEBE I would not be thy executioner.
I fly thee, for I would not injure thee.
10   Thou tell'st me there is murder in mine eye:
'Tis pretty, sure, and very probable,
That eyes, that are the frail'st and softest things,
Who shut their coward gates on atomies,
Should be called tyrants, butchers, murderers.
15   Now I do frown on thee with all my heart,
And if mine eyes can wound, now let them kill thee.
Now counterfeit to swoon, why now fall down,

---

44 **complained of** lamented over   49 **pageant** spectacle, scene   53 **mark** observe   54 **remove** move
3.5   5 **Falls** lets fall   6 **But … pardon** without begging pardon first (a traditional practice)   7 **he …
lives** the executioner who earns his living until he dies   11 **pretty** ingenious   13 **coward gates** i.e. eyelids
atomies atoms, specks   17 **counterfeit** pretend

Or if thou canst not, O, for shame, for shame,
Lie not, to say mine eyes are murderers.

20 Now show the wound mine eye hath made in thee:
Scratch thee but with a pin, and there remains
Some scar of it. Lean but upon a rush,
The cicatrice and capable impressure
Thy palm some moment keeps. But now mine eyes,

25 Which I have darted at thee, hurt thee not,
Nor, I am sure, there is no force in eyes
That can do hurt.

SILVIUS O dear Phoebe, If ever — as that ever may be
        near —
You meet in some fresh cheek the power of fancy,

30 Then shall you know the wounds invisible
That love's keen arrows make.

PHOEBE But till that time
Come not thou near me: and when that time comes,
Afflict me with thy mocks, pity me not,

35 As till that time I shall not pity thee.

ROSALIND And why, I pray you? Who might be your   *Steps forward*
        mother,
That you insult, exult, and all at once,
Over the wretched? What though you have no
        beauty —
As, by my faith, I see no more in you

40 Than without candle may go dark to bed —
Must you be therefore proud and pitiless?
Why, what means this? Why do you look on me?
I see no more in you than in the ordinary
Of nature's sale-work. 'Od's my little life,

45 I think she means to tangle my eyes too!
No, faith, proud mistress, hope not after it:
'Tis not your inky brows, your black silk hair,
Your bugle eyeballs, nor your cheek of cream
That can entame my spirits to your worship.

50 You foolish shepherd, wherefore do you follow her,   *To Silvius*
Like foggy south, puffing with wind and rain?
You are a thousand times a properer man
Than she a woman. 'Tis such fools as you

---

22 rush waterside plant   **23 cicatrice** scar   **capable impressure** palpable impression   **29 fancy** love
31 keen sharp   **38 What though** what does it matter   **40 Than … bed** i.e. than ought to go to bed in
darkness so that your lover will not see you   **43 ordinary** common condition   **44 sale-work** ready-made
goods of inferior quality   **'Od's** (may) God save   **45 tangle** ensnare   **48 bugle** glass beads, usually black
51 south south wind   **wind and rain** i.e. sighs and tears   **52 properer** more handsome, finer

That makes the world full of ill-favoured children.
55   'Tis not her glass but you that flatters her,
        And out of you she sees herself more proper
        Than any of her lineaments can show her.
        But mistress, know yourself: down on your knees,
        And thank heaven, fasting, for a good man's love;
60   For I must tell you friendly in your ear,
        Sell when you can, you are not for all markets.
        Cry the man mercy, love him, take his offer:
        Foul is most foul, being foul to be a scoffer.
        So take her to thee, shepherd. Fare you well.
65 PHOEBE Sweet youth, I pray you chide a year together:
        I had rather hear you chide than this man woo.
    ROSALIND He's fallen in love with your foulness— and   *Aside or to*
        she'll fall in love with my anger. If it be so, as fast as   *Phoebe/To*
        she answers thee with frowning looks, I'll sauce her   *Silvius*
70   with bitter words.— Why look you so upon me?   *To Phoebe*
    PHOEBE For no ill will I bear you.

    ROSALIND I pray you do not fall in love with me,
        For I am falser than vows made in wine.
        Besides, I like you not. If you will know my house,
75   'Tis at the tuft of olives, here hard by.
        Will you go, sister? Shepherd, ply her hard.
        Come, sister. Shepherdess, look on him better,
        And be not proud: though all the world could see,
        None could be so abused in sight as he.
80   Come, to our flock. *Exeunt [Rosalind, Celia and Corin]*
    PHOEBE Dead Shepherd, now I find thy saw of might,
        'Who ever loved that loved not at first sight?'
    SILVIUS Sweet Phoebe—
    PHOEBE Ha, what say'st thou, Silvius?
85 SILVIUS Sweet Phoebe, pity me.
    PHOEBE Why, I am sorry for thee, gentle Silvius.
    SILVIUS Wherever sorrow is, relief would be.
        If you do sorrow at my grief in love,
        By giving love your sorrow and my grief
90   Were both extermined.
    PHOEBE Thou hast my love. Is not that neighbourly?

---

55 glass mirror   **57 lineaments** facial features   **62 Cry** beg   **63 Foul … scoffer** ugliness is most
hideous when it is rough and abusive   **65 together** uninterruptedly   **69 sauce** rebuke   **73 in wine** when
drunk   **75 tuft of olives** clump of olive trees   **hard** close   **76 ply** urge   **79 abused in sight** deceived in
his perception   **81 Dead Shepherd** i.e. Christopher Marlowe (murdered in 1593), from whose poem *Hero
and Leander* the ensuing quotation is taken   **saw** maxim, saying   **of might** powerful, convincing
90 extermined exterminated   **91 love … neighbourly** refers to the biblical instruction to 'love thy
neighbour as thyself'

SILVIUS I would have you.

PHOEBE Why, that were covetousness.

Silvius, the time was that I hated thee;

95 And yet it is not that I bear thee love,

But since that thou canst talk of love so well,

Thy company, which erst was irksome to me,

I will endure; and I'll employ thee too.

But do not look for further recompense

100 Than thine own gladness that thou art employed.

SILVIUS So holy and so perfect is my love,

And I in such a poverty of grace,

That I shall think it a most plenteous crop

To glean the broken ears after the man

105 That the main harvest reaps. Loose now and then

A scattered smile, and that I'll live upon.

PHOEBE Know'st thou the youth that spoke to me

erewhile?

SILVIUS Not very well, but I have met him oft,

And he hath bought the cottage and the bounds

110 That the old carlot once was master of.

PHOEBE Think not I love him, though I ask for him:

'Tis but a peevish boy, yet he talks well.

But what care I for words? Yet words do well

When he that speaks them pleases those that hear.

115 It is a pretty youth, not very pretty.

But sure he's proud, and yet his pride becomes him;

He'll make a proper man. The best thing in him

Is his complexion. And faster than his tongue

Did make offence his eye did heal it up.

120 He is not very tall, yet for his years he's tall.

His leg is but so-so, and yet 'tis well.

There was a pretty redness in his lip,

A little riper and more lusty red

Than that mixed in his cheek. 'Twas just the

difference

125 Betwixt the constant red and mingled damask.

There be some women, Silvius, had they marked him

In parcels as I did, would have gone near

To fall in love with him. But, for my part,

---

93 covetousness refers to the Tenth Commandment which prohibits coveting one's neighbour's goods
97 erst formerly   **102 poverty** deficiency   **104 ears** i.e. of corn   **107 erewhile** a short time ago
109 bounds land   **110 carlot** churl, peasant   **112 peevish** silly, foolish/spiteful   **118 complexion** face/
appearance   **123 lusty** lively   **125 constant** unchanging   **damask** pink or light red   **127 parcels**
bits, parts

I love him not nor hate him not. And yet
130   Have more cause to hate him than to love him:
For what had he to do to chide at me?
He said mine eyes were black and my hair black,
And, now I am remembered, scorned at me.
I marvel why I answered not again.
135   But that's all one: omittance is no quittance.
I'll write to him a very taunting letter,
And thou shalt bear it. Wilt thou, Silvius?
SILVIUS Phoebe, with all my heart.
PHOEBE I'll write it straight:
140   The matter's in my head and in my heart.
I will be bitter with him and passing short.
Go with me, Silvius.   *Exeunt*

Act 4 Scene 1   *running scene 9 continues*

Enter Rosalind, and Celia and Jaques
JAQUES   I prithee, pretty youth, let me be better
acquainted with thee.
ROSALIND They say you are a melancholy fellow.
JAQUES I am so. I do love it better than laughing.
5   **ROSALIND** Those that are in extremity of either are
abominable fellows, and betray themselves to every
modern censure worse than drunkards.
JAQUES Why, 'tis good to be sad and say nothing.
ROSALIND Why then, 'tis good to be a post.
10   **JAQUES** I have neither the scholar's melancholy, which
is emulation, nor the musician's, which is fantastical,
nor the courtier's, which is proud, nor the soldier's,
which is ambitious, nor the lawyer's, which is politic,
nor the lady's, which is nice, nor the lover's, which is
15   all these: but it is a melancholy of mine own,
compounded of many simples, extracted from many
objects, and indeed the sundry contemplation of my
travels, in which my often rumination wraps me in a
most humorous sadness.
20   **ROSALIND** A traveller! By my faith, you have great
reason to be sad: I fear you have sold your own lands

133 am remembered remember   **134 again** back   **135 omittance** ... **quittance** not having done so
does not mean I never shall   **139 straight** straight away   **141 passing** excessively   **4.1**   **6 betray**
expose   **7 modern censure** commonplace judgement   **8 sad** Rosalind quibbles on the sense of 'massive,
solid'   **9 post** stout pole   **11 emulation** envy of those who are superior   **fantastical** fanciful, extravagant
13 politic crafty   **14 nice** fastidious   **16 simples** ingredients (literally, medicinal herbs)   **17 sundry**
varied   **18 often** frequent   **19 humorous** moody

to see other men's; then to have seen much and to
have nothing is to have rich eyes and poor hands.

JAQUES Yes, I have gained my experience.

Enter Orlando

25 ROSALIND And your experience makes you sad: I had
rather have a fool to make me merry than experience
to make me sad, and to travel for it too.

ORLANDO Good day and happiness, dear Rosalind!

JAQUES Nay, then, God buy you, an you talk in blank
30 verse.   [*Exit*]

ROSALIND Farewell, Monsieur Traveller: look you lisp
and wear strange suits, disable all the benefits of your
own country, be out of love with your nativity, and
almost chide God for making you that countenance
35 you are; or I will scarce think you have swam in a
gondola. Why, how now, Orlando, where have you
been all this while? You a lover? An you serve me
such another trick, never come in my sight more.

ORLANDO My fair Rosalind, I come within an hour of my
40 promise.

ROSALIND Break an hour's promise in love? He that will
divide a minute into a thousand parts and break but
a part of the thousand part of a minute in the affairs
of love, it may be said of him that Cupid hath clapped
45 him o'th'shoulder, but I'll warrant him heart-whole.

ORLANDO Pardon me, dear Rosalind.

ROSALIND Nay, an you be so tardy, come no more in my
sight. I had as lief be wooed of a snail.

ORLANDO Of a snail?

50 ROSALIND Ay, of a snail, for though he comes slowly, he
carries his house on his head; a better jointure, I
think, than you make a woman. Besides, he brings
his destiny with him.

ORLANDO What's that?

55 ROSALIND Why, horns, which such as you are fain to be
beholding to your wives for: but he comes armed in
his fortune and prevents the slander of his wife.

---

27 **travel** voyage/take pains   29 **an** if   31 **lisp** put on a foreign accent   32 **strange suits** foreign
clothes   **disable** disparage   33 **nativity** birth (i.e. nationality)   35 **swam** floated, travelled   44 **clapped
him o'th'shoulder** merely tapped him/arrested him   45 **heart-whole** essentially unaffected, with the heart
unengaged   51 **jointure** marriage settlement that provided for the wife in the event of her husband's
death   55 **horns** of a snail/of a cuckold   **fain** obliged   56 **beholding** indebted   **armed ... fortune** i.e. as
a **snail**, naturally possessed of horns   57 **prevents the slander** forestalls the disrepute

ORLANDO Virtue is no horn-maker, and my Rosalind is
virtuous.

60   **ROSALIND** And I am your Rosalind.

CELIA It pleases him to call you so, but he hath a
Rosalind of a better leer than you.

ROSALIND Come, woo me, woo me, for now I am in a
holiday humour and like enough to consent. What
65   would you say to me now, an I were your very very
Rosalind?

ORLANDO I would kiss before I spoke.

ROSALIND Nay, you were better speak first, and when
you were gravelled for lack of matter, you might take
70   occasion to kiss. Very good orators, when they are
out, they will spit. And for lovers lacking — God
warn us! — matter, the cleanliest shift is to kiss.

ORLANDO How if the kiss be denied?

ROSALIND Then she puts you to entreaty, and there
75   begins new matter.

ORLANDO Who could be out, being before his beloved
mistress?

ROSALIND Marry, that should you, if I were your
mistress, or I should think my honesty ranker than
80   my wit.

ORLANDO What, of my suit?

ROSALIND Not out of your apparel, and yet out of your
suit. Am not I your Rosalind?

ORLANDO I take some joy to say you are, because I
85   would be talking of her.

ROSALIND Well, in her person, I say I will not have you.

ORLANDO Then, in mine own person, I die.

ROSALIND No, faith, die by attorney. The poor world is
almost six thousand years old, and in all this time
90   there was not any man died in his own person,
videlicet, in a love-cause. Troilus had his brains
dashed out with a Grecian club, yet he did what he
could to die before, and he is one of the patterns of
love. Leander, he would have lived many a fair year

62 **leer** complexion, appearance   64 **holiday humour** festive mood   65 **very** true   69 **gravelled**
stumped   71 **out** at a loss for words   72 **warn** protect, warrant   **cleanliest shift** most skilful
measure   76 **Who … out** Rosalind goes on to play with the sense of 'denied vaginal entry'   79 **honesty**
chastity   **ranker** more corrupt   81 **of my suit** out of my courtship/clothing   88 **by attorney** by proxy (as
opposed to 'in person')   91 *videlicet* 'namely' (Latin)   **Troilus** lover of Cressida, who proved faithless to
him; he was killed by Achilles during the Trojan war   93 **die** may play on the sense of 'experience
orgasm'   **patterns** models   94 **Leander** in classical mythology, Leander regularly swam across the river
Hellespont to see his lover **Hero of Sestos**, until one night he drowned

95   though Hero had turned nun, if it had not been for a
        hot midsummer night, for, good youth, he went but
        forth to wash him in the Hellespont and being taken
        with the cramp was drowned. And the foolish
        chroniclers of that age found it was 'Hero of
100   Sestos'. But these are all lies: men have died from
        time to time and worms have eaten them, but not for
        love.

ORLANDO I would not have my right Rosalind of this
        mind, for I protest her frown might kill me.

105 **ROSALIND** By this hand, it will not kill a fly. But come,
        now I will be your Rosalind in a more coming-on
        disposition. And ask me what you will, I will grant it.

ORLANDO Then love me, Rosalind.

ROSALIND Yes, faith, will I, Fridays and Saturdays and
110   all.

ORLANDO And wilt thou have me?

ROSALIND Ay, and twenty such.

ORLANDO What sayest thou?

ROSALIND Are you not good?

115 **ORLANDO** I hope so.

ROSALIND Why then, can one desire too much of a good
        thing? Come, sister, you shall be the priest and marry
        us. Give me your hand, Orlando. What do you say,
        sister?

120 **ORLANDO** Pray thee marry us.

CELIA I cannot say the words.

ROSALIND You must begin, 'Will you, Orlando —'

CELIA Go to. Will you, Orlando, have to wife this
        Rosalind?

125 **ORLANDO** I will.

ROSALIND Ay, but when?

ORLANDO Why now, as fast as she can marry us.

ROSALIND Then you must say 'I take thee, Rosalind, for
        wife.'

130 **ORLANDO** I take thee, Rosalind, for wife.

ROSALIND I might ask you for your commission, but I do
        take thee, Orlando, for my husband. There's a girl
        goes before the priest, and certainly a woman's
        thought runs before her actions.

---

95 though even if   **99 found it** concluded the cause   **103 right** real   **106 coming-on** agreeable,
encouraging   **109 Fridays and Saturdays** days on which Christians abstained from eating meat
112 twenty twenty more   **123 Go to** expression of impatient dismissal   **127 fast** firmly/quickly
131 commission authority   **133 goes** … **priest** proceeds with the service more quickly than the priest

135 ORLANDO So do all thoughts: they are winged.

ROSALIND Now tell me how long you would have her after you have possessed her.

ORLANDO Forever and a day.

ROSALIND Say 'a day', without the 'ever'. No, no,
140 Orlando. Men are April when they woo, December when they wed. Maids are May when they are maids, but the sky changes when they are wives. I will be more jealous of thee than a Barbary cock-pigeon over his hen, more clamorous than a parrot against rain,
145 more new-fangled than an ape, more giddy in my desires than a monkey. I will weep for nothing, like Diana in the fountain, and I will do that when you are disposed to be merry. I will laugh like a hyena, and that when thou art inclined to sleep.

150 ORLANDO But will my Rosalind do so?

ROSALIND By my life, she will do as I do.

ORLANDO O, but she is wise.

ROSALIND Or else she could not have the wit to do this: the wiser, the waywarder. Make the doors upon a
155 woman's wit and it will out at the casement. Shut that and 'twill out at the key-hole. Stop that, 'twill fly with the smoke out at the chimney.

ORLANDO A man that had a wife with such a wit, he might say 'Wit, whither wilt?'

160 ROSALIND Nay, you might keep that check for it till you met your wife's wit going to your neighbour's bed.

ORLANDO And what wit could wit have to excuse that?

ROSALIND Marry, to say she came to seek you there. You shall never take her without her answer, unless you
165 take her without her tongue. O, that woman that cannot make her fault her husband's occasion, let her never nurse her child herself, for she will breed it like a fool.

ORLANDO For these two hours, Rosalind, I will leave
170 thee.

ROSALIND Alas, dear love, I cannot lack thee two hours.

---

137 possessed married/had sex with   **143 Barbary cock-pigeon** male pigeon thought to be from Barbary (north Africa)   **144 against** before, in anticipation of   **145 new-fangled** fond of novelty, easily distracted by new things   **147 Diana … fountain** the goddess was a fairly popular figure to adorn fountains   **154 waywarder** more obstinate, wilful   **Make** shut   **155 wit** possible play on the sense of 'genitals'   **casement** window   **159 'Wit, whither wilt?'** Wit, where are you going? (proverbial; refers to one with 'wandering' wits)   **160 check** rebuke   **164 take** catch/possess sexually   **166 fault** error (plays on the sense of 'vagina')   **husband's occasion** excuse to attack her husband (plays on the sense of 'sexual business, opportunity for use')   **167 nurse** breastfeed

ORLANDO I must attend the duke at dinner. By two
o'clock I will be with thee again.

ROSALIND Ay, go your ways, go your ways. I knew what
175 you would prove: my friends told me as much, and I
thought no less. That flattering tongue of yours won
me. 'Tis but one cast away, and so, come, death! Two
o'clock is your hour?

ORLANDO Ay, sweet Rosalind.

180 **ROSALIND** By my troth, and in good earnest, and so God
mend me, and by all pretty oaths that are not
dangerous, if you break one jot of your promise or
come one minute behind your hour, I will think you
the most pathetical break-promise and the most
185 hollow lover and the most unworthy of her you call
Rosalind that may be chosen out of the gross band of
the unfaithful: therefore beware my censure and
keep your promise.

ORLANDO With no less religion than if thou wert indeed
190 my Rosalind: so adieu.

ROSALIND Well, time is the old justice that examines all
such offenders, and let time try. Adieu. *Exit [Orlando]*

CELIA You have simply misused our sex in your love-
prate: we must have your doublet and hose plucked
195 over your head, and show the world what the bird
hath done to her own nest.

ROSALIND O coz, coz, coz, my pretty little coz, that thou
didst know how many fathom deep I am in love! But
it cannot be sounded: my affection hath an unknown
200 bottom, like the Bay of Portugal.

CELIA Or rather, bottomless, that as fast as you pour
affection in, it runs out.

ROSALIND No, that same wicked bastard of Venus that
was begot of thought, conceived of spleen and born of
205 madness, that blind rascally boy that abuses
everyone's eyes because his own are out, let him be
judge how deep I am in love. I'll tell thee, Aliena, I

---

177 but … away only one abandoned woman   **183 behind your hour** late   **184 pathetical** miserable,
deplorable   **186 gross** whole/inferior   **187 censure** condemnation/judgement   **189 religion** faithfulness
192 try test/judge   **193 simply misused** absolutely abused   **love-prate** love-talk   **195 what … nest**
proverbially, the bird fouls its own nest (**nest** also plays on the sense of 'vagina')   **198 fathom** six
feet   **199 sounded** measured, penetrated   **203 bastard of Venus** Cupid, son of Venus by Mars (or,
variously, Mercury or Jupiter), not by her husband Vulcan   **204 begot** conceived   **thought** fancy
spleen impulse   **205 blind** Cupid was traditionally depicted as sightless   **abuses** deceives

cannot be out of the sight of Orlando: I'll go find a
shadow and sigh till he come.

210   CELIA And I'll sleep.   *Exeunt*

Act 4 Scene 2   *running scene 10*

Enter Jaques and Lords [as] foresters

JAQUES Which is he that killed the deer?

FIRST LORD Sir, it was I.

JAQUES Let's present him to the duke like a Roman
conqueror. And it would do well to set the deer's
5   horns upon his head for a branch of victory. Have
you no song, forester, for this purpose?

SECOND LORD Yes, sir.

JAQUES Sing it: 'tis no matter how it be in tune, so it
make noise enough.
Music, song

10   LORDS   What shall he have that killed the deer?
His leather skin and horns to wear.
Then sing him home,
The rest shall bear this burden:
Take thou no scorn to wear the horn,
15   It was a crest ere thou wast born,
Thy father's father wore it,
And thy father bore it.
The horn, the horn, the lusty horn,
Is not a thing to laugh to scorn.   *Exeunt*

Act 4 Scene 3   *running scene 11*

Enter Rosalind and Celia

ROSALIND How say you now? Is it not past two o'clock?
And here much Orlando!

CELIA I warrant you, with pure love and troubled brain,
he hath ta'en his bow and arrows and is gone forth to
5   sleep.
Enter Silvius   *With a letter*
Look, who comes here.

SILVIUS My errand is to you, fair youth.   *To Rosalind*
My gentle Phoebe bid me give you this:
I know not the contents, but — as I guess

209 **shadow** shade   4.2   **5 branch** wreath (plays on the sense of 'subdivision of a deer's horn')   **13 bear
this burden** sing this refrain/bear the cuckold's horns   **18 lusty** lively/lustful   4.3   **2 here much
Orlando** 'much Orlando there is to be seen here' (said in irony)

10   By the stern brow and waspish action
        Which she did use as she was writing of it —
        It bears an angry tenor; pardon me,
        I am but as a guiltless messenger.

ROSALIND Patience herself would startle at this letter   *Reads letter*
15   And play the swaggerer. Bear this, bear all:
        She says I am not fair, that I lack manners.
        She calls me proud, and that she could not love me,
        Were man as rare as phoenix. 'Od's my will!
        Her love is not the hare that I do hunt.
20   Why writes she so to me? Well, shepherd, well,
        This is a letter of your own device.

SILVIUS No, I protest, I know not the contents.
        Phoebe did write it.

ROSALIND Come, come, you are a fool
25   And turned into the extremity of love.
        I saw her hand. She has a leathern hand,
        A freestone-coloured hand. I verily did think
        That her old gloves were on, but 'twas her hands.
        She has a huswife's hand, but that's no matter:
30   I say she never did invent this letter,
        This is a man's invention and his hand.

SILVIUS Sure, it is hers.

ROSALIND Why, 'tis a boisterous and a cruel style.
        A style for challengers. Why, she defies me,
35   Like Turk to Christian. Women's gentle brain
        Could not drop forth such giant-rude invention,
        Such Ethiope words, blacker in their effect
        Than in their countenance. Will you hear the letter?

SILVIUS So please you, for I never heard it yet,
40   Yet heard too much of Phoebe's cruelty.

ROSALIND She Phoebes me. Mark how the tyrant writes:
          'Art thou god to shepherd turned,   *Read*
          That a maiden's heart hath burned?'
        Can a woman rail thus?
45 **SILVIUS** Call you this railing?

ROSALIND 'Why, thy godhead laid apart,   *Read*
          Warr'st thou with a woman's heart?'

---

10 waspish spiteful   **11 use** employ, adopt   **15 swaggerer** quarreller, blusterer   **18 phoenix** mythical Arabian bird that was consumed by fire every 500 years, then resurrected from the ashes; only one existed at a time   **'Od's** God is   **21 device** devising   **22 protest** declare, vow   **26 leathern** leathery, rough   **27 freestone-coloured** brownish-yellow   **freestone** sandstone or limestone   **verily** truly   **29 huswife's** housewife's (i.e. hard and coarse)   **31 invention** style   **hand** handwriting   **33 boisterous** violent, rough   **36 giant-rude** extremely rough   **37 Ethiope** Ethiopian (i.e. black)   **41 Phoebes** i.e. is cruel to   **46 apart** aside

Did you ever hear such railing?
              'Whiles the eye of man did woo me,
50   That could do no vengeance to me.'
Meaning me a beast.
              'If the scorn of your bright eyne
              Have power to raise such love in mine,
              Alack, in me what strange effect
55   Would they work in mild aspect!
              Whiles you chid me, I did love.
              How then might your prayers move!
              He that brings this love to thee
              Little knows this love in me;
60   And by him seal up thy mind,
              Whether that thy youth and kind
              Will the faithful offer take
              Of me and all that I can make,
              Or else by him my love deny,
65   And then I'll study how to die.'

SILVIUS Call you this chiding?

CELIA Alas, poor shepherd!

ROSALIND Do you pity him? No, he deserves no pity. Wilt
thou love such a woman? What, to make thee an
70   instrument and play false strains upon thee? Not to
be endured! Well, go your way to her, for I see love
hath made thee a tame snake, and say this to her:
that if she love me, I charge her to love thee. If she
will not, I will never have her unless thou entreat for
75   her. If you be a true lover, hence, and not a word, for
here comes more company.   *Exit Silvius*
Enter Oliver

OLIVER Good morrow, fair ones: pray you, if you know,
Where in the purlieus of this forest stands
A sheep-cote fenced about with olive trees?

80   **CELIA** West of this place, down in the neighbour bottom.
The rank of osiers by the murmuring stream
Left on your right hand brings you to the place.
But at this hour the house doth keep itself,
There's none within.

---

50 **vengeance** harm   52 **eyne** eyes   55 **aspect** gaze (with astrological connotations)   57 **prayers**
entreaties   60 **by … mind** i.e. employ Silvius to bring me your decision in a sealed letter   61 **kind**
nature   63 **make** offer   70 **instrument** tool/musical instrument   **strains** melodies   72 **snake** i.e. drudge
78 **purlieus** borders   80 **neighbour bottom** nearby valley   81 **rank of osiers** row of willows
82 **Left** passed by

85 **OLIVER** If that an eye may profit by a tongue,
         Then should I know you by description,
         Such garments and such years: 'The boy is fair,
         Of female favour, and bestows himself
         Like a ripe sister. The woman low
90   And browner than her brother.' Are not you
         The owner of the house I did inquire for?
    CELIA It is no boast, being asked, to say we are.
    OLIVER Orlando doth commend him to you both,
         And to that youth he calls his Rosalind
95   He sends this bloody napkin. Are you he?   *Shows bloody*
    ROSALIND I am. What must we understand by this?   *handkerchief*
    OLIVER Some of my shame, if you will know of me
         What man I am, and how, and why, and where
         This handkercher was stained.
100 **CELIA** I pray you tell it.
    OLIVER When last the young Orlando parted from you,
         He left a promise to return again
         Within an hour, and pacing through the forest,
         Chewing the food of sweet and bitter fancy,
105   Lo, what befell! He threw his eye aside,
         And mark what object did present itself:
         Und'r an old oak, whose boughs were mossed
            with age
         And high top bald with dry antiquity,
         A wretched ragged man, o'ergrown with hair,
110   Lay sleeping on his back; about his neck
         A green and gilded snake had wreathed itself,
         Who with her head nimble in threats approached
         The opening of his mouth. But suddenly,
         Seeing Orlando, it unlinked itself,
115   And with indented glides did slip away
         Into a bush, under which bush's shade
         A lioness, with udders all drawn dry,
         Lay couching, head on ground, with catlike watch
         When that the sleeping man should stir; for 'tis
120   The royal disposition of that beast
         To prey on nothing that doth seem as dead.
         This seen, Orlando did approach the man
         And found it was his brother, his elder brother.

---

88 **favour** appearance/face **bestows** acquits 89 **ripe** mature/elder **low** short 93 **commend him** i.e.
offers his respectful greetings 95 **napkin** handkerchief 99 **handkercher** handkerchief 104 **fancy**
love 108 **bald** i.e. leafless 111 **gilded** gold 114 **unlinked** uncoiled 115 **indented** undulating
118 **couching** stretched out/hidden 119 **When that** for the time when

CELIA O, I have heard him speak of that same brother,
125   And he did render him the most unnatural
          That lived amongst men.
OLIVER And well he might so do,
          For well I know he was unnatural.
ROSALIND But to Orlando: did he leave him there,
130   Food to the sucked and hungry lioness?
OLIVER Twice did he turn his back and purposed so,
          But kindness, nobler ever than revenge,
          And nature, stronger than his just occasion,
          Made him give battle to the lioness,
135   Who quickly fell before him, in which hurtling
          From miserable slumber I awaked.
CELIA Are you his brother?
ROSALIND Was't you he rescued?
CELIA Was't you that did so oft contrive to kill him?
140 **OLIVER** 'Twas I, but 'tis not I. I do not shame
          To tell you what I was, since my conversion
          So sweetly tastes, being the thing I am.
ROSALIND But, for the bloody napkin?
OLIVER By and by.
145   When from the first to last betwixt us two,
          Tears our recounts had most kindly bathed,
          As how I came into that desert place:
          In brief, he led me to the gentle duke,
          Who gave me fresh array and entertainment,
150   Committing me unto my brother's love,
          Who led me instantly unto his cave,
          There stripped himself, and here upon his arm
          The lioness had torn some flesh away,
          Which all this while had bled; and now he fainted
155   And cried, in fainting, upon Rosalind.
          Brief, I recovered him, bound up his wound,
          And after some small space, being strong at heart,
          He sent me hither, stranger as I am,
          To tell this story, that you might excuse
160   His broken promise, and to give this napkin,
          Dyed in this blood, unto the shepherd youth
          That he in sport doth call his Rosalind.   *Rosalind faints*
CELIA Why, how now, Ganymede? Sweet Ganymede!
OLIVER Many will swoon when they do look on blood.

125 **render him** describe him as   129 **to** with regard to   132 **kindness** feelings of kinship   133 **just occasion** justifiable reason   135 **hurtling** tumult   143 **for** what about   146 **recounts** accounts of events **kindly** naturally/affectionately   149 **array** clothing **entertainment** welcome, provision   156 **Brief** in short **recovered** revived   157 **space** time

165 **CELIA** There is more in it. Cousin Ganymede!

OLIVER Look, he recovers.

ROSALIND I would I were at home.

CELIA We'll lead you thither.— I pray you, will you take
him by the arm?   *They get Rosalind*

170 **OLIVER** Be of good cheer, youth. You a man! You lack a   *to her feet*
man's heart.

ROSALIND I do so, I confess it. Ah, sirrah, a body would
think this was well counterfeited! I pray you tell your
brother how well I counterfeited. Heigh-ho!

175 **OLIVER** This was not counterfeit: there is too great
testimony in your complexion that it was a passion of
earnest.

ROSALIND Counterfeit, I assure you.

OLIVER Well then, take a good heart and counterfeit to
180 be a man.

ROSALIND So I do. But, i'faith, I should have been a
woman by right.

CELIA Come, you look paler and paler. Pray you draw
homewards. Good sir, go with us.

185 **OLIVER** That will I, for I must bear answer back
How you excuse my brother, Rosalind.

ROSALIND I shall devise something: but I pray you
commend my counterfeiting to him. Will you go?

Exeunt

Act 5 Scene 1   *running scene 11 continues*

Enter Clown [Touchstone] and Audrey

TOUCHSTONE We shall find a time, Audrey. Patience,
gentle Audrey.

AUDREY Faith, the priest was good enough, for all the old
gentleman's saying.

5 **TOUCHSTONE** A most wicked Sir Oliver, Audrey, a most
vile Martext. But, Audrey, there is a youth here in
the forest lays claim to you.

AUDREY Ay, I know who 'tis: he hath no interest in me
in the world. Here comes the man you mean.

Enter William

10 **TOUCHSTONE** It is meat and drink to me to see a clown.
By my troth, we that have good wits have much to
answer for. We shall be flouting: we cannot hold.

---

172 a body anyone   **176 passion of earnest** genuine emotion   **5.1   3 old gentleman's** i.e. Jaques'
8 interest in right to/share in   **10 clown** rustic   **12 flouting** mocking   **hold** resist, stop

WILLIAM Good ev'n, Audrey.

AUDREY God ye good ev'n, William.

15 **WILLIAM** And good ev'n to you, sir.

TOUCHSTONE Good ev'n, gentle friend. Cover thy head, cover thy head. Nay, prithee be covered. How old are you, friend?

WILLIAM Five and twenty, sir.

20 **TOUCHSTONE** A ripe age. Is thy name William?

WILLIAM William, sir.

TOUCHSTONE A fair name. Wast born i'th'forest here?

WILLIAM Ay, sir, I thank God.

TOUCHSTONE 'Thank God'. A good answer. Art rich?

25 **WILLIAM** Faith, sir, so-so.

TOUCHSTONE 'So-so' is good, very good, very excellent good. And yet it is not, it is but so-so. Art thou wise?

WILLIAM Ay, sir, I have a pretty wit.

TOUCHSTONE Why, thou sayest well. I do now
30 remember a saying: 'The fool doth think he is wise, but the wise man knows himself to be a fool.' The heathen philosopher, when he had a desire to eat a grape, would open his lips when he put it into his mouth, meaning thereby that grapes were made to
35 eat and lips to open. You do love this maid?

WILLIAM I do, sir.

TOUCHSTONE Give me your hand. Art thou learnèd?

WILLIAM No, sir.

TOUCHSTONE Then learn this of me: to have is to have,
40 for it is a figure in rhetoric that drink, being poured out of a cup into a glass, by filling the one doth empty the other. For all your writers do consent that *ipse* is he. Now, you are not *ipse*, for I am he.

WILLIAM Which he, sir?

45 **TOUCHSTONE** He, sir, that must marry this woman: therefore, you clown, abandon — which is in the vulgar 'leave' — the society — which in the boorish is 'company' — of this female — which in the common is 'woman', which together is: abandon the
50 society of this female, or, clown, thou perishest. Or, to thy better understanding, diest; or, to wit, I kill thee, make thee away, translate thy life into death, thy

---

14 **God ye** God give you   16 **Cover thy head** i.e. put on your hat (which William has respectfully removed)   24 **God'. A good** Touchstone may mock William's rustic accent   37 **learnèd** educated   40 **figure** figure of speech, device   42 *ipse* 'he himself' (Latin)   47 **vulgar** vernacular   **boorish** coarse speech   49 **common** vulgar tongue   51 **to wit** that is to say

55

liberty into bondage. I will deal in poison with thee, or in bastinado, or in steel; I will bandy with thee in faction; I will o'errun thee with policy. I will kill thee a hundred and fifty ways: therefore tremble and depart.

AUDREY Do, good William.

WILLIAM God rest you merry, sir.   *Exit*

Enter Corin

60

CORIN Our master and mistress seeks you. Come, away, away!

TOUCHSTONE Trip, Audrey, trip, Audrey.— I attend, I attend.   *Exeunt*

Act 5 Scene 2   *running scene 11 continues*

Enter Orlando and Oliver   *Orlando with his*

ORLANDO Is't possible that on so little acquaintance you   *arm in a sling* should like her? That but seeing, you should love her? And loving, woo? And wooing, she should grant? And will you persever to enjoy her?

5

OLIVER Neither call the giddiness of it in question, the poverty of her, the small acquaintance, my sudden wooing, nor her sudden consenting. But say with me, I love Aliena. Say with her that she loves me; consent with both that we may enjoy each other. It shall be

10

to your good, for my father's house and all the revenue that was old Sir Rowland's will I estate upon you, and here live and die a shepherd.

Enter Rosalind

ORLANDO You have my consent. Let your wedding be tomorrow: thither will I invite the duke and all's

15

contented followers. Go you and prepare Aliena; for look you, here comes my Rosalind.

ROSALIND God save you, brother.

OLIVER And you, fair 'sister'.

ROSALIND O my dear Orlando, how it grieves me to see

20

thee wear thy heart in a scarf!

ORLANDO It is my arm.

---

54 **bastinado** beating with a stick   **bandy** fight   **in faction** in insults   55 **o'errun** … **policy** overwhelm you with cunning   59 **rest** keep   62 **Trip** skip (plays on the sense of 'succumb sexually')   **attend** follow/ accompany   **5.2   4 persever** persevere   11 **estate** settle   14 **all's** all his   15 **contented** willing   17 **brother** i.e. brother-in-law   18 **'sister'** i.e. responding to Orlando calling Ganymede 'Rosalind' (unless Oliver sees through the disguise and realizes that it really is Rosalind)   20 **scarf** i.e. sling

ROSALIND I thought thy heart had been wounded with
the claws of a lion.

ORLANDO Wounded it is, but with the eyes of a lady.

25   ROSALIND Did your brother tell you how I counterfeited
to swoon when he showed me your handkerchief?

ORLANDO Ay, and greater wonders than that.

ROSALIND O, I know where you are: nay, 'tis true. There
was never anything so sudden but the fight of two
30   rams and Caesar's thrasonical brag of 'I came, saw,
and overcame.' For your brother and my sister no
sooner met but they looked, no sooner looked but
they loved, no sooner loved but they sighed, no
sooner sighed but they asked one another the reason,
35   no sooner knew the reason but they sought the
remedy: and in these degrees have they made a pair
of stairs to marriage, which they will climb
incontinent, or else be incontinent before marriage;
they are in the very wrath of love and they will
40   together: clubs cannot part them.

ORLANDO They shall be married tomorrow, and I will bid
the duke to the nuptial. But O, how bitter a thing it is
to look into happiness through another man's eyes!
By so much the more shall I tomorrow be at the
45   height of heart-heaviness, by how much I shall think
my brother happy in having what he wishes for.

ROSALIND Why then, tomorrow I cannot serve your
turn for Rosalind?

ORLANDO I can live no longer by thinking.

50   ROSALIND I will weary you then no longer with idle
talking. Know of me then, for now I speak to some
purpose, that I know you are a gentleman of good
conceit: I speak not this that you should bear a good
opinion of my knowledge, insomuch I say I know you
55   are. Neither do I labour for a greater esteem than
may in some little measure draw a belief from you, to
do yourself good and not to grace me. Believe then, if
you please, that I can do strange things: I have, since
I was three year old, conversed with a magician,

28 where you are what you mean   30 thrasonical boastful, vainglorious   36 degrees puns on the sense
of 'steps'; also refers to the rhetorical device of climax Rosalind uses as her verbs link together and move the
sentence forward   pair flight   38 incontinent at once (sense then shifts to 'unchaste')   39 wrath full
passion   41 bid invite   47 serve your turn act as a substitute (puns on the sense of 'satisfy you sexually')
53 conceit understanding, intelligence   54 insomuch inasmuch as   55 Neither … me nor am I trying
to gain greater approval from you other than that which is necessary to enable you to trust me enough to
help you; I am not seeking my own promotion

60   most profound in his art and yet not damnable. If you
      do love Rosalind so near the heart as your gesture
      cries it out, when your brother marries Aliena, shall
      you marry her. I know into what straits of fortune
      she is driven, and it is not impossible to me, if it
65   appear not inconvenient to you, to set her before
      your eyes tomorrow, human as she is, and without
      any danger.
ORLANDO Speak'st thou in sober meanings?
ROSALIND By my life, I do, which I tender dearly, though
70   I say I am a magician: therefore, put you in your best
      array, bid your friends, for if you will be married
      tomorrow, you shall, and to Rosalind, if you will.
Enter Silvius and Phoebe
      Look, here comes a lover of mine and a lover of hers.
PHOEBE Youth, you have done me much ungentleness,
75   To show the letter that I writ to you.
ROSALIND I care not if I have. It is my study
      To seem despiteful and ungentle to you.
      You are there followed by a faithful shepherd.
      Look upon him, love him: he worships you.
80 PHOEBE Good shepherd, tell this youth what 'tis to love.
SILVIUS It is to be all made of sighs and tears,
      And so am I for Phoebe.
PHOEBE And I for Ganymede.
ORLANDO And I for Rosalind.
85 ROSALIND And I for no woman.
SILVIUS It is to be all made of faith and service,
      And so am I for Phoebe.
PHOEBE And I for Ganymede.
ORLANDO And I for Rosalind.
90 ROSALIND And I for no woman.
SILVIUS It is to be all made of fantasy,
      All made of passion and all made of wishes,
      All adoration, duty, and observance,
      All humbleness, all patience and impatience,
95   All purity, all trial, all observance,
      And so am I for Phoebe.

60 **not damnable** i.e. not practising black magic   61 **gesture** ... **out** manner proclaims   63 **straits** confined places   65 **inconvenient** unsuitable   66 **human** ... **is** i.e. the real Rosalind, not a spirit conjured up by black magic   68 **sober** serious   69 **tender** value   71 **array** clothing   74 **ungentleness** discourtesy   76 **study** purpose   77 **despiteful** cruel, scornful   86 **service** devotion   93 **observance** due respect/service

PHOEBE And so am I for Ganymede.
ORLANDO And so am I for Rosalind.
ROSALIND And so am I for no woman.
100   PHOEBE If this be so, why blame you me to love you?   *To Rosalind*
SILVIUS If this be so, why blame you me to love you?   *To Phoebe*
ORLANDO If this be so, why blame you me to love you?
ROSALIND Who do you speak to? 'Why blame you me to
love you?'
105   ORLANDO To her that is not here, nor doth not hear.
ROSALIND Pray you no more of this. 'Tis like the howling
of Irish wolves against the moon.—
I will help you if I can.—   *To Silvius*
I would love you, if I could.—   *To Phoebe*
110   Tomorrow meet me all together.—   *To all*
I will marry you, if ever I marry woman, and I'll be   *To Phoebe*
married tomorrow.—
I will satisfy you, if ever I satisfied man, and you shall   *To Orlando*
be married tomorrow.—
115   I will content you, if what pleases you contents you,   *To Silvius*
and you shall be married tomorrow.—
As you love Rosalind, meet.—   *To Orlando*
As you love Phoebe, meet.— And as I love no   *To Silvius*
woman, I'll meet. So fare you well:
120   I have left you commands.
SILVIUS I'll not fail, if I live.
PHOEBE Nor I.
ORLANDO Nor I.   *Exeunt*

Act 5 Scene 3   *running scene 11 continues*

Enter Clown [Touchstone] and Audrey
TOUCHSTONE Tomorrow is the joyful day, Audrey:
tomorrow will we be married.
AUDREY I do desire it with all my heart, and I hope it is
no dishonest desire to desire to be a woman of the
5   world. Here come two of the banished duke's pages.
Enter two Pages
FIRST PAGE Well met, honest gentleman.
TOUCHSTONE By my troth, well met. Come, sit, sit, and a
song.

---

113 satisfy content (plays on the sense of 'sexually satisfy')   **121 fail** be absent   **5.3   4 dishonest**
unchaste   **woman … world** i.e. married (plays on the sense of 'sexually experienced')   **6 honest**
honourable

SECOND PAGE We are for you. Sit i'th'middle.   *They sit*

10 **FIRST PAGE** Shall we clap into't roundly, without
          hawking or spitting or saying we are hoarse, which
          are the only prologues to a bad voice?
    SECOND PAGE I'faith, i'faith, and both in a tune, like two
          gypsies on a horse.
                    Song
15   It was a lover and his lass,
               With a hey, and a ho, and a hey nonino,
             That o'er the green cornfield did pass
               In the spring-time, the only pretty ring-time,
             When birds do sing, hey ding a ding, ding.
20   Sweet lovers love the spring.
             And therefore take the present time,
               With a hey, and a ho, and a hey nonino,
             For love is crownèd with the prime
               In spring-time, etc.

25   Between the acres of the rye,
               With a hey, and a ho, and a hey nonino,
             These pretty country folks would lie
               In spring-time, etc.

             This carol they began that hour,
30   With a hey, and a ho, and a hey nonino,
             How that a life was but a flower
               In spring-time, etc.

    TOUCHSTONE Truly, young gentlemen, though there
          was no great matter in the ditty, yet the note was
35   very untunable.
    FIRST PAGE You are deceived, sir: we kept time, we lost
          not our time.
    TOUCHSTONE By my troth, yes: I count it but time lost to
          hear such a foolish song. God buy you, and God
40   mend your voices! Come, Audrey.   *Exeunt*

---

10 clap into't roundly begin immediately   **11 hawking** throat clearing   **12 only** usual   **13 in a tune**
keeping time/in unison   **18 ring-time** time for giving or exchanging rings (i.e. wedding season)   **21 take**
seize/enjoy   **23 prime** spring/height of perfection   **24 etc.** i.e. repeat chorus   **29 carol** song   **34 ditty**
lyrics   **note** music, tune   **35 untunable** unmelodious

Act 5 Scene 4

Enter Duke Senior, Amiens, Jaques, Orlando, Oliver, Celia

DUKE SENIOR   Dost thou believe, Orlando, that the boy
    Can do all this that he hath promisèd?

ORLANDO I sometimes do believe and sometimes do not,
    As those that fear they hope and know they fear.

Enter Rosalind, Silvius and Phoebe

5   **ROSALIND** Patience once more, whiles our compact is
    urged:
    You say, if I bring in your Rosalind, you will bestow   *To Duke Senior*
    her on Orlando here?

DUKE SENIOR That would I, had I kingdoms to give with
    her.

ROSALIND And you say, you will have her, when I bring   *To Orlando*
    her?

10 **ORLANDO** That would I, were I of all kingdoms king.

ROSALIND You say, you'll marry me, if I be willing?   *To Phoebe*

PHOEBE That will I, should I die the hour after.

ROSALIND But if you do refuse to marry me,
    You'll give yourself to this most faithful shepherd?

15 **PHOEBE** So is the bargain.

ROSALIND You say, that you'll have Phoebe, if she will?   *To Silvius*

SILVIUS Though to have her and death were both one
    thing.

ROSALIND I have promised to make all this matter even.
    Keep you your word, O duke, to give your daughter,

20   You yours, Orlando, to receive his daughter.
    Keep you your word, Phoebe, that you'll marry me,
    Or else refusing me, to wed this shepherd.
    Keep your word, Silvius, that you'll marry her
    If she refuse me. And from hence I go,

25   To make these doubts all even.

Exeunt Rosalind and Celia

DUKE SENIOR I do remember in this shepherd boy
    Some lively touches of my daughter's favour.

ORLANDO My lord, the first time that I ever saw him
    Methought he was a brother to your daughter:

30   But, my good lord, this boy is forest-born,
    And hath been tutored in the rudiments

5.4   **5 compact** agreement   **urged** presented formally   **18 make** ... **even** smooth out all these
matters   **27 lively** lifelike/striking   **touches** qualities/features   **favour** appearance/face   **31 rudiments**
basics

Of many desperate studies by his uncle,
Whom he reports to be a great magician,

Enter Clown [Touchstone] and Audrey

Obscurèd in the circle of this forest.

35 JAQUES There is, sure, another flood toward, and these
couples are coming to the ark. Here comes a pair of
very strange beasts, which in all tongues are called
fools.

TOUCHSTONE Salutation and greeting to you all!

40 JAQUES Good my lord, bid him welcome: this is the
motley-minded gentleman that I have so often met in
the forest. He hath been a courtier, he swears.

TOUCHSTONE If any man doubt that, let him put me to
my purgation. I have trod a measure, I have flattered

45 a lady, I have been politic with my friend, smooth
with mine enemy, I have undone three tailors, I have
had four quarrels, and like to have fought one.

JAQUES And how was that ta'en up?

TOUCHSTONE Faith, we met, and found the quarrel was

50 upon the seventh cause.

JAQUES How seventh cause? Good my lord, like this
fellow.

DUKE SENIOR I like him very well.

TOUCHSTONE God 'ild you, sir, I desire you of the like. I

55 press in here, sir, amongst the rest of the country
copulatives, to swear and to forswear, according as
marriage binds and blood breaks. A poor virgin, sir,
an ill-favoured thing, sir, but mine own, a poor
humour of mine, sir, to take that that no man else

60 will. Rich honesty dwells like a miser, sir, in a poor
house, as your pearl in your foul oyster.

DUKE SENIOR By my faith, he is very swift and
sententious.

TOUCHSTONE According to the fool's bolt, sir, and such

65 dulcet diseases.

---

32 **desperate** dangerous   34 **Obscurèd** concealed   **circle** surroundings/magic circle   35 **toward**
approaching   37 **tongues** languages   41 **motley-minded** foolish-minded   44 **purgation** test   **measure**
stately dance   45 **politic** crafty   **smooth** seemingly amiable   46 **undone** ruined, bankrupted   47 **like to
have** almost   48 **ta'en up** settled   54 **'ild** yield (i.e. reward)   **desire ... like** wish you the same
56 **copulatives** people being joined in marriage (with play on 'those engaged in copulation')   57 **blood
breaks** passion declines   59 **humour** inclination, whim   60 **honesty** chastity/virtue   61 **foul** dirty
62 **swift** quick-witted   63 **sententious** given to utter pointed sayings   64 **fool's bolt** 'a fool's bolt is soon
shot' (proverbial; phallic and ejaculatory connotations)   **bolt** short, thick arrow   65 **dulcet diseases**
sweet afflictions

JAQUES But, for the seventh cause. How did you find the quarrel on the seventh cause?

TOUCHSTONE Upon a lie seven times removed — bear your body more seeming, Audrey — as thus, sir: I did
70   dislike the cut of a certain courtier's beard. He sent me word, if I said his beard was not cut well, he was in the mind it was: this is called the Retort Courteous. If I sent him word again it was not well cut, he would send me word, he cut it to please himself: this is
75   called the Quip Modest. If again it was not well cut, he disabled my judgement: this is called the Reply Churlish. If again it was not well cut, he would answer, I spake not true: this is called the Reproof Valiant. If again it was not well cut, he would say I
80   lied: this is called the Countercheck Quarrelsome: and so to the Lie Circumstantial and the Lie Direct.

JAQUES And how oft did you say his beard was not well cut?

TOUCHSTONE I durst go no further than the Lie
85   Circumstantial, nor he durst not give me the Lie Direct, and so we measured swords and parted.

JAQUES Can you nominate in order now the degrees of the lie?

TOUCHSTONE O sir, we quarrel in print, by the book, as
90   you have books for good manners. I will name you the degrees: The first, the Retort Courteous: the second, the Quip Modest: the third, the Reply Churlish: the fourth, the Reproof Valiant: the fifth, the Countercheck Quarrelsome: the sixth, the Lie
95   with Circumstance: the seventh, the Lie Direct. All these you may avoid but the Lie Direct, and you may avoid that too, with an 'if'. I knew when seven justices could not take up a quarrel, but when the parties were met themselves, one of them
100   thought but of an 'if', as, 'If you said so, then I said so', and they shook hands and swore brothers. Your 'if' is the only peacemaker. Much virtue in 'if'.

JAQUES Is not this a rare fellow, my lord? He's as good at anything and yet a fool.

---

69 seeming seemingly   **as** for instance   **72 in the mind** of the opinion   **76 disabled** disparaged
80 Countercheck rebuke   **81 Circumstantial** told indirectly through circumstances or details
86 measured swords checked that the length of the swords was the same (a necessary preparation for duelling)   **87 nominate** name   **89 in print** in a precise manner   **98 take up** settle   **101 swore brothers** vowed devoted friendship   **103 rare** extraordinary/splendid

105 **DUKE SENIOR** He uses his folly like a stalking-horse and
        under the presentation of that he shoots his wit.
        Enter Hymen, Rosalind and Celia. Still music
     HYMEN Then is there mirth in heaven,
          When earthly things made even
          Atone together.
110   Good duke, receive thy daughter,
          Hymen from heaven brought her,
          Yea, brought her hither,
          That thou mightst join her hand with his
          Whose heart within his bosom is.
115 **ROSALIND** To you I give myself, for I am yours.—   *To Duke Senior*
          To you I give myself, for I am yours.   *To Orlando*
     DUKE SENIOR If there be truth in sight, you are my
          daughter.
     ORLANDO If there be truth in sight, you are my Rosalind.
     PHOEBE If sight and shape be true,
120   Why then, my love adieu!
     ROSALIND I'll have no father, if you be not he.—   *To Duke Senior*
          I'll have no husband, if you be not he.—   *To Orlando*
          Nor ne'er wed woman, if you be not she.   *To Phoebe*
     HYMEN Peace, ho! I bar confusion:
125   'Tis I must make conclusion
          Of these most strange events.
          Here's eight that must take hands
          To join in Hymen's bands,
          If truth holds true contents.—
130   You and you no cross shall part;—   *To Orlando and Rosalind*
          You and you are heart in heart.—   *To Oliver and Celia*
          You to his love must accord,   *To Phoebe*
          Or have a woman to your lord.—
          You and you are sure together,   *To Touchstone and Audrey*
135   As the winter to foul weather.—
          Whiles a wedlock-hymn we sing,
          Feed yourselves with questioning,
          That reason wonder may diminish
          How thus we met, and these things finish.

105 stalking-horse horse behind which a hunter concealed himself in order to get within easy range of the
game **106 presentation** show *Hymen* god of marriage (commonly depicted as a young man carrying a
torch); sometimes played as a god, sometimes as a part enacted by Amiens or another courtier *Still*
subdued/soft **107 mirth** joy **108 made even** are reconciled **109 Atone** unite **119 shape** appearance,
physical form **124 bar** prohibit **128 bands** bonds, i.e. marriage **130 cross** adversity **132 accord**
agree **133 lord** husband **134 sure** securely bound **137 questioning** conversation/inquiry

Song

140   Wedding is great Juno's crown,
          O, blessèd bond of board and bed!
          'Tis Hymen peoples every town,
          High wedlock then be honourèd:
          Honour, high honour and renown,
145   To Hymen, god of every town!

DUKE SENIOR O my dear niece, welcome thou art to me!   *To Celia*
          Even daughter, welcome, in no less degree.

PHOEBE I will not eat my word, now thou art mine,   *To Silvius*
          Thy faith my fancy to thee doth combine.

Enter Second Brother [Jaques de Bois]

150 **JAQUES DE BOIS** Let me have audience for a word or two:
          I am the second son of old Sir Rowland,
          That bring these tidings to this fair assembly.
          Duke Frederick, hearing how that every day
          Men of great worth resorted to this forest,
155   Addressed a mighty power, which were on foot,
          In his own conduct, purposely to take
          His brother here and put him to the sword:
          And to the skirts of this wild wood he came;
          Where, meeting with an old religious man,
160   After some question with him, was converted
          Both from his enterprise and from the world,
          His crown bequeathing to his banished brother,
          And all their lands restored to them again
          That were with him exiled. This to be true,
165   I do engage my life.

DUKE SENIOR Welcome, young man.
          Thou offer'st fairly to thy brothers' wedding:
          To one his lands withheld, and to the other
          A land itself at large, a potent dukedom.
170   First, in this forest, let us do those ends
          That here were well begun and well begot:
          And after, every of this happy number
          That have endured shrewd days and nights with us
          Shall share the good of our returnèd fortune,
175   According to the measure of their states.

---

140 **Juno** queen of the gods and goddess of marriage   141 **board and bed** food and lodging   142 **peoples** populates   148 **thou** i.e. Silvius   149 **fancy** love   **combine** unite   155 **Addressed** prepared   **power** army   156 **In ... conduct** under his own leadership   161 **world** secular life/material interests   165 **engage** pledge   167 **offer'st fairly** contribute finely   169 **at large** of full size   170 **do those ends** accomplish those aims   172 **every** every one   173 **shrewd** hard   175 **states** ranks, status

Meantime, forget this new-fall'n dignity
And fall into our rustic revelry.
Play, music! And you, brides and bridegrooms all,
With measure heaped in joy, to th'measures fall.

180 **JAQUES** Sir, by your patience. If I heard you rightly,
The duke hath put on a religious life
And thrown into neglect the pompous court?

JAQUES DE BOIS He hath.

JAQUES To him will I: out of these convertites
185 There is much matter to be heard and learned.—
You to your former honour I bequeath,   *To Duke Senior*
Your patience and your virtue well deserves it.—
You to a love that your true faith doth merit.—   *To Orlando*
You to your land and love and great allies.—   *To Oliver*
190 You to a long and well-deservèd bed.—   *To Silvius*
And you to wrangling, for thy loving voyage   *To Touchstone*
Is but for two months victualled. So, to your
    pleasures.
I am for other than for dancing measures.

DUKE SENIOR Stay, Jaques, stay.

195 **JAQUES** To see no pastime, I. What you would have
I'll stay to know at your abandoned cave.   *Exit*

DUKE SENIOR Proceed, proceed.— We'll begin these
    rites,
As we do trust they'll end, in true delights.   *They dance*

[*Exeunt all but Rosalind*]

ROSALIND It is not the fashion to see the lady the
200 epilogue, but it is no more unhandsome than to see
the lord the prologue. If it be true that good wine
needs no bush, 'tis true that a good play needs no
epilogue. Yet to good wine they do use good bushes,
and good plays prove the better by the help of good
205 epilogues. What a case am I in then, that am neither
a good epilogue nor cannot insinuate with you in the
behalf of a good play! I am not furnished like a
beggar, therefore to beg will not become me. My way
is to conjure you, and I'll begin with the women. I
210 charge you, O women, for the love you bear to men,

176 **new-fall'n** newly received   179 **With** … **joy** in abundant joy   **th'measures** stately dances
180 **patience** permission   182 **pompous** vainglorious/ceremonious   184 **convertites** converts
189 **allies** relatives   192 **but** … **victualled** only has sufficient supplies for two months
200 **unhandsome** faulty in appearance/inappropriate   201 **good** … **bush** proverbial: something of good
quality needs no advertising as its merits speak for themselves   202 **bush** tavern sign (originally a small
bush)   205 **case** state/predicament   206 **insinuate with** work on/stealthily win the favour of
207 **furnished** dressed   209 **conjure** entreat/put a spell on

to like as much of this play as please you. And I
charge you, O men, for the love you bear to women
— as I perceive by your simpering, none of you hates
them — that between you and the women the play
215   may please. If I were a woman, I would kiss as many
of you as had beards that pleased me, complexions
that liked me and breaths that I defied not. And I am
sure, as many as have good beards or good faces or
sweet breaths will, for my kind offer, when I make
220   curtsy, bid me farewell.   *Exit*

---

214 the play *As You Like It*/sexual dalliance   **215 If** ... **woman** in Shakespeare's England all parts were
played by male actors   **217 liked** pleased   **defied** despised   **220 bid me farewell** i.e. applaud/shout
approvingly

TEXTUAL NOTES

F = First Folio text of 1623, the only authority for the play
F2 = a correction introduced in the Second Folio text of 1632
F3 = a correction introduced in the Third Folio text of 1664
Ed = a correction introduced by a later editor
SH = speech heading (i.e. speaker's name)

List of parts = Ed

1.1.107 she = F3. F = hee   **157 SH OLIVER** = F2. *Not in* F
1.2.3 yet I were = Ed. F = yet were   **55 SH TOUCHSTONE** = Ed. F = *Clow. (then Clo. throughout)*   **79 SH CELIA** = Ed. F = *Ros.*
1.3.78 her = F2. F = per   **122 be** = F2. F = by
2.1.51 much = F2. F = must
2.3.10 some = F2. F = seeme   **16 SH ORLANDO** = F2. *Not in* F   **30 SH ORLANDO** = F2. F = *Ad.*   **72 seventeen** = Ed. F = seauentie
2.4.41 thy = Ed. F = they   **wound** = F2. F = would   **69 you, friend** = F2. F = your friend   **74 travel** = F3. F = trauaile
2.5.1 SH AMIENS = Ed. *Not in* F
2.7.38 brain = Ed. F = braive   **88 comes** = F2. F = come   **186 The** = F. Ed = Then   **202 master** = F2. F = masters
3.2.26 good = Ed. F = pood   **124 this a** = Ed. F = *this*   **144 her** = Ed. F = *his*   **234 forth such** = F2. F = forth   **258 more** = *modernization of* F's moe   **355 deifying** = F2. F = defying   **363 are** = F2. F = art   **374 accoutrements** *spelled* accoustrements *in* F
3.3.89 SH TOUCHSTONE = F2. F = *Ol.*
3.4.27 of a = F2. F = of
3.5.22 Lean but = F2. F = Leane   **107 erewhile** = Ed. F = yere-while
4.1.1 me be = F2. F = me   **17 my** = F2. F = by   **27 travel** = F3. F = trauaile   **100 Sestos** = F2. F = Cestos   **148 hyena** = Ed. F = Hyen   **159 wilt** = F3. F = wil't   **202 in, it** = F2. F = in, in
4.2.2 SH FIRST LORD = Ed. F = *Lord*   **7 SH SECOND LORD** = Ed. F = *Lord.*   **10 SH LORDS** = Ed. *Not in* F
4.3.8 bid = F2. F = did bid   **148 In** = F2. F = I
5.1.36 sir = F2. F = sit   **55 policy** = F2. F = police
5.2.7 nor her = Ed. F = nor   **26 swoon** = Ed. F = sound   **31 overcame** = F2. F = overcome   **103 Who** = Ed. F = Why
5.3.18 ring = Ed. F = *rang*
5.4.80 lied = Ed. F = lie   **81 to the** = F2. F = ro   **113 her** = F3. F = his   **150 SH JAQUES DE BOIS** = Ed. F = *2.Bro.*   **163 them** = Ed. F = him   **171 were** = F2. F = vvete

SCENE-BY-SCENE ANALYSIS

ACT 1 SCENE 1

Lines 1–28: Orlando complains to Adam about his eldest brother's treatment of him. Orlando has inherited 'but poor a thousand crowns' and, while their other brother is at university, Oliver keeps Orlando at home, unoccupied. He tells Adam that he 'begins to mutiny', but admits that he cannot see any 'wise remedy' for his circumstances. He sees Oliver approaching and tells Adam to 'Go apart' and watch how Oliver scolds and abuses him.

Lines 29–83: Orlando responds insolently to Oliver's questions, saying that he has nothing to do, and has not been taught any useful occupation. Oliver asserts his place as 'the first-born', introducing the theme of social position and status. Orlando acknowledges this but argues that, although his brother has inherited their father's estate and title, they have both inherited his 'blood', establishing the theme of lineage and inheritance. Their argument becomes physical and Adam steps in. Orlando repeats his complaints, but Oliver sends him off, telling the 'old dog' Adam to go too. Offended, Adam observes that their father would not have spoken to him in such a way.

Lines 84–167: Oliver calls for Charles, 'the duke's wrestler'. He asks for news of the court, and Charles, setting the background for the play, says that there is only 'old news': Duke Senior remains banished by his usurping younger brother, Duke Frederick, along with 'three or four' of his lords who have remained faithful; a brotherly rift that echoes the discord between Orlando and Oliver. The old duke and his followers are living in the Forest of Arden, 'like the old Robin Hood of England' in 'the golden world', an allusion that acknowledges the play's mythological qualities and its roots in traditional romantic narratives. Charles reports that Duke Senior's daughter, Rosalind, remains at court. He describes how her cousin Celia, Duke Frederick's daughter, loves Rosalind so much that she would have 'died' had she been separated from her, an image of female unity that contrasts with the discordant male relationships presented so far. The conversation moves to Charles' forthcoming wrestling match. Charles has heard that Orlando intends to disguise himself and wrestle against him. He says that if Orlando does fight, he must 'foil' him, but he is worried about the disgrace to Oliver. Oliver thanks Charles but tells him that his brother is 'a secret and villainous contriver'. He warns him that Orlando means to defeat him 'by some treacherous device', and advises Charles to break his brother's neck. Oliver's soliloquy reveals how he hates Orlando for the good qualities that make people prefer him. He hopes that Charles will kill Orlando.

ACT 1 SCENE 2

Lines 1–138: In an exchange that reveals their love for each other, Celia encourages Rosalind to 'be merry' despite the banishment of her father. Rosalind argues that she is already trying to 'show more mirth' than she is 'mistress of', raising the theme of disguise/concealment. Celia promises that one day she will restore Rosalind to her true status. Rosalind tries to be merry as Celia requests and begins to 'devise sports' for their entertainment, asking 'what think you of falling in love?', thereby introducing the key theme of the play: love in its various forms. As Celia and Rosalind banter about love, revealing their quick wit, they are interrupted by Touchstone. The jester joins in the ladies' witty exchange, quipping about wise fools and foolish wise men (reinforcing a wider theme of 'exchanged roles' and raising a key motif of fools and foolishness). They are joined by Monsieur Le Beau, who tells them of the 'sport' at the wrestling match, a language choice that echoes Rosalind's earlier use of the term in conjunction with love, creating a parallel between sport and courtship. Le Beau reports that Charles has defeated three men and there is to be another bout. Celia and Rosalind decide to watch.

Lines 139–249: The ladies comment on Charles' youthful challenger (the disguised Orlando). Duke Frederick has tried to dissuade him from fighting, and suggests that the ladies may be able to 'move him'. Orlando thanks the ladies but insists that he will fight, declaring that his 'place' in the world 'may be better supplied' by someone else if he dies. Orlando defeats Charles and reveals that he is 'the youngest son of Rowland de Bois'. Frederick's attitude changes: he and Orlando's father were enemies. When Frederick has left, Rosalind explains that de Bois was a loyal friend of her father. Celia is ashamed of Duke Frederick's 'rough and envious' behaviour and praises Orlando. Rosalind gives him a chain from round her neck as a favour, a gesture that reinforces ideas of courtly romance. The ladies take their leave and Orlando tries to stop them. Rosalind, clearly smitten with Orlando, stays briefly to tell him that he has 'overthrown / More than [his] enemies'.

Lines 250–282: Orlando realizes that he, too, is 'overthrown', and says that 'passion' rendered him unable to talk to Rosalind. Le Beau urges Orlando to leave. He explains that Duke Frederick is temperamental. Orlando asks about the two ladies. Le Beau describes Celia and reveals that the other lady is 'daughter to the banished duke'. He adds that the love between the two of them is 'dearer than the natural bond of sisters', again presenting a female love to contrast with the male enmity seen so far. He explains that Frederick has recently 'ta'en displeasure' against Rosalind because the people 'praise her for her virtues', creating a parallel between Rosalind and Orlando, who is disliked by Oliver for similar reasons. Le Beau warns that Frederick's 'malice' against Rosalind 'Will suddenly break forth'. He leaves Orlando musing on 'heavenly Rosalind'.

ACT 1 SCENE 3

Lines 1–90: Celia questions whether Rosalind can have fallen in love with Orlando 'on such a sudden'. They are interrupted by Duke

Frederick who abruptly tells Rosalind that she is banished from the court. Bewildered, Rosalind asks for an explanation and Frederick replies that she is her 'father's daughter, there's enough', a statement that reinforces the theme of inheritance, as does Rosalind's retort that 'Treason is not inherited'. Celia pleads with her father, claiming that she and Rosalind are 'coupled and inseparable'. Frederick is unmoved, saying that Celia is a 'fool' and reiterating Rosalind's banishment before he leaves.

Lines 91–142: Celia announces that her father has banished them both – she and Rosalind are 'one' and cannot be 'sundered'. She suggests that they go into the forest to find Rosalind's father. Rosalind points out that two 'Maids' such as themselves would be in danger, as 'Beauty provoketh thieves sooner than gold'. Celia suggests they disguise themselves 'in poor and mean attire' for safety. Rosalind agrees, deciding that she will disguise herself as a man, with a 'swashing and a martial outside' to conceal her 'hidden woman's fear', emphasizing the theme of disguise/concealment and raising the issue of gender identity. She announces that she will be called 'Ganymede', and Celia chooses 'Aliena' as her new identity. They decide to take Touchstone with them.

ACT 2 SCENE 1

The action moves from the court to the country, one of several binaries in the play, including male/female and hate/love, as well as the oppositions within and between characters: pairs of warring brothers and the division of various characters between their disguised selves and true identities.

Duke Senior compares the 'sweet' life in the forest with the 'painted pomp' of the 'envious court'. The language used to describe the forest by the duke and others reinforces the idyllic, pastoral nature of the setting, but there are also constant reminders of the realities and troubles of human existence, a tension sustained throughout the play. The duke suggests that they go hunting but is troubled that the 'native' citizens of the forest, the deer, are to be usurped and killed 'in their own confines', an image that echoes his own deposition by his brother. A lord describes how the 'melancholy Jaques' watched a dying deer and wept while moralizing on the human condition. Duke Senior is entertained by Jaques' somewhat excessive and affected moralizing and suggests that they go to find him.

ACT 2 SCENE 2

Duke Frederick has discovered that Celia has fled with Rosalind. One lord reveals that Touchstone has gone with them; another reports that Celia's waiting woman overheard them discussing Orlando and suspects that he is 'surely in their company'. Frederick sends for Orlando, and, if he cannot be found, for Oliver.

ACT 2 SCENE 3

Orlando is met by Adam who warns him he should leave immediately. He reports that Oliver is so jealous of his brother that he plans to kill him. Orlando replies that he has nowhere to go and no money. Adam offers all the money he has saved for his old age and suggests that he goes with him. Much moved by Adam's goodness, Orlando agrees.

ACT 2 SCENE 4

Rosalind (as Ganymede), Celia (as Aliena) and Touchstone arrive in the Forest of Arden. Celia and Touchstone are weary, but Rosalind is 'merry' in spirit. She argues that, since she is disguised as a man, she must be brave, 'as doublet and hose ought to show itself courageous to petticoat', raising issues of gender but also the extent to which 'disguise' creates or conceals identity. Two shepherds enter and the others stand aside to listen. The theme of love is raised again, as Silvius tells Corin how much he loves Phoebe. When Corin sympathizes, Silvius claims that Corin is too old to know how he feels and can never have loved as he does. Silvius leaves, still lamenting, and Rosalind sympathizes with him, seeing a parallel between his love and hers for Orlando. Touchstone, too, recalls past love, but with cynical, bawdy, humour, concluding that 'so is all nature in love mortal in folly'. Touchstone's prosaic attitude is compounded by Celia, who is thinking only of food. They ask Corin to take them where they can rest and feed. He explains that he cannot help them himself: he is only 'shepherd to another man', introducing an anti-pastoral element of realism and reinforcing the play's concerns with social position and status. He offers to take them to his master's cottage which is for sale. Rosalind offers to buy the 'cottage, pasture and the flock'.

ACT 2 SCENE 5

Amiens sings a song emphasizing the pleasant idleness of the pastoral setting. Jaques asks Amiens to carry on singing, but he refuses, as it will make Jaques melancholy. Revealing his affected nature, Jaques says he enjoys being melancholy, and Amiens continues. Jaques contributes a final, cynical, verse, suggesting that anyone who leaves the 'wealth and ease' of the court for the country is an 'ass'. Amiens goes to call Duke Senior to a banquet.

ACT 2 SCENE 6

Adam is weak from hunger. Orlando carries him, promising to find food and shelter.

ACT 2 SCENE 7

Lines 1–88: Duke Senior searches for Jaques. He appears and describes a meeting he has had with a 'motley fool' (Touchstone). He is filled with admiration for Touchstone's apparently profound reflections on time and humanity and expresses his own desire to be 'a fool', saying he is 'ambitious for a motley coat'. Ironically, Jaques is often 'foolish', but he also comes close to fulfilling the traditional, dramatic role of the fool: providing observation on the events of the play and the human condition, but his self-importance and affectation hinder his insight. As Duke Senior and Jaques debate with each other, Orlando enters.

Lines 89–169: Orlando draws his sword and demands food, saying that 'bare distress' prevents him from 'the show / Of smooth civility', suggesting, perhaps, that manners and courtliness are a 'disguise' for basic human instincts. When the duke gently invites him to 'Sit down and feed', Orlando apologizes. He adds that he must fetch Adam, declaring that he will not eat until his servant has. While he is gone, the duke comments that they are not the only ones to be unhappy, observing that 'This wide and universal theatre / Presents more woeful pageants than the scene / Wherein we play in.' Continuing the meta-theatrical theme, Jaques compares human existence to theatrical performance: 'All the world's a stage / And all the men and women merely players'. As he comments on the last 'scene', old age, Orlando returns, carrying the elderly Adam on his back.

Lines 170–204: Orlando thanks Duke Senior, and a song is sung as they eat. The duke tells Orlando that, if he is really the son of 'good Sir Rowland', then he is 'truly welcome'.

ACT 3 SCENE 1

Duke Frederick refuses to believe that Oliver has not seen Orlando. He orders him to find his brother dead or alive within the year or face banishment. The duke seizes control of Oliver's estate until Orlando is found. Oliver tells the duke that he has never loved Orlando, at which Frederick ironically brands him a 'villain', confiscates his lands and banishes him.

ACT 3 SCENE 2

Lines 1–86: Lovesick Orlando has written poems to Rosalind and is hanging them on trees in the forest. In highly conventional poetic language he praises 'The fair, the chaste and unexpressive' Rosalind and declares his intention to carve her name 'on every tree'. As he leaves, Corin and Touchstone enter, discussing the differences between court and country. Touchstone provides a neat summary, providing arguments and counter-arguments for both. Corin returns this 'philosophy' with his prosaic observations, such as the 'great cause of the night is lack of the sun'. He observes, however, that court and country are two mutually exclusive spheres, emphasizing the notion that the courtly characters' sojourn in the woods is an unreal, artificial episode. As they wrangle, Rosalind arrives (still in disguise as Ganymede).

Lines 87–249: Rosalind is reading a poem in praise of herself that she has found on another tree. Touchstone satirizes the verse and Celia enters, reading another long poem that even Rosalind describes as a 'tedious homily of love'. Sending Touchstone and Corin away, they discuss the poems, agreeing they are badly written, but Rosalind is anxious to know who wrote them. Celia teases her for a while before revealing that it was Orlando. Rosalind bombards Celia with questions, deeply regretting that she is disguised in 'doublet and hose'. They see Orlando and Jaques approaching and stand aside.

Lines 250–426: Orlando accuses Jaques of being 'either a fool or a cipher', and Jaques criticizes Orlando for being in love. Jaques leaves and Rosalind decides to speak to Orlando, retaining her disguise as Ganymede. She engages him in a witty exchange and he observes that her accent is 'finer' than most shepherds, drawing attention to the limitations of disguise. Rosalind turns the conversation to a man who 'haunts the forest' and 'abuses' the trees by carving the name 'Rosalind' on them, adding she wishes that she could meet this lovesick 'fancy-monger', so that she could offer him 'some good counsel'. Orlando admits that he is the one who is 'so love-shaked' and asks what the 'remedy' is. Rosalind, as Ganymede, argues that 'Love is merely a madness' and suggests that 'he' can cure Orlando by pretending to be Rosalind and showing how 'inconstant' women are. Orlando arranges to call every day at the cottage.

ACT 3 SCENE 3

Touchstone is courting Audrey. They are accompanied by Jaques, who interjects cynical comments on their courtship, adding to the humour already created by the disparity between Touchstone's wordy philosophies and Audrey's limited understanding and forthright declarations. Touchstone has arranged for a country clergyman, Sir Oliver Martext, to marry them in the forest, but he refuses unless there is someone to give the bride away. Jaques offers to do this, but succeeds in convincing Touchstone that he should be married in a church, not 'under a bush like a beggar'. Despite Touchstone's cynical argument that an irregular marriage service will make it easier for him to leave his wife, he agrees, and they abandon the confused Sir Oliver.

ACT 3 SCENE 4

Rosalind is distressed that Orlando has not kept his appointment, and Celia cynically suggests that he is not in love after all. Rosalind reveals how she met her father, Duke Senior, in the forest and that he questioned her, believing her to be Ganymede. Corin arrives to invite them to observe a meeting between Silvius and Phoebe: 'a pageant truly played' between 'true love' and 'proud distain'. The metatheatrical circumstance of the dual 'audience' is compounded by Rosalind's suggestion that she may become 'a busy actor in their play'.

ACT 3 SCENE 5

Lines 1–80: Silvius begs Phoebe to love him, but she scornfully rejects him. Rosalind emerges and berates Phoebe for her cruelty. She argues that Phoebe is fortunate to be loved by the shepherd, particularly when she is so unattractive. Deceived by Rosalind's disguise, however, Phoebe promptly falls in love with 'Ganymede'.

Lines 81–142: Denying any love for Ganymede to Silvius, Phoebe pretends that she wishes she had 'answered' his criticisms. She decides to write a letter which she gets Silvius to deliver.

ACT 4 SCENE 1

Lines 1–30: Jaques approaches Ganymede in order to become 'better acquainted'. He expounds his melancholy philosophy. Rosalind is unimpressed and observes that she would 'rather have a fool' to make her laugh. Orlando arrives, and Jaques leaves.

Lines 31–192: Orlando plays along with the pretence that Ganymede is Rosalind, creating dramatic irony, and blurring the boundaries of gender and sexuality as he woos a woman disguised as a man pretending to be a woman. Rosalind chides him for being late, claiming that a true lover would never 'Break an hour's promise'. She invites Orlando to 'woo' her as he would Rosalind, then proceeds to counter all of his arguments. She then changes tack, and suggests that she be 'Rosalind in a more coming-on disposition'. She sets up a mock wedding between them, with Aliena playing the part of the priest, before arguing that Orlando would soon tire of Rosalind: 'Maids are May when they are maids, but the sky changes when they are wives'. She describes the changeable and jealous nature of wives and, although her arguments generate humour, they also demonstrate a realistic attitude to love and relationships that counters the play's overtly poetic romanticism. Orlando announces he has to leave to dine with Duke Senior, but promises to return in two hours.

Lines 193–210: Celia complains that Rosalind has 'misused' the female sex, but Rosalind merely responds by saying that she is 'deep . . . in love' with Orlando, and is going to 'find a shadow and sigh' until he returns.

ACT 4 SCENE 2

Jaques and the lords have killed a deer, which they plan to present to Duke Senior. They sing a humorous song to celebrate the occasion.

ACT 4 SCENE 3

Lines 1–76: Rosalind and Celia are discussing the fact that Orlando is late again when they are interrupted by Silvius with a letter from

Phoebe (for Ganymede). He warns them that the letter 'bears an angry tenor'. Rosalind accuses Silvius of writing the letter and reads it aloud. Silvius is confused: the letter does not seem chiding but romantic. Rosalind encourages Silvius to be more forceful and sends a message to Phoebe that Ganymede will not love her unless she loves Silvius.

Lines 77–188: Oliver arrives seeking Ganymede and Aliena, and Celia tells him that that is who they are. Her increased participation in the dialogue hints at her interest in Oliver, who hands Rosalind a bloody handkerchief. He says it was sent by Orlando. When questioned, Oliver admits that the story will reveal his 'shame'. He describes how Orlando was heading back to the cottage when he saw a 'wretched ragged man' asleep under a tree. Orlando saved the man's life from a snake, before realizing that it was 'his elder brother'. Seeing a lioness also preparing to attack, Orlando, with 'kindness, nobler ever than revenge', fought the lion and saved his brother again. The ladies realize that the man they are speaking to is Oliver, who has 'oft contrived to kill' Orlando. Oliver shamefully confesses and then describes the brothers' reconciliation, which culminated in Orlando taking Oliver to Duke Frederick's cave. Once there, Orlando's wounds were revealed, and he fainted, calling out 'Rosalind'. When he had recovered, he sent Oliver to find Ganymede, 'that he in sport doth call his Rosalind', to excuse his broken promise, with the handkerchief as proof. Rosalind faints, and, ironically, Oliver observes that she 'lack[s] a man's heart'. Despite Rosalind's explanation that she is 'counterfeiting', Oliver seems unconvinced, but accompanies them back to the cottage.

ACT 5 SCENE 1

Touchstone and Audrey meet William, another suitor of Audrey's. Touchstone tells him to give up Audrey or he will kill him. William agrees.

ACT 5 SCENE 2

Oliver admits he is in love with the shepherdess, Aliena, and Orlando questions that he should be so 'on so little acquaintance', echoing Celia's comments to Rosalind in Act 1 scene 3. Oliver declares his intention to renounce his inheritance in favour of Orlando, marry Aliena, and 'live and die a shepherd' in the forest. Orlando agrees. Rosalind arrives, still dressed as Ganymede, and Oliver greets her as 'fair "sister"', although it is uncertain whether he is joining in the pretence or has seen through her disguise. He goes to find Aliena. Ironically, Rosalind and Orlando discuss the suddenness of Oliver and Aliena's love, and Orlando announces that the wedding will be the next day. Ganymede then promises to produce Rosalind, so that Orlando can be married at the same time. Phoebe and Silvius arrive, and Phoebe berates Ganymede for showing her letter to Silvius. After a comic, circular dialogue, 'like the howling of Irish wolves against the moon', emphasizing the confusions between the four characters, Rosalind promises to make Ganymede marry Phoebe the next day if he should ever 'marry woman'.

ACT 5 SCENE 3

Touchstone and Audrey are also to be married the next day. As they talk, they are interrupted by two pages who sing a romantic song that Touchstone describes as 'foolish'.

ACT 5 SCENE 4

Lines 1–106: Duke Senior and Orlando discuss whether Ganymede can do all that 'he hath promisèd'. They are joined by Rosalind (still as Ganymede), Silvius and Phoebe. Having ensured that everyone will keep their promises, she leaves with Celia, vowing to 'make these doubts all even'. As the duke and Orlando innocently discuss Ganymede's resemblance to Rosalind, Touchstone and Audrey arrive. While they wait for the others to return, Touchstone philosophizes on the nature of quarrels, a reminder of the tensions that existed at the beginning of the play and which are moving towards resolution, and expounds the virtue of 'if' (thereby allowing time for Rosalind's costume change).

Lines 107–198: Rosalind and Celia return as themselves, accompanied by Hymen, god of marriage, whose presence reinforces the play's unrealistic qualities. Hymen announces that he will 'bar confusion', and joins all of the lovers: Orlando and Rosalind, Oliver and Celia, Touchstone and Audrey, and Silvius and Phoebe. As the duke welcomes his daughter and niece to the forest, Oliver and Orlando's other brother, also called Jaques, appears with important news. He explains that Duke Frederick has undergone a spiritual conversion and has relinquished his lands to the rightful ruler, Duke Senior. This, with the revelation of everyone's true identities, restores the social order, and ends the courtiers' stay in the forest pastoral. Jaques questions Jaques de Bois, and resolves to join Duke Frederick, who has become a hermit, and remain in the forest. He leaves, and all the rest join in a dance.

Lines 199–220: The epilogue is spoken by Rosalind, who acknowledges that it is unusual for 'the lady' to do this, before urging the audience to be as pleased with the play as they are with the opposite sex.

AS YOU LIKE IT IN PERFORMANCE: THE RSC AND BEYOND

The best way to understand a Shakespeare play is to see it or ideally to participate in it. By examining a range of productions, we may gain a sense of the extraordinary variety of approaches and interpretations that are possible – a variety that gives Shakespeare his unique capacity to be reinvented and made 'our contemporary' four centuries after his death.

We begin with a brief overview of the play's theatrical and cinematic life, offering historical perspectives on how it has been performed. We then analyse in more detail a series of productions staged over the last half-century by the Royal Shakespeare Company. The sense of dialogue between productions that can only occur when a company is dedicated to the revival and investigation of the Shakespeare canon over a long period, together with the uniquely comprehensive archival resource of promptbooks, programme notes, reviews and interviews held on behalf of the RSC at the Shakespeare Birthplace Trust in Stratford-upon-Avon, allows an 'RSC stage history' to become a crucible in which the chemistry of the play can be explored.

Finally, we go to the horse's mouth. Modern theatre is dominated by the figure of the director, who must hold together the whole play, whereas the actor must concentrate on his or her part. The director's viewpoint is therefore especially valuable. Shakespeare's plasticity is wonderfully revealed when we hear directors of highly successful productions answering the same questions in very different ways. And in the case of *As You Like It*, which offers Shakespearean comedy's largest female role, it is equally essential to hear the voice of an actor who has played the part: we provide that of Naomi Frederick.

FOUR CENTURIES OF *AS YOU LIKE IT*: AN OVERVIEW

The stage history of *As You Like It* has been dominated by the succession of talented actors who have played the demanding role of Rosalind. The identity of the boy-actor who originated the part is not known, although the scholar T. W. Baldwin speculated on the original casting of Shakespeare's company, the Chamberlain's Men, suggesting Richard Burbage played Orlando, with Henry Condell as Oliver, John Heminges as Duke Senior, Richard Cowley as William, Thomas Pope as Jaques, Robert Armin as Touchstone and Shakespeare himself as Adam.[1] This last is based on an anecdote recorded by the eighteenth-century scholar William Oldys in which an elderly Stratfordian claimed to have seen the poet playing a part in which as a 'decrepit old man, he wore a long beard, and appeared so weak and drooping and unable to walk, that he was forced to be supported and carried by another person to a table, at which he was seated among some company, who were eating, and one of them sung a song'.[2] Another anecdote has Lady Mary Herbert, Countess of Pembroke (sister of Sir Philip Sidney), writing to her son, William, telling him to bring James I with him to Wilton House to see *As You Like It*, adding: 'we have the man Shakespeare with us'.[3]

Tantalizing as these possibilities remain, the fact is that there is no recorded performance of the play in the seventeenth century, although scholars agree that it was written in 1599 or early 1600, making it one of the first plays to be performed in the newly-built Globe Theatre. In 1723 Charles Johnson staged an adaptation entitled *Love in a Forest*,[4] which, in accordance with eighteenth-century notions of social decorum, eliminated Touchstone and other lower-class characters, had Orlando and Charles fight a duel with rapiers rather than engage in a wrestling match, borrowing lines from *Richard II*, and made Jaques fall in love with Celia using Benedick's lines from *Much Ado about Nothing*. Touchstone's recapitulated speech on the Degrees of the Lie, which allows for Rosalind's costume-change in the last act, was replaced by *A Midsummer Night's Dream*'s play-within-a-play, 'Pyramus and Thisbe'.

Shakespeare's *As You Like It* was successfully revived, with minor cuts, at Drury Lane in 1740, after which it became one of the most popular plays on the London stage. Rival productions in the following decade starred Hannah Pritchard at Covent Garden and Margaret (Peg) Woffington at Drury Lane. Theatre historian Anthony Vaughan credits Pritchard's Rosalind as a prime motive for the renewed interest in Shakespeare alongside David Garrick's efforts to popularize his plays.[5] Her performance was admired for its liveliness and spirited delivery. Thomas Arne composed the music for Amiens' 'Under the Greenwood Tree' and 'Blow, Blow, Thou Winter Wind', as well as the 'Cuckoo song' ('When daisies pied') from *Love's Labour's Lost* to be sung by Celia. The performance, with dancing after Acts 1, 3 and 4, was followed by a pantomime of *Robin Goodfellow*.

Hannah Pritchard, principally known as a character actress, was described by John Hill as possessing the 'ductility of mind' that enabled her to play Rosalind 'with finesse'.[6] Her rival, Peg Woffington, was famous for her beauty, 'racy love-life'[7] and 'great sensibility'.[8] Both played the part in a way later characterized as the 'spirited hoyden'.[9] Sarah Siddons, the greatest tragic actress of the period, failed in the role due in part to her refusal to wear male costume as Ganymede. Her brother, John Philip Kemble, who had played Orlando in his youth, chose to play Jaques and thus established a performance tradition for subsequent actor-managers. He cut and pasted the text in line with contemporary notions of decorum as well as reducing the number of scene changes.

Ann Barry, Maria Macklin and Mary Ann Yates scored notable triumphs, but the finest Rosalind of the late eighteenth century was Dorothy (or Dora) Jordan who played the part regularly from 1787 to 1814 in London and the provinces, despite her frequent pregnancies.[10] Dorothy Jordan was mistress of the Duke of Clarence (later King William IV) and bore him at least ten illegitimate children. Despite her scandalous lifestyle, many attested to her warmth, charm and general high spirits:

> though she was neither beautiful, nor handsome, nor even pretty, nor accomplished, nor 'a lady', nor anything conventional or *comme il faut* whatsoever, yet was so pleasant, so cordial, so natural, so full of spirits, so healthily constituted in mind and body, had such a shapely leg withal, so charming a voice, and such a happy and happy-making expression of countenance, that she appeared something superior to all those requirements of acceptability, and to hold a patent from nature herself for our delight and good opinion.[11]

In her account of the play's stage history, Cynthia Marshall draws attention to differences between modern attitudes to gender fluidity and performance style and those of the eighteenth century, concluding that 'performance style was presentational rather than representational; viewers came to the theatre to see feminine display, not convincing gender transformation'.[12] Thus the so-called 'breeches parts', in which a woman played a man and wore masculine attire which revealed her figure and legs, were extremely popular.

William Charles Macready's 1842 production at Drury Lane was 'one of his most beautiful "illustrations" of Shakespeare' and 'a significant event in the stage history of the play' since Macready 'restored the true text' (as far as time and public morality permitted) in what then seemed to be a revolutionary manner.[13] Ironically, his production 'initiated both the major trend in nineteenth-century stagings of *As You Like It* – visual spectacle – and the problem with it – a lack of emphasis on the Shakespearean verse'.[14] Macready himself played Jaques with Samuel Phelps as Adam and Louisa Nisbett as the last of the 'hoydenish' Rosalinds. Tastes were changing, though, and the part was subsequently taken over by Helen Faucit in a romantic interpretation of the role she carried on playing until her retirement in 1879. Faucit's Rosalind reflected the Victorian ideal of womanhood: 'The essential qualities of Miss

Faucit's *Rosalind* were innate nobility, purity of mind, acute sensibility, a joyous temperament, sustained, consistent identification with the character, and womanly loveliness.'[15]

Charles Kean's productions were noted for the historical accuracy of their lavish pictorial stagings. His 1851 *As You Like It* at the Princess's Theatre included 'avenues of trees, rustic bridges, and running brooks'.[16] Kean himself played Jaques with his wife (Ellen Tree) as Rosalind. It was her performance in an earlier production at the Park Theater, New York, in 1836 that was responsible for the play's popularity in America. The greatest American actress of the period, Charlotte Cushman, had played Rosalind in London to considerable acclaim. Cushman had famously played Romeo to her sister's Juliet, and her performance of Rosalind was felt to be especially convincing in the part of Ganymede: 'the transformation from woman to man had the same effect on her as on the famed Tiresias...Her mind became masculine as well as her outward semblance.'[17] Cushman went on to reprise the role successfully in New York in 1849.

Helena Modjeska played Rosalind in another critically and financially successful production Booth's Theater, New York, in 1882. The distinguished Polish-born actress was principally known, like Helen Faucit, for playing tragic parts and, in the same way as Faucit, she made a distinction between the Rosalind of Act 1 and her subsequent liberation in the Forest of Arden:

> Of these opening scenes, quite without significance to an actress without imagination, Mme. Modjeska makes a little domestic drama...With her entry among the green boles of Arden the pathos of her part is ended. Thenceforward all is comedy...And Modjeska is singularly brilliant. She sparkles with merriment. She throws off epigrams like a spray of diamonds. She flirts and frolics, prattles and plays. Never under the shade of these melancholy boughs had roamed so gay a creature. Never had these foresters, fleeting the time so carelessly, as they did in the golden world, had among them a youth so trim in limb, so dapper in bearing, so merry in humour.[18]

The London revival at the St James's Theatre in 1885 by John Hare and W. H. Kendal again emphasized spectacle, with a set which included 'cascading water, ferns in a forested glade, "sunlight effects" produced by electric lighting, and stage grass manufactured from dyed feathers sewn into mats'.[19] 'The first act was played on the terraced garden of a medieval chateau'[20] in costumes based on Froissart's chronicles. While some admired the lavish sets and costumes, most critics agreed with the *Theatre*'s assessment that its appeal was to those 'devoid of imaginative and poetic ideas...To the true lovers of Shakespeare...the play is the *first* thing to be considered; secondarily, the manner in which it is caparisoned and bedecked.'[21]

The quest for authenticity and realist staging continued in Barry Sullivan's 1879 production at the Stratford Festival. The American actress, Mary Anderson, who played Rosalind in the inaugural production of the Shakespeare Memorial Theatre, later recalled how:

> The stage was decorated with blossoms from Shakespeare's garden; the flowers used by Rosalind and Celia, as well as the turnip gnawed by Audrey, had been plucked near Ann Hathaway's cottage; the deer carried across the stage in the hunting chorus had been shot in Charl[e]cote Park for the occasion – so I was told – by one of the Lacys.[22]

Augustin Daly's productions were also famous for spectacle and display. His *As You Like It*, which opened in New York in 1889 before transferring to London and then touring America, was one of the most successful. The set made '[e]specially effective use' of 'a revolving panorama of forest, which not only presents a variety of charming pictures, but conveys an impression of great spaces, and suggests in a striking manner the freedom and seclusion of the life in Arden'.[23] However, the show's greatest asset was its leading lady:

> Ada Rehan played Rosalind in a style peculiarly her own. It was not Shakespearean, and it was not poetic to any marked degree, but it was delightfully animated, piquant and feminine...she was a most attractive figure in her doublet and hose, and her

1. Ada Rehan as Rosalind in 1889: 'a precursor of the New Woman'.

love-scenes with Orlando were full of roguish humor and a very pretty audacity, tempered by little touches of womanly tenderness and apprehension, as in the episode of the bloody napkin. There can be no doubt that she won the warm favor of her audience.[24]

She even managed to win the approval of George Bernard Shaw, one of Daly's severest critics.[25] Marshall argues that her 'restless movement registered a vigorous style of feminine behaviour – a precursor of the New Woman'.[26]

Daly's success caused Henry Irving to shelve plans for a production at the Lyceum, so Rosalind was one of the few major female Shakespearean characters Ellen Terry never had an opportunity of playing.[27] Seeing the play in terms of lavish theatrical spectacle was still evident in Oscar Ashe's production at His Majesty's in 1907 which featured 'two thousand pots of ferns' plus 'large clumps of bamboo' and 'cartloads of last autumn's leaves'.[28] Ashe himself played Jaques, with his wife, Lily Brayton, as a more 'straightforward'[29] Rosalind than usual. Meanwhile, at Stratford 'productions entered a kind of time warp. A popular favourite, the play was staged sixteen times between 1894 and 1915, usually under the direction of Frank Benson.'[30] Despite the fact that Benson used a fuller text with fewer cuts and alterations, his productions had come to seem conventional:

> As the play most emphatically linked to the Stratford area, *As You Like It* became especially encrusted with tradition, of which the stuffed stag was emblematic: it was not seen as an increasingly moth-eaten prop but as a relic linked to Shakespeare himself.[31]

This changed with Nigel Playfair's 'experimental' production of 1919 when the theatre reopened after the First World War. Playfair had been influenced by the work of Harley Granville-Barker who had worked with William Poel and the Elizabethan Stage Society and their attempts to reproduce the original stagings of Shakespeare's plays. Playfair used an uncut text with only one interval and a simple set and costumes on a limited budget and a very tight schedule. Critical response was positive:

> The basis of the staging is obviously some illuminated manuscript of the early fifteenth century, perhaps not altogether unaffected by the Omega style in drawing. The forest, for instance, is

ruthlessly simplified, while the costumes are all 15th century, and very brilliant and exciting they are, even in the dim lighting affected by the modern stage artist. Mr. C. Lovat Fraser, who has designed it all, has, at any rate, vigour, and his daring mixture of styles certainly throws up the player against the scene.[32]

Rosalind was especially well received: 'Miss Athene Seyler takes the part at a tremendous rate, but the delicacy and perfection of her technique wonderfully brings out the invincible gaiety and tenderness which lie in Rosalind.'[33] But it was too much for the conservative local populace, as Nigel Playfair reported:

> When I came into my hotel . . . people turned their backs and got up and walked from the room . . . the rest of the cast fared little better; they were cut and cold-shouldered everywhere. When Lovat Fraser was walking in the street, a woman came up to him and shook her fist in his face. 'Young man,' she said impressively, 'how dare you meddle with our Shakespeare?'[34]

Edith Evans' Rosalind was the highlight of early twentieth-century productions from the Old Vic in 1926 to the New Theatre in 1937; as the critic J. C. Trewin put it in his review of the latter with Michael Redgrave as Orlando, she was 'Rosalind herself'.[35] Katherine Hepburn played Rosalind in Michael Benthall's production at New York's Cort Theater in 1950, but despite its successful run most critics agreed with Brooks Atkinson that 'There is too much Yankee in Miss Hepburn for Shakespeare's glades and lyric fancies' and she was ill-served by the 'literal and ponderous' production style.[36]

Glen Byam Shaw staged the play at Stratford in 1952 and 1957. The key on each occasion was the passing of the seasons from a wintry opening to the gradual arrival of spring. The London *Times* observed: 'It is hard to imagine Touchstone consenting to set out for the forest before spring had come'; it also necessitated 'the Duke and his fellow exiles enjoying an al fresco meal of fruit in the snow' with 'only their costumes, which are in the elegant fashion of the French court of Louis XVI, all silk and lace, to keep them warm'.[37] Nevertheless, critics were won over and Margaret Leighton's Rosalind and Laurence Harvey's Orlando were generally approved. Peggy Ashcroft, who had not succeeded in Harcourt Williams' experimental 1932 production at the Old Vic, was described in 1957 as 'quiveringly alive...an exquisitely light-hearted performance',[38] while another critic thought 'It would be difficult to find a better Orlando for this Rosalind than Richard Johnson. Here is a hero of manly charm, as handsome as he is sensitive, and surely irresistible to any woman of discernment.'[39] Wendy Toye 'breathed some life into what had become a moribund play'[40] at the Old Vic two years later, with strong performances by Barbara Jefford as Rosalind, Maggie Smith as Celia and Judi Dench as Phoebe. But the most successful and influential production of the mid-twentieth century was Michael Elliott's for the Royal Shakespeare Company in 1961 with Vanessa Redgrave as Rosalind, which is discussed in detail below.

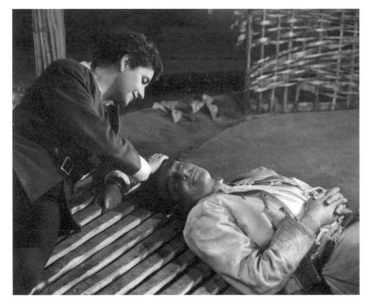

2. Glen Byam Shaw production, 1957, with Peggy Ashcroft as Rosalind and Richard Johnson as Orlando – 'A hero of manly charm, as handsome as he is sensitive, and surely irresistible to any woman of discernment'.

Overseas productions less wedded to the English pastoral tradition were often more ambitiously experimental. Jaques Copeau's at the Théâtre de l'Atelier in Paris in 1934 was marked by '[a]rchitectural décor and intellectual sophistication';[41] an Italian version of the production was staged in the Boboli Gardens in 1937. Moscow's Maria Yermolova Theatre mounted a 1940 production with a 'Robin Hood theme' in which 'pastoral received less emphasis than social critique'.[42] The Italian filmmaker Luchino Visconti's 1948 production at the Teatro Eliseo in Rome featured surrealist designs by Salvador Dalí. In 1954 Hans Schalla directed a production for the German Shakespeare Society with Touchstone as 'master of ceremonies'. Liviu Ciulei's 'famously avant-garde production at Bucharest's Teatrul Bulandra in 1961 ... emphasised ... fantasy and theatricality'.[43]

The work of Polish academic Jan Kott's *Shakespeare, Our Contemporary* (1964) influenced European productions such as Roberto Ciulli's 'coldly clinical staging' in Cologne in 1974 in which 'love could not operate, and was not meant to'[44]. Romanian director Petrica Ionescu's 1976 production at Bochum featured an all-male cast in a set 'suggesting a vandalized slaughterhouse or a war-damaged factory, with burst pipes, torn-off tiles and heaps of rubble.'[45] Marshall argues that the most successful experiment was Peter Stein's 1977 Berlin production which 'discovered a way to expose the pastoral's political charge without destroying the structure of fantasy.'[46] Staged before the fall of the Berlin Wall, 'attending the play required audiences to venture outside the city, lending peculiar resonance for a Berlin audience surrounded by the GDR' involving an hour-long bus drive to the CCC Film Studios where the first act was staged, after which the audience were 'actually hounded from the hall by the sound of barking dogs playing over the sound system.' There was then a fifteen-minute walk to 'Arden' which 'passed through a dark, gusty maze, with dangling vines, dripping water, and occasional surprises such as a wild bear.'[47]

The changing cultural climate of the 1960s had introduced radical ideas about sexuality and the social construction of gender and a desire to explore the dark side of Shakespeare's comedies. Clifford Williams' 1967 all-male National Theatre production at the Old Vic provoked much critical comment. Despite Williams' disclaimer, most saw the influence of Kott's ideas on the production. Opinions were divided about 'Ralph Koltai's plastic décor – dangling transparent tubes and dappled overhead cut-outs, and a variety of silver boots, PVC macs, and tattered regimentals.'[48] Williams was on record as saying 'underlying all the love scenes between Orlando and Rosalind there is an incredible incandescent purity.'[49] Most critics however thought the production sexless; more than one described Ronald Pickup playing Rosalind as 'beaky', 'long-legged' and 'nonerotic'[50], although others recognised how his performance grew:

> toward the end, Pickup softens the queerness into something quite close to girlhood. By the time Shakespeare's touching quartet arrives, he can read Rosalind's 'I for no woman' with a double meaning both effective and moving. And from then to the end he is wonderful, reading the epilogue as it had never been read before . . .[51]

The cast included Anthony Hopkins as Audrey '(the funniest of all performances)'[52] and Robert Stephens as Jaques. Buzz Goodbody's 1973 RSC production was a deliberate attempt to 'win the play back for women'.[53]

Conventional productions built around a star actress were still current; Maggie Smith's Rosalind formed 'the comic mainspring of the production'[54] in Robin Phillips' production at the Stratford Festival Ontario in 1977. John Dexter, who had walked out on the National's all-male version, directed their next in 1979 based on anthropologist J. G. Frazer's *The Golden Bough* and dominated by a Tree of Life on which was strewn flowers and a red garland of the innards from the slaughtered deer of Act 4. William was smeared with the deer's blood and crowned with its antlers, while

> other actors gathered round him wearing beautifully expressive deer masks. In the finale, the stage was completely surrounded by these 'deer', with William as an antlered Hymen, naked except

for fronds of leaves – a rustic god with whom Rosalind had joined forces to provide the 'rites' for her wedding.[55]

Productions since then have veered between radical explorations of the play's politics, gender and sexuality, and a view of it as a quintessentially English romp through the countryside. The first of many open-air performances was staged at Coombe House, Kingston-upon-Thames, in June 1885, and it was performed in the 1933 inaugural season at the Open Air Theatre in London's Regent's Park. It remains a popular choice for outdoor venues with local groups. The possibilities such outdoor productions offer, particularly their democratic potential, have been capitalized on in America, notably in Joseph Papp's 1973 production at the Delacorte Theater in New York's Central Park, which featured pop singer Meat Loaf as Amiens and film star Raul Julia as Orlando.[56] Rural Australia was the setting for Sydney's Nimrod Theatre production in 1983 and an 'aboriginal "second" shadowed Charles in the wrestling match; "topsy-haired" Audrey too was "part Negro or aboriginal or Islander"'.[57]

In Cheek by Jowl's 1991 production the director, Declan Donnellan, claimed that the 'all-male cast forces the audience to tread a tightrope of willed belief, a quintessentially theatrical act of faith'.[58] *City Limits* thought he used the actors 'to polymorphously perverse and liberating effect: every tug of affection, in any direction, is unloosed to be played explicitly'.[59] The production was well received, although not all critics found its exploration of sexual ambiguity liberating. The performance of the black actor Adrian Lester as Rosalind was subtly playful:

> The extraordinary thing about Adrian Lester was that, with his beautiful voice and grace of movement, when he played the female Rosalind playing at being the male Ganymede he seemed more like a woman playing a man than a man playing a woman. And when he played at Rosalind playing Ganymede playing Rosalind, one simply gave up trying to work out in one's mind whether one thought he was a woman playing a man playing a woman or a man playing a woman playing a man playing a woman.[60]

After her Oscar for *Shakespeare in Love*, in which she briefly played both Romeo and Juliet, Gwyneth Paltrow successfully took on Rosalind in Barry Edelstein's 1999 production at the Williamstown Theater 'as an ungainly youth in knickers and spectacles, his peaked cap worn backward on the head, like an aw-shucks version of Huckleberry Finn'.[61] In Lucy Bailey's 1999 promenade-type production at the Globe Theatre, some of the action was played in the yard among spectators who 'needed streetwise skills to leap backward on a surface littered with discarded soda cans, as the wicked Duke's followers strong-armed them out of the way to make room for the wrestling match at ground level'.[62] It was nevertheless 'a friendly and satisfying production' in which the 'one scary element' was Rosalind herself, 'in an unusual and fascinating performance by Anastasia Hille, who apparently wanted to turn the play into something more complex, more female-oriented', in a production that 'otherwise took the title of the play as a key to its interpretation'.[63]

The opportunities that film offers for realism, including Orlando's fight with the lion, were quickly recognized, and two early silent film versions were made by Kalem (1908) and Vitagraph (1912). Paul Czinner's 1936 film, with the distinguished Austrian actress Elisabeth Bergner and featuring a young Laurence Olivier as Orlando, blended 'realism and fantasy in odd and charming ways'[64] to a score by William Walton. In her 1992 film, Christine Edzard 'sought to evoke the spirit of Arden in a different place: the urban wasteland of London's docksides'.[65] Critics were divided: one argued that 'the film can only be fully appreciated when assessed in its own avant-garde terms as a postmodern experiment attendant upon, and sensitive to, a *fin-de-siècle* moment',[66] while others regretted its 'puritanical denial of visual pleasure'.[67] Despite praising the non-theatrical doubling of Orlando and Oliver, Marshall concludes that 'The disjunction between the Shakespearean language and the modern setting creates more strain than the rejection of pastoral convention.'[68] Several stage versions have been recorded for television, including an adaptation of the 1946 Regent's Park staging and the RSC's 1953 version with Margaret Leighton and Laurence Harvey, as well as Michael Elliott's 1961 production with Vanessa Redgrave. The BBC Shakespeare version directed by Basil Coleman was set at Glamis Castle in Scotland, but despite Helen Mirren's 'intelligent Rosalind', the naturalistic scenery dominated the small screen.

AT THE RSC

'Well, this is the Forest of Arden'

> Shakespeare's fantasy is a device to put us off our guard so that when he makes one of his sudden dives into truth our unpreparedness renders the unexpected vision all the more striking. In Shakespeare, reality and artifice are not two opposing modes but 'sphere-born, harmonious sisters', indispensable the one to the other.[69]

One of the major difficulties with *As You Like It* in performance seems to be the successful depiction of real feeling in an environment based on an artificial literary construct, the pastoral – melding naturalism with artificiality and making it believable.

In Michael Elliott's 1961 production the designer created a complete environment for the actors to play in, focusing, like so many in the past, on the idea of Arden as a second Eden, an idealistic idyll:

> [Richard] Negri's set is a steep green breast of a hill; from its top a mighty tree soars up and out of sight; branches jut from it like elephant tusks, supporting flat palettes of leaves. For the first scene or two I found the steepness of the rake distracting . . . but soon the set began to reveal its remarkable possibilities. For scene changes, patterns could be projected on to the ground: the grille of an iron gate in a courtyard, the dappled pattern of sunlight through the leaves of the forest. Superb groupings could be formed without any blatant use of 'levels'. And characters could converse lying flat on their backs – which (quite apart from its theatrical novelty) is precisely what one does in a forest glade. By the end of the evening I was in no doubt that, from Epping to the Schwarzwald, this was the knoll where I would pitch my ideal picnic. And what better definition could there be of Arden.[70]

Despite this, there were early indications that something darker was emerging from the subconscious forest world:

> Most strikingly, the killing of the deer became a crucial symbolic set-piece which acted as a critique of naïve pastoralism and affected the characterisation of the court-in-exile. By staging the stalking of the prey, its killing amid bestial cries from men momentarily turned to wolves, Mr Elliott gives point to Jaques' wincing – and suggests a reason for his melancholy, the old nightmare of the horns.[71]

Thus Elliott brought into question the idea of man the 'natural superior' and the masculine attributes on which a patriarchal social order is based.

The depiction of the hunting episode in this production was a precursor to an increased emphasis in the last half of the twentieth century on 'elements of pain and violence'[72] in the play. Not only has the duke's court become a place of genuine tyranny, but the forest, too, has been seen as a place of foreboding rather than a pastoral idyll. In the RSC's 1967 production, director David Jones

> never once lets us forget the play's reliance on the disruptive yet sustaining natural world . . . This Arden is black and cold; we first see the Duke and his compatriots shivering in sheep-coats, stamping upon the ground in order to forget the discomforts of exile. Jones makes a great deal of the deer-hunting scene which he transforms into a frightening ritual in which the men of Arden stain each other with blood.[73]

Nature proves as unforgiving as the court in winter and brings out man's baser instincts. Away from society and Christian restraints, the men revert back to pagan behaviour with a mock hunting initiation rite suggestive of manhood and fertility. Conversely, in Adrian Noble's 1985 production the hunting scene heralded the sexual initiation of Celia:

> Fiona Shaw's Celia gained from the production's clearest idea. The brief hunting episode ('What shall he have that killed the

deer?') that follows her line 'And I'll sleep' at the end of IV.i was interpreted as her dream. Jaques drew a bloodstained sheet across her as she slept, and the lords then pursued her around the stage as if she were the hunted deer. She had obviously had an erotic dream, a sexual awakening, and was therefore especially receptive to Oliver on his arrival, a point reinforced by the little laugh of sexual shock at his reference to the snake from which Orlando had saved him.[74]

Ritual was also portrayed as a positive force for healing and communion in the 1980 production, which climaxed with 'a pagan love-in and fertility-feast involving the cast as a whole'.[75] It moved

> from winter towards May Day (bringing a transformation of Farrah's set from a fleece-lined box to a sunny glade carpeted with spring flowers); it, too, is rooted in folklore which pervades the stage at the garlanded finale under Corin's hymen.[76]

> And so with the stage adorned with colourful blossom and foliage a cart appears, pulled by the forest lords, chariot-style . . . Celia, Rosalind, dressed as girls again. All is resolved and all presumably live happily ever after, as in all fairy tales. To celebrate, the cast dance and sing. It's a sort of fertility dance, rather like a Morris dance on the local village green, the audience clap to the beat and finally Rosalind delivers her epilogue to a sea of smiling, happy faces.[77]

Certain festivals and calendar dates were important to the Elizabethans – Midsummer, Harvest Home, Twelfth Night, New Year and, of course, May Day. Terry Hands' reference to these modified pagan rituals emphasized the elements of the play that bring about a heightened awareness of the relationship between man and nature. They also brought to mind how these festivals acted as a release-valve for human behaviour, especially sexuality. Inhibition was freed for celebration – Rosalind can free herself from the social restraints, strictures and expectations inflicted on women. Festive licence, while seemingly transgressing social boundaries, served in reality to underscore the underlying

3. Terry Hands production, 1980: ritual in the play 'climaxed with a pagan love-in and fertility feast involving the cast as a whole'.

expectations about appropriate behaviour demanded in everyday life. At the end of the play the status quo is resumed, but with a sense of hope rather than oppression.

The psychological aspects of the play were given a less subtle treatment in Noble's 1985 production which reinterpreted the idea of the Elizabethan pastoral, transforming the 'forest of Arden into a dream crossed Jungian testing-ground where true selves are discovered':

Arden is a state of mind, a psychic Garden of Eden which lies just behind the civilised courtly world. At court Duke Frederick is a malicious despot; he banishes his brother Duke Senior and then Rosalind from the kingdom. But the moment he steps through his reflection in the looking-glass he finds himself in Arden and it is the same actor (Joseph O'Conor) who plays both the dukes. The set, which consists of a large chamber, the mirror, a clock and a few chairs and tables, hardly changes except for the introduction of dust covers which are made, ingeniously, to billow and soar during a dream snow storm.[78]

Through the looking-glass, personalities were magically transformed, and what was described as the 'lunar beauty'[79] of the set offered possibilities for play and imagination:

> Noble's Arden was a dream-like version of the ducal court, with dustsheets covering the furniture...An enormous white silk cloth trailed behind the exiles as they arrived in Arden, obliterating the court furniture and providing 'possibilities for transformation into a hiding-place, a wedding-canopy'... Touchstone pulled it up about himself and Audrey to suggest bed clothes; she arranged it like a wedding dress; and when Rosalind encouraged Orlando to 'woo me, woo me', she likewise fabricated a dress from the stage cloth...for Noble the set was meant to release the actors so that characters might be explored in new ways. Not only is Arden 'a realm of imagination', but the production's emphasis shifted increasingly from stage effects 'towards making its characters' inner lives more visible'.[80]

In 2000, Kaffe Fassett's highly artificial set was based on tapestries created by Elizabethan women, depicting 'wonderful forests with palm trees and lionesses, great big flowers and tiny little stags and a big caterpillar and two people in love...'.[81] Arden was not a literal forest, but one created from the imagination of Rosalind: '*As you Like It* demonstrates not only "the green world", but also the manner in which that green world exists in our consciousness, namely the timeless world of play.'[82]

Artificiality, music and fun were the keynotes for the 1973 and 1977 productions which pastiched and updated the pastoral form. In 1977 this took the form of Trevor Nunn's eighteenth-century fantasy that included elements of baroque opera. The RSC main stage was adapted by designer John Napier 'to look like a late 17th century stage, with rows of lines and flats leading back, as it were, to infinity':[83]

> A toy proscenium stands within the proscenium proper; its curtain rises not on Act 1, scene 1, but on a musical scena in the manner of Purcell....Trevor Nunn, the director takes

every chance to introduce dancing or singing. They are dancing at the Bad Duke's court before Celia and Rosalind draw aside for their initial confidences. At the end, Hymen descends from heaven in a cloud and steals some of Rosalind's best lines while Rosalind, who has presumably contrived his arrival with real and not pretend magic, gets married with the other country copulatives.[84]

Critical of the artificiality of this approach, John Peter commented: 'There was poor old Shakespeare applying all his skill and sophistication to turning the rigid pastoral form into warm human drama; and here comes Trevor Nunn and turns it back into elaborate artifice.'[85]

In Buzz Goodbody's 1973 production, metallic 'tubular trees replaced the "melancholy boughs" of more conventional settings'.[86] As one critic described the effect of Christopher Morley's design, its 'pattern of dangling metal pipes for the forest background suggests that someone has disembowelled the Albert Hall organ above the stage'.[87] Many reviewers accused the production of never aiming

at even remotely credible behaviour among evolved human beings; for her the whole silly fable is an opportunity for three hours of high and low comedy ... [Goodbody] offers us a rock-and-roll setting by Guy Woolfenden of 'It was a lover' sung by two small boys with a tea-chest skiffle base. ('Same to you,' says one of them when Touchstone bids 'God mend your voices.') Derek Smith essays Touchstone as a music hall comic in distant descent from Max Miller ... After the final joining of all the copulatives, rock-and-roll breaks out again in a dancing epithalamium; streamers are thrown ... towards the audience, and a rain of coloured paper hearts falls from the ceiling.[88]

Despite its superficially bright and bouncy façade the production did not shirk at portraying the underlying threat of violence:

Frederick's court had 'the touchy atmosphere of Hitler's bunker', and while Duke Senior by contrast ruled over a place 'pretty cosy for a forest camp, with armchairs and the best wineglasses' ...

this Duke reached for a gun when he spoke of hunting, not a picturesque bow and arrow.[89]

Bringing references of political tyranny up-to-date,

John Caird's ... production in 1989 alluded to the recent collapse of communist regimes in Eastern Europe, showing Duke Frederick's court as a monument of oppressive totalitarian architecture, which had to be painfully dismantled by the dissident exiles to reveal the forest floor below. This production also literalized the Forest of Arden's 'winter and rough weather', showing the refugees making their escape through blizzards. Even in Arden they wore heavy greatcoats and huddled together for warmth, which somewhat hampered the expressiveness of their gestures and movement.[90]

Love and the Politics of Gender

The naturalness, the unforced understanding of her playing, the passionate, breathless conviction of it, the depth of feeling and the breadth of reality – this is not acting at all, but living, being, loving ... If the word enchantment has any meaning, it is here.[91]

This was how Bernard Levin described Vanessa Redgrave's landmark performance as Rosalind. He was echoed by a plethora of male critics who were equally beguiled by her rendition of the character:

Her performance is a triumph. For the first few scenes it looked as if she was going to seem gawky in the part, but I suspect she intended it. Her Rosalind, very properly is mewed up in court clothes. As soon as she gets into the forest she expands, throws her arms wide to the air, and frolics up and down Negri's hill like one of shepherd Corin's long-legged lambs. Between the leaps she pants out Rosalind's euphuistic conceits with all the excitement of someone who has just found that she too can play the game of fashionable wit. In every way the forest of Arden is a place of discovery for her.[92]

Most male critics failed to mention how Redgrave's performance forced the audience to recognize that

> [Rosalind] is also a character thrown on her own resources when exiled by an authoritarian state. It seems entirely appropriate that Redgrave, between the Stratford season and the London revival,

4. Vanessa Redgrave's landmark performance as Rosalind in 1961: 'Arden is a place of discovery for her'.

became a political activist, for what she was demonstrating on the Stratford stage was literally 'actresses' liberation.[93]

In Arden, expressions of love and the flouting of gender stereotypes become political statement, an active reaction against the tyrannical court and the strictures of society. As in *A Midsummer Night's Dream*, the forest acts as a place of catharsis, of self-discovery where lessons can be learnt and hopefully taken back into society.

In Trevor Nunn's 1977 production Rosalind and Orlando were, in part, drawn together by their desire to lead a different type of life than the one offered to them:

> Peter McEnery's ravaged Orlando in a West Country accent [adopted as a sign of his neglected education] is far from the orthodox mooning lover, and seems at times to be desperately trying to break out of the conventions that surround him, and Kate Nelligan's bursting and exuberant Rosalind – all darting hands and flying ringlets – has precisely the kind of humanity that these conventions try and control. What the play says finally is that humanity, love and simplicity must triumph over corruption.[94]

Similarly, in David Thacker's 1992 production,

> Samantha Bond's Rosalind and Peter de Jersey's Orlando set themselves up interestingly against convention. Both of them have to fight to keep their hold upon life. De Jersey's Orlando, no cool hero he, is almost at the end of his emotional tether in the hostile court; Miss Bond's precarious Rosalind, threatened with banishment, is overwhelmed rather than comforted by Phyllida Hancock's bland Celia.[95]

The friendship between Celia and Rosalind is central to the dynamic of the play. In Adrian Noble's 1985 modern dress production, Juliet Stevenson (Rosalind) and Fiona Shaw (Celia) explained how,

> To liberate Shakespeare's women from the confines of literary and theatrical tradition requires an analysis of the nature and effects of those social structures which define and contain them – the opening of this play sees Rosalind and Celia already contained

within a structure that is oppressive and patriarchal, namely the court of Duke Frederick, Celia's father. The modern dress decision served to remind us that such structures are by no means 'ancient history', and that the freedom and self-definition that the two girls are seeking remain prevalent needs for many of their contemporaries today.[96]

In some recent productions Celia's role has been given added poignancy with the suggestion that she, too, is in love with Orlando. In Terry Hands' 1980 production Sinead Cusack as Celia did 'much to bring an unrewarding part to life by suggesting that she too fancies Orlando, is jealous of, if good humouredly resigned to his preference for Rosalind, and doesn't altogether relish her role as gooseberry at their flirtations'.[97] In Dominic Cooke's 2005 production,

Amanda Harris, in a brilliantly detailed performance, turns Celia into a myopic closet romantic, who equally fancies Orlando but lacks her cousin's emotional audacity. Their relationship wittily becomes a microcosm of the play's fascination with antithetical, yet linked, worlds.[98]

Unlike Celia, Rosalind is given a unique opportunity, the freedom to behave as she wishes when she dons a male identity. Juliet Stevenson's Rosalind in 1985

delightedly shuffles off her limiting female apparel to prove a manipulative, teasing and sexually curious young woman – and it would be interesting to think that this is, in part, a play about how we are defined by gender – certainly Stevenson's performance substantiates this idea.[99]

The difficulty with having a woman play Rosalind is that we can never quite believe that Orlando is fooled by the deception. Most actresses maintain such a large element of their femininity, or resort to exaggerated male swaggering, that it wouldn't fool anyone. There is a suspension of belief required that doesn't quite bring about the frisson which it would have done in Shakespeare's day when all female roles were played by men. Stevenson's performance, although not widely applauded, did bring out a sense of equality between Rosalind and Orlando, by being convincing as Ganymede:

> The one really successful feature of this messy production was the masterly partnership of Juliet Stevenson and Hilton McRae as Rosalind and Orlando. For once, the two parts were equally matched. They were the same kind of people, warm, direct, impulsive: Orlando attacked Oliver at one moment yet hugged him generously the next; Rosalind vehemently assured Duke Frederick that she and her father were not traitors. With her contemporary unisex hairstyle and white suit, Miss Stevenson was equally convincing as boy and girl. Her baggy trousers followed the latest fashion but also suggested that she was in part a clown: she used a bowler hat and cane like a cabaret artiste to illustrate the 'divers paces' of Time. She transformed this directorial gambit by her own grace and timing, and because she so securely communicated the crucial point that it is through mockery and deception that Rosalind expresses her love. At 'I can live no longer by thinking,' Orlando momentarily glimpsed, through eyes dimmed with tears, the features of Rosalind, not just Ganymede, reflected in the water as she looked over his shoulder; and when he subsequently cried passionately 'Why blame you me to love you?' he caught exactly both the game and the underlying emotional intensity. In the mock marriage, their mutual declarations 'I take thee, Rosalind...I do take thee, Orlando' were heartfelt and gave the impression of an equal relationship.[100]

The costuming used for many Rosalinds has actually emphasized her sexuality, as if Arden has accentuated her femininity through male disguise. Michael Billington said of Buzz Goodbody's 1973 production:

> this is a play of enormous sexual ambiguity in which man woos girl-dressed-as-boy. But any hint of sexual equivocation is knocked on the head by Eileen Atkins's minimal attempt to disguise her femininity as Rosalind. Indeed, with her headband,

fringed blouse and crutch hugging jeans, she seemed even more seductive as Ganymede than before.[101]

Likewise, in 1996, Niamh Cusack in her disguise as Ganymede looked, 'with her long honey-gold tresses, unequivocally feminine'.[102] The obviousness of Rosalind's disguise does alter audiences' reactions to the central relationship, as does the sense of Orlando's awareness that Ganymede is, indeed, a girl in disguise. This awareness is often built into performances, as in 2005, when Lia Williams was

> so overcome with the romping giddiness of love and with the licence granted by her male mufti that she's always in danger of going too far. She allows, for example, a finger to rove up Orlando's chest and it's no surprise that the pair find themselves in a prolonged kiss, leaving [Barnaby] Kay to shore up his heterosexual credentials afterwards in a very funny, dazed macho strut. In this interpretation, Rosalind is rumbled when she faints into the arms of Orlando's brother, Oliver, who becomes aware of her breasts. It's clear that he passes this information on to the hero, who hence emerges here as a man of great empathy and tolerance. His tacit acceptance of the trick imparts an added charge to the line: 'I can live no longer by thinking' and Williams's Rosalind duly accords it the respect of a lengthy pensive silence.[103]

It appears that productions are more likely to fail when Rosalind suppresses her sexuality through disguise. Peter Holland commented of David Thacker's 1992 production:

> Samantha Bond's Rosalind belonged to the tradition aptly defined by Lindsay Duguid: '[She] is wholesome and pert with her slightly husky actress's voice and her gamine gestures (legs apart, arms akimbo, hands in pockets, and so on). The English actress playing Rosalind is a gender all her own' . . . If this was Rosalind in a limbo of gender it was also Rosalind without sexuality. For in a play so full of sexual desire the production saw only clichéd romance, epitomised by the long hard look between Celia and Oliver at the end of 4.3 or their rapt attention of each other in 5.4.[104]

From what we can glean from the wildly divergent opinions of Sophie Thompson's exuberant performance as Rosalind in 1989, she emphasized the sexual immaturity of a young woman discovering sex for the first time:

> The result is very different from the romantic heroines of yore. Her Rosalind is part waif, part tomboy, a naïve, gawky girl who can mug and fool, tickle an irritating friend, but also play purposeful games when the time comes. With that bewildered heart-throb, Flynn's Orlando, you feel she is testing the sexual waters, readying herself for a plunge that may one day end her, as she claims, 'fathoms deep in love'.[105]

What's so Funny?

The major problem in producing the play today lies not in Orlando and Rosalind, whose relationship, for all its fantastic context, seems to have an everlasting modernity, but in finding satisfactory modern equivalents for these sixteenth-century variety turns.[106]

In *As You Like It* 'the love action is supervised by the counter-clowns Touchstone and Jaques.'[107] Like many elements in the play, these two characters offer us a 'juxtapositions of opposites':[108] Touchstone the professional clown, and Jaques the natural melancholic, punctuate the play with opposing witticisms. Unfortunately, comedy does have a tendency to date, and Touchstone, more than most Shakespearean comic roles, does not seem to have stood the test of time. B. A. Young of the *Financial Times*, having witnessed many productions of *As You Like It*, stated: 'it would take [Buster] Keaton himself to persuade me that Touchstone is funny'.[109]

David Tennant, who played the part in 1996, eventually discovered humour in the role, but on initial inspection of the character, he concluded:

> I could see that Touchstone was supposed to be funny in terms of the structure of the play, the tone of his scenes, and the fact that everyone keeps going on about how hilarious he is. Jaques

in particular, an otherwise miserable sod, when confronted with Touchstone, finds his 'lungs began to crow like Chanticleer' [2.7.30] and yet I could find nothing in the part to make me even smile...long speeches heavy with obscure double entendres and long tracts of cool philosophy, but nothing obviously funny.[110]

The actor playing Touchstone often has to resort to obvious visual gags, or crude humour in order to get a laugh from the audience. In Adrian Noble's 1985 production an onstage pool offered the inevitability of a pratfall. One reviewer commented:

Worst of all...is the strip cartoon, slapstick routines provided by Nicky Henson's Touchstone....Henson ends up in a pool at least three times, and provides a most laboured and unfunny illustration of the 'lie seven times removed' speech, in which the rest of the cast are made...to join in. His routine ends with a chorus of mock farts.[111]

5. An initial impression of cool philosophy rather than obvious humour: David Tennant as Touchstone, with Arthur Cox as Corin, in Stephen Pimlott's 1996 production.

Paul Chahidi in the RSC's 2005 production managed to make Touchstone funny, successfully engaging the audience, which he had 'eating out of his hand'.[112] Nevertheless, he, too, had to find humour in visual gags and asides added to what Shakespeare has supplied: 'Paul Chahidi is that rarest of things, a genuinely funny Touchstone, never more entertaining than in an inspired routine when he treads in something nasty in the forest':[113] '[He] works wonders with the thankless role of Touchstone...[but] can't resist milking his chatty relationship with front-row spectators.'[114]

Buzz Goodbody updated the character in an attempt to give the audience a contemporary equivalent: 'Certainly the director, Buzz Goodbody, was not one for half measures. Touchstone, court-jester, became the television comedian, who has transmigrated from the music hall to the new medium.'[115] In the same production (1973), modern literary references informed Richard Pasco's widely applauded performance as Jaques. He portrayed him as 'one of those hypochondriacal patients of Dr Chekhov who are in mourning for their life':[116]

In a seedily smart suit, wispy-haired, fiddling with gold-rimmed spectacles, he diffuses the bulbous fragility of an alcoholic, precariously cured, whose self-disgust still expresses itself in rapid apprehension and exuberant fancy. He enriches the Ages of Man speech by making each age a self-contained antithesis, with a twist in the tail. He signals recognition of each predictable folly with a most delicate play of feature, points each deflationary line with a musical accuracy which is a joy in itself. He gives an enormously enjoyable performance, like many a Jaques before him; and like all fine rather than merely exciting players, he expands one's understanding of human nature.[117]

Because the comedy does not often work with modern audiences, directors have added an extra dimension to both Touchstone and Jaques by emphasizing their similarities rather than their differences. In 1961,

Mr Max Adrian and Mr Colin Blakely are a Jaques and a Touchstone who seem to take a genuine pleasure in each other's company. The egoist's wisdom, it has been said, is half fooling, as Touchstone's fooling is half wisdom, and both seem delightedly aware of their true relations.[118]

In Terry Hands' 1980 production the characters of Touchstone and Jaques ran parallel to each rather than being opposites. Derek Godfrey's Jaques demonstrated a talent for clowning and also revealed a lustful side, showing he was equally under Arden's influence:

a close bond develops between these two. From the moment when Derek Godfrey, instead of simply reporting his meeting with a fool in the forest, launches into his own clown routine. This being a performance show, Joe Melia's Touchstone is a whole-time performer as much as Audrey's balding lover as when called upon to do a turn for the Duke...Much more surprising but thoroughly in keeping with the fertility motif, Jaques is shown falling for Rosalind who half-succumbs to being folded in his cloak before her real lover arrives on the scene and the sound of youthful laughter drives Jaques back into solitude.[119]

In the majority of productions Jaques as the melancholic is also the outsider of the pastoral world, the world of love. In productions that emphasized 'the tyrannical rule of Duke Frederick's court as either a fascist or a communist dictatorship...Jaques was shown either as...a political dissident or a student agitator'.[120] His separateness from the other characters in the play was taken to an interesting extreme in John Caird's 1989 production:

The whole world seemed a show put on for [Jaques] benefit; indeed, at times he took a seat in the front of the stalls to watch the parade of folly, leaping back onto the stage at, for instance, [3.3.67] to help Touchstone get married. The bitterness of his out-of-place dignity turned his report on Touchstone into a brutal language that this Touchstone would not have used...his final comments to Touchstone [5.4.191–2] were inordinately vicious, provoking a response of genuine distress from Touchstone himself.[121]

The way in which Jaques was costumed and lit also added an extra dimension of sinister foreboding to the character, giving him a darkly metaphysical presence:

> a suave, crisply spoken Jaques, with elegant overcoat, trilby hat, and walking cane, separating him sharply from his ragged co-mates in exile. He had an unforgettable moment as he stood still and silent upstage behind Hymen, his dark clothes lost against the background, top lighting catching his cheek-bones and giving him a startling cadaverous look for this 'last scene of all'. [122]

Jaques, is also often portrayed as a timeless figure or, indeed, like Rosalind, a character at odds with the society in which he finds himself. In 1992, Michael Siberry played

> a dark, elegant, superbly spoken Jaques ... a handsome, battered man in early middle age, majestically embittered and revelling in it with the relish of an exhibitionist. His revulsion at the slaughter of animals is quite genuine, which only reminds you that Shakespeare was writing for an age which found pleasure in their public torture and killing. Even Queen Elizabeth preferred bear-baiting to stage plays. Once again, the dramatist is light years ahead of his time.[123]

The tendency for modern productions to focus on the darker elements in the play has sometimes gone too far, draining the comedy of its humour, vitality and passion. Steven Pimlott's 1996 production provided

> few laughs and almost no delight. Touchstone (David Tennant) works hard to make some sour humour out of Arden ... Niamh Cusack plays Rosalind as if she has been told to avoid all playfulness, and Rachel Joyce as Celia declines all chances of wryness in her commentaries on the follies of lovers.[124]

John Woodvine, however, was praised as 'a wonderfully grave, sententious Jacques whose seven-ages-of-man speech acquires unusual poignancy when he discovers that old Adam has quietly expired'.[125]

What is often described as Shakespeare's most accessible and enjoyable comedy throws some decidedly difficult curves for the modern director. The frequency with which the play is revived in the modern repertoire attests to its popularity with audiences, but has resulted in very idiosyncratic approaches, turning a pleasing comedy into a melancholy tale of exile and isolation, a feminist tract or modern psychodrama. As Penny Gay points out 'a final loss of directorial innocence . . . is the hallmark of most modern productions.' In our postmodern culture, directors know that there is no such thing as a simple 'trust in the given material'.[126]

THE DIRECTOR'S CUT: INTERVIEWS WITH DOMINIC COOKE AND MICHAEL BOYD

Dominic Cooke was born in 1966 and educated at the University of Warwick. His *Arabian Nights* (1998) won a TMA/Equity Award for Best Show for Young People after it was produced at The Young Vic and on tour in 1998. He was Associate Director first at the Royal Court Theatre and then with the Royal Shakespeare Company, where his productions included *Cymbeline*, *Macbeth*, John Marston's *The Malcontent*, the acclaimed *As You Like It* (with Lia Williams as Rosalind) that he talks about here and an equally acclaimed rendition of Arthur Miller's *The Crucible*. He was nominated for an Evening Standard Theatre Award in 2003 for Best Director. In 2007 he returned to the Royal Court, Britain's leading venue for new theatre writing, as Artistic Director.

Michael Boyd was born in Belfast in 1955, educated in London and Edinburgh and completed his MA in English Literature at Edinburgh University. He trained as a director at the Malaya Bronnaya Theatre in Moscow. He then went on to work at the Belgrade Theatre in Coventry, joining the Sheffield Crucible as Associate Director in 1982. In 1985 Boyd became founding Artistic Director of the Tron Theatre in Glasgow, becoming equally acclaimed for staging new writing and innovative productions of the classics. He was Drama

Director of the New Beginnings Festival of Soviet Arts in Glasgow in 1999. He joined the RSC as an Associate Director in 1996 and has since directed numerous productions of Shakespeare's plays. He won the Laurence Olivier Award for Best Director for his version of the *Henry VI* plays in the RSC's 'This England: The Histories' in 2001. He took over as Artistic Director of the RSC in 2003 and oversaw the extraordinarily successful Complete Works Festival in 2006–07. His own contribution to this was a cycle of all eight history plays, from *Richard II* through to *Richard III*, with the same company of actors. This transferred to London's Roundhouse Theatre in 2008 and won multiple awards. He talks here about his 2009 production of *As You Like It* in The Courtyard Theatre in Stratford-upon-Avon, with Katy Stephens as Rosalind.

It's very much a play of two worlds – the court and the country. How did you and your designer set about conveying that?

DC: We were more interested in the connections between the two worlds than their differences. The set remained the same throughout; we had a very large tree which served both for an urban garden and the middle of a forest. The tree was an evergreen, so it could also work through the seasons, which was an important feature of the production. We moved from winter to summer to autumn, so that the end of the play felt like harvest-time. We started the play at Christmas, with the tree as a Christmas tree. We chose Christmas because it is a time where loss is keenly felt. Rosalind has lost her father, and this was a time where she would usually be with him, so her memories of him brought on the melancholy she felt at the start of the play. Family conflicts often happen at Christmas too, so the Oliver/Orlando row was put into context. We were also interested in the summer-holiday quality to the third act of the play, as Ganymede tutors Orlando. The only way that we emphasized the different worlds visually was through costume. The court was a night-time world of formal evening dress, Arden was a cross between a summer holiday and *Lord of the Flies*. The transformation from court into country was done by the actors

6. Dominic Cooke production, 2005: Duke Senior's exiles return to the harsh but honest reality of nature.

who doubled as the dukes and the respective courts. As we first moved into the Forest of Arden, to take us into Duke Senior's 'Now, my co-mates and brothers in exile' speech, the actors took their tops off as it snowed, as if Duke Senior's celebrating the honest, harsh reality of nature as opposed to the artificial, deceitful world of the Court.

MB: The court is often portrayed as deeply unattractive, but Tom Piper, the designer, and I felt that the dukedom should look as if it was worth fighting for. We also wanted it to boast of the purity and the reformed colour palate of a 'new broom' revolutionary court. Two uninterrupted rectangles of very pale parquet against which the restrictive choreography and black Elizabethan dress of Frederick's world could be seen to be striking as well as oppressive.

Arden then became a subversive dismantling of the too-perfect court, a humanizing reinvention of its constituent parts through poor theatre improvisation.

The received idea of Arden is sentimental and decorative, but Shakespeare talks of winter, rough weather, exile, and a hard-earned subsistence. Frederick's troops are attacking the woods, and animals are hunted and slain not for sport but for 'venison'.

As the exiled world reinvents for us how best to live, the high collars and corsets disappear and gradually the visual world moves from the rigid uniformity of Renaissance Protestant revolution to a colourful pluralism of contemporary dress.

A careful reading of the text suggests that Arden is not a single place: Corin seems to be a farmer on the fringes of the forest, faced with real economic problems, whereas the duke and his men hunting the stag seem to be in deep, perhaps more mythic, woodlands (Robin Hood and all that). Was this an angle you explored?

DC: With Arden, Shakespeare is contrasting the myth of the pastoral idyll with the reality of the hardship of country life. We played the cold weather in the early Arden scenes, showing how difficult it is to actually survive in the wild, especially for the exiles, used to the creature comforts of the court. We imagined a shift from winter to summer before Act 3 scene 1, which is where we placed the interval.

I was very interested in the conflict between Duke Senior's idealization of the life of the exiled court and Jaques' cynicism. For me, every scene of *As You Like It* contrasts a romantic with a realistic view of life, and that exists as much in the court as in the country scenes. Duke Senior's opening speech expresses the notion that by throwing off the shackles of civilization it is possible to reveal an inner authenticity, free of 'painted pomp', whereas Jaques' view is that life is a series of different performances – as expressed in his 'seven ages of man' speech – and there is no 'inner core': the idea that you can throw off civilization and become this pure being, to him, is just a sentimental myth, a political ideology to make the exiles feel that their lot, which is pretty miserable, is actually a happy one. Also, Duke Senior has a difficult political situation on his hands. We learn from

Charles the wrestler that the forest lords have 'thrown themselves into voluntary exile', but when they get to Arden they find that they've exposed themselves to 'winter and rough weather', so Duke Senior's optimism could also be read as an attempt to convince them that it's all going to be worth it and they should stick with him. I suppose that makes Amiens his chief propagandist.

MB: The woods of Corin, Silvius and Phoebe are comically overlaid with idealized, mythic notions of courtly love every bit as much as Ferdinand's 'inner' forest is in search of the mythic simplicities of the 'golden age'. Both sets of forest-dwellers live in actual hardship, and from the word go there is a busy traffic between them: Orlando, Touchstone, Jaques, Rosalind and Ferdinand all meet long before the wedding. The main distinction (even if in part the result of disguise) is one of class.

Banishment, a usurping brother (and uncle), envy, and the abuse of authority all surface in the opening act of this comedy, and Rosalind's situation at the beginning of the play is very close to Hamlet's. Tragic court, comic Arden, then? Or is it more complex than that?

DC: For me, it is more complex. I think Shakespeare is interested in both simultaneously subverting and supporting all those conventional notions of court as false and country as authentic. There's always a dialectic, a duality being played out in *As You Like It*. In the court there is warmth in the intimate relationship between Celia and Rosalind surviving against the odds. There's loyalty in Touchstone and even Le Beau. While the world of the court is performative, Arden is in some respects even more so. Here, for example, Rosalind is in the permanent state of performing Ganymede. Equally, the country is as full of pain and loss as the court. The first time we see anyone talk about love in Arden it's Silvius, and he's in agony. We played Silvius' pain very strongly in our production, the terrible despair and torture of what Phoebe's doing to him. Arden's also a place of great physical hardship: Corin talks about how hard his life is. What's continually subverted is the sentimental cliché that the country is 'nice' – Shakespeare, after all, was a country boy himself and knew that country life and country people can be far from nice. It can be a cruel and dangerous place.

MB: Rosalind is our Hamlet as we would like it. Written around the same time as her less fortunate brother Hamlet, and her other sibling Henry V, Rosalind comes at civil strife and injustice and a world out of joint from a different angle. Perhaps she is blessed that as a woman she was not 'born to set it right', and can therefore behave more like an artist, more like Shakespeare: the 'powerless' subversive. She is also allowed a more fully explored exile from court than Hamlet, and *As You Like It* accordingly invites us to explore the alternatives to the misery of rule by Claudius and Frederick.

Where do you think Jaques' melancholy stems from?

DC: I speculated that he is someone who had suffered a loss in love that he's never recovered from. Clearly, the play is concerned with the different ways human beings go about trying to find love. For me, Jaques is the cynic who was once the lover. He was once the Orlando figure, and that's why he despises Orlando so much: because Orlando represents something that he has crushed within himself – the loving, open-hearted, vulnerable young man who will, in Jaques eyes, inevitably get hurt. He cannot tolerate romantic views in anyone, especially in Duke Senior and Orlando.

To me it's significant that the two characters that Shakespeare invented that weren't in the source text were Jaques and Touchstone, who are the cynics, the anti-romantics. This was very significant in my understanding of the play. The elements that Shakespeare's added to the story are the minor notes, the voices of dissent, the anti-pastoral elements. So it is useful to look at what he was trying to do with those characters tonally. In the early court scenes between Celia and Rosalind, Rosalind frequently expresses a romantic view of love and Celia undercuts it. The same dynamic continues in Arden – Jaques is introduced as a foil for Duke Senior, to undercut and puncture the duke's romantic view of man as a pure being with an essence and a moral core; Jaques' melancholy is a minor note that cuts against that because it speaks of loss, of human frailty and the inevitability of death.

MB: Rosalind gives the ungenerous answer to this question in her encounter with Jaques. She steps effortlessly into the shoes of the little boy in *The Emperor's New Clothes*, and strips Jaques naked with startling clarity. He is revealed as a lonely, would-be monk who thinks he can find truth in ascetic gestures, but who still yearns for company, the court and pretty youths.

Elsewhere, we, like the duke's exiled court, find ourselves utterly drawn to what this melancholic has to say about brief mortality, and the wicked and venal nature of the world. That said, the self-importance of the usual treatment of Jaques in the English tradition is surprising, and possibly due to the reputation of the role as a 'star part' for important actors.

And what on earth is going on with the other Jaques, the middle brother who suddenly appears at the end? Why did Shakespeare call him Jaques as well? Just lazy writing on Shakespeare's part? It's not exactly a rewarding part for an actor, is it?

DC: Shakespeare is often interested in the number three in his plays; the classic example being *A Midsummer Night's Dream*, where everything's structured around three worlds. The number three in drama is very potent. It implies a beginning, a middle and an end. In the story of *As You Like It*, Oliver is the beginning, Orlando the middle and Jaques de Bois is the end. Perhaps the reason he's called Jaques is that the other Jaques disappears out of the play at the point that he comes in. And the original Jaques disappears because hope wins over and so the minor notes are no longer necessary. The new Jaques brings in a crucial message of hope: transformation is possible, although hard-won.

MB: Jaques de Bois completes the family and the picture of Britain: Orlando in exiled opposition; Oliver, the traitor to his family's heritage; and Jaques, the secret recusant, allowed to study at university but keeping his faith, and waiting for the return of the 'true king'.

Practically speaking, what devices did you use for the cross-dressing of Rosalind?

DC: The main focus was in the physicality and attitude of the character rather than the costume, which we kept simple. Because we were focusing on the continuums between court and country, one of the first decisions Lia [Williams – Rosalind], Rae [Smith – Designer] and I came to about the way Rosalind should look, was that she shouldn't have a wig. Originally we were going to have long tresses in the court, then Lia's own short hair would be revealed in the country. But we felt it was useful to leave as much of the job of the transformation to the actor and her physical life, rather than using the more obvious visual sign that long hair equals 'girl' and short hair equals 'boy'. We gave Rosalind a quite formal, classical evening dress in the court. In Arden, she wore a pair of brown jeans, a white shirt with a pair of braces, and boots, so there was a slightly ragamuffin, scruffy feeling about her clothes. Lia also had padding between her legs which helped her stand, move and feel like a male.

MB: Strangely enough, we let Katy's hair down for Ganymede. We also threw away the court collar and corset and gave her a small moustache which made her look like a cross between Antonio Banderas and Katharine Hepburn. Dharmesh Patel wore a wig of even longer hair as Amiens, to afford us a currency of young men with long hair.

And, more profoundly, did your Rosalind become more herself when she was Ganymede?

DC: I don't really know what this question means. I think the play is partly dealing with how authentic you can be as a person, and what does authenticity mean? Do human beings have a core to them, a moral centre, or is life a series of different acts played out, a performance? I don't think the play comes down on one side or the other. What is undoubtedly true is that by performing and being artificial she discovers the authenticity of Orlando's feelings. Her disguise allows her to explore Orlando's feelings for her in safe parameters.

MB: Katy came to rehearsals very confident of her ability to inhabit a young pugnacious male, and it came as a shock to us all to discover that Rosalind was at her most profoundly feminine as Ganymede.

Entered into as a self-protective act of male impersonation, Ganymede becomes a powerful and disturbing disinhibitor that reveals and transforms Rosalind more profoundly than any forest could. Dreams and demons which were inexpressible for a courtly woman of the time come tumbling out to anticipate centuries of gender struggle, striking us as astonishingly contemporary and scaring the pants off both Celia and Orlando.

Is Orlando worthy of Rosalind? Linguistically and psychologically, hers does seem to be the stronger part.

DC: I read James Shapiro's book *1599* while I was in rehearsal, and that was a big influence on me. His argument is that Orlando knows from the word go that Ganymede is Rosalind in disguise. I felt that this would make the playing of the Orlando–Rosalind scenes rather arch and overcomplicated. But I was struck by the idea that Orlando knows that Ganymede is Rosalind as he goes into the final scene. I think there is textual justification for this. Also, if Orlando starts the final scene unaware that Ganymede is in fact Rosalind, he's both very much behind Rosalind and behind the audience, and therefore never her equal. For me it was important that he was her equal, otherwise her choice is brought into question by an audience, in a way that makes the play unsatisfying. It feels like a bad match that couldn't possibly survive. Our eventual supposition – and like all Shakespeare interpretations, it is open to question – was that, in the 'bloody handkerchief' scene, when Oliver picks up Ganymede after she's fainted, he discovers through physical contact with her that she's a woman. I think this is supported by the text: he calls her 'Rosalind' at the end of the scene, for example, rather than 'Ganymede'. We speculated that between this scene and the scene where Orlando tells Rosalind that he 'can live no longer by thinking', Oliver has told Orlando what he's discovered. This seems justified by Orlando's complete change of mood in relation to Ganymede – he's had enough of the mind games. However, he has learned that role-play, improvisation and an element of performance are a crucial part of keeping a relationship alive; it's not all about pinning poems on trees. A successful marriage is built on each partner agreeing to improvise together, to play a variety of roles with conviction, to have flexibility. This is what he has learned from Rosalind, and in our production it became clear through the way he played along when she said 'I have, since I was three year old, conversed with a magician'. Therefore, he was a knowing participant in this conspiracy rather than a dupe. This completed Rosalind and Orlando's journey together. He has learned his lesson and they are now ready to go into marriage together as equals. I was really pleased with this aspect of the production, because I thought it did solve one of the problems of the play, of 'Well, why is she marrying that guy, he's so naive?'

MB: She should be so lucky. Phoebe is not the only woman in *As You Like It* who is 'not for all markets'. The disgraced daughter of a defeated duke, spirited and wanton, and far too intelligent for the average male ego, Rosalind will almost certainly have to look abroad and probably trade down for a husband. In Orlando she has found a man whom she desires on sight, who shares her moral strength, and who surpasses her in potency and sense of wonder. His name is an anagram not just of his father's but of the great Roland of chivalric legend. His lyric verses are imperfect, but that's a manly failing. He has the open heart, the wit and the playfulness to spar as an equal with Rosalind on fire as Ganymede. It is true that the action which ultimately makes him more than worthy of Rosalind takes place offstage: it is Orlando's love, courage and physical strength when faced with the lion and Oliver

7. Michael Boyd production, 2009: Orlando as a match for Rosalind, 'He has the open heart, the wit and the playfulness to spar as an equal with Rosalind'.

that turns the fortunes of the play and even mystically disarms the troops of Frederick. Orlando in the theatre depends heavily on his Oliver to return the favour as he recounts the tale of Orlando's Christ-like sacrifice of his own blood to cleanse the sins of the world.

How do you see the balance in the relationship between Rosalind and Celia?

DC: We made a decision very early on that Celia is the more naive of the two when it comes to the opposite sex. We went down the line that she was a very learned, slightly swotty, bookish girl, who preferred the company of other girls and hadn't discovered boys yet. This played well because it allowed Celia's deflating responses to Rosalind to be based on her lack of experience in love. She is not really interested in boys until she meets Oliver, where everything changes. Tellingly, from that point in the play she's silent. It's as if she's now been bitten by the romantic bug and has nothing more to say. There's a major shift in the relationship between Rosalind and Celia when

Rosalind falls in love with Orlando, and as the love between Rosalind and Orlando deepens, life becomes quite fraught and painful for Celia. She feels excluded. She's given up everything for Rosalind – her home, her family – and now it feels like Rosalind's abandoned her. But she's also intrigued by the strange transformation her friend is undergoing. Celia's story is about letting go of Rosalind and, on some psychic level, making space for Oliver.

MB: Celia is the daughter of the younger brother and talks of being too young to appreciate Rosalind at the time of Frederick's coup. So she's probably younger that Rosalind, even though her voice at court is older and more pragmatic; the voice of authority and merry competence compared with Rosalind's hesitant and volatile start.

I enjoyed the youth and frailty of Mariah Gale in our production, which is repressed at court and covered with a determined optimism, then revealed as hopelessly out of its depth in the forest as Katy's older Rosalind sings and bleeds as an adult woman on fire with desire. Celia is brittle but in charge of her father's court, and, after a delightful burst of bossy grand-dame behaviour, has to sit quietly and learn from Rosalind how to be ready for love when it strikes in the shape of Oliver.

In what ways was Touchstone a touchstone in your production?

DC: In the first half of the play in the court I think he is, because he's saying the unsayable, speaking the truth in a world where the truth is dangerous. He's someone that Rosalind and Celia can trust to tell them the truth. Within the court world he does what Jaques does within Duke Senior's court, which is to provide the minor notes, undercutting the myths of power that are being propagated. Once Touchstone's let loose in the country, however, his story becomes much more about his pursuit of Audrey, his physical drives.

MB: He was Celia's prickly touchstone at court, licensed to offend her with stinging reminders of the injustice and hypocrisy of her father's court, even after being silenced by her father, the duke.

He became the audience's antiheroic touchstone in the forest, allowed to moan at discomfort, selfishly make the most of it with Audrey, and long for home.

At the end of the play Hymen asserts that the audience's 'wonder may diminish', yet, with the highest marriage count of any Shakespearean comedy, the play's neat conclusion can still appear implausible. How did you set about making each coupling believable for the audience?

DC: Each of the romantic stories that leads towards those weddings has a specific and detailed journey, each with very clear turning points. It felt crucial to reveal the detail of those journeys in performance, so that when everything comes together at the end it feels natural rather than contrived. To help this we made the Hymen section of the final scene ritualistic. Hymen's entrance, with Hymen played by Corin, was a quite formal ritual that, in our minds, Rosalind had cooked up. This gave the ending a kind of magic and stopped it from feeling like a playwright trying to tie things up and make them neat. Equally, each of the marriage blessings is different – there's texture there, so that when you look closely at what's happening, Shakespeare isn't creating a happy-ever-after ending for the play. It's far more nuanced.

There's always an element of magic at the end of Shakespeare's comedies. He isn't writing naturalistically. Frequently, he's referring to the ritual of theatre in a knowing way. There are many references to the theatre and role-play in *As You Like It*. For example, you have a girl playing a boy – and of course in the Jacobean theatre it would have been a boy playing a girl playing a boy, so you get that double level of irony and theatricality. Because plays were performed in the open air, and therefore without the division between audience and performers that there is in a contemporary theatre, the audience were constantly reminded that they were watching a performance. So events that might read as contrived or artificial in performances are joyously theatrical. None of the plays are documentaries; they're dealing with archetypes, a distillation of human experience. The gesture of the plays is always mythic, so to do them completely realistically is wrong, I think. There is a difference between being truthful and being realistic, and that distinction is crucial to an understanding of how to perform Shakespeare's plays.

MB: It is Rosalind's vivid and moving account of Oliver and Celia's incontinent dash to the altar that sells it to us as the most natural and enviable thing in the world. In our case we had a real young couple in love offstage (who were also excellent in their understudy roles as Orlando and Rosalind), which made Katy Stephen's job even easier. Forbes Masson as Jaques implied bitterly that Oliver was marrying power and money, but the audience didn't believe him.

The entire audience is meant to fall instantly in love with William, and did in our production with Dyfan Dwyfor, but Sophie Russell's surreal Audrey and Richard Katz's Da Da Touchstone were clearly meant for each other, and will quite possibly prove Jaques' prediction of a short-lived marriage wrong.

Jimmy Tucker's Act 5 breakthrough as Silvius was to move from plaintive pastoral minor key to full-on physical passion the moment that Ganymede was revealed as a woman. He did a Benedick on Phoebe and literally stopped her mouth, earning her eleventh-hour conversion with physical masterfulness.

I don't for one moment buy the idea that Orlando rumbles Rosalind before the wedding, and he does have a lot to reassess on the instant of Rosalind's self-revelation, but his is the most unconditional male love in Shakespeare, and in any case it's clear to him that he has passed any covert test set for him by Rosalind disguised as that pretty youth.

PLAYING ROSALIND: AN INTERVIEW WITH NAOMI FREDERICK[*]

Naomi Frederick, born in 1976, has worked on stage and in film and television. Trained at RADA, she has played Celia in *As You Like It* for the RSC, where she also appeared in John Fletcher's sequel to

[*] This interview is based on an extract from Globe Education's annual Adopt An Actor project at Shakespeare's Globe (www.globe-education.org).

The Taming of the Shrew, *The Tamer Tamed*. She was Isabella in Complicite's *Measure for Measure* that played at the National Theatre in London, where she was also Lady Percy (Hotspur's wife) in the two parts of *Henry IV*. She talks here about playing Rosalind in the summer of 2009 in Thea Sharrock's production of *As You Like It* on the stage of the reconstructed open-air Elizabethan theatre in London, Shakespeare's Globe.

What was your first encounter with the play?

As You Like It was the first Shakespeare I ever saw. I was twelve, and it was a production done by the sixth form at the school I was going to, and I was taken along specially. I fell in love with Celia and Rosalind instantly. I remember thinking initially that Celia was the main part (I think that happens for a lot of people – it appears to be Celia's play at the start) and I wanted to be her.

As luck would have it, I played Celia in a production for the RSC in 2003. So I know the play and it is one of my favourites – I love this play! It's about love, living, and the things that count in life.

And your first impression of the character of Rosalind?

As rehearsals began, I didn't know what I would make of Rosalind: having played Celia, I knew quite a lot about Rosalind, but only through Celia's eyes. I had to spend very little time relearning those scenes, because Rosalind's words were almost as familiar as Celia's, having heard them and having had to respond to them in the previous production.

Of course, what you absolutely underestimate is the different perspective – Rosalind's perspective is entirely different from Celia's. Her journey is so different: Rosalind is somebody who has to leave where she lives because otherwise she'll be killed. She has lost her father; she then has to leave behind somebody she has just fallen in love with, and to dress up as a boy to protect herself. She is a victim of circumstance, but she has the wit and the heart to turn the play around. All the tricks and games that she sets up come to an end when she decides that the most important thing is to be able to tell Orlando that she loves him.

How do you see her key relationships in the early part of the play?

At the start, Rosalind's most important relationship is with Celia. It's a wonderful relationship; it's that special friendship with somebody who is your own sex and your own age. They've grown up together, they know each other inside out and they adore each other. But they are at a particular point in their lives when something quite catastrophic has just happened: Celia's father has just banished Rosalind's father. So Rosalind, who was brought up as the princess, is now not the princess any more and is not the heir to the throne: Celia is. It is a remarkable testament to the strength of their friendship that not even Rosalind's banishment can drive them apart – they stick together.

Duke Frederick has taken over very recently and Rosalind has been through a lot. She has lost her father – maybe only in the last week? – so she doesn't know who she is, or what her position is. She is yearning to be loved. When this young guy Orlando comes in and is about to be the next one to be demolished in a wrestling match, she can't bear it. She thinks, 'That's ridiculous! It's a mistake: this beautiful young man shouldn't be attempting a fight.' And at the point when he explains his reasons for fighting, not least because of his respect for the memory of his own father and his loyalty to his family name, she falls in love with him in an instant.

I don't have any scenes with my father until the very end, which is interesting. In Act 1, the absence of Rosalind's father is the reason for Rosalind's destitution. Her father meant the world to her, and she and Celia head for the Forest of Arden in order to try to find him. But when Orlando arrives in the forest, all Rosalind's attentions turn to him and she forgets her father. That is an illustration of how huge her passion for Orlando must be: it has usurped her love for her father. Can this be the same girl that we saw at the beginning of the play?

What is Rosalind's perception of love?

I think we get clues from Rosalind early on that she is ready for love – she's got men on the brain! When Celia is trying to cheer her up, Rosalind agrees to try and have some fun, and her first suggestion is that they have a chat about falling in love. Then, when she and Celia are joking about Nature and Fortune, Rosalind says that Fortune deals a really bad hand to women and that men have it much easier! So it seems that she is thinking about men and maybe even finding a husband.

When Orlando appears, it's a sexual attraction at first, and then it becomes something even fuller. She sees he has a beautiful heart and stands for beautiful things. His speech explaining why he wants to wrestle ('I shall do my friends no wrong, for I have none to lament me') alerts her to his hidden depths. There is a meeting of their souls at that moment. Then Orlando wins the wrestling! And then it turns out that he is the son of Sir Rowland – whom her dad worshipped more than any other human being that ever lived. So for Rosalind, this boy is about as special as they come.

When Rosalind is banished, the rug is pulled from under her feet and she's lost again. Even though she hadn't established a relationship with Orlando, she's left with a wound that she doesn't know how to heal. She's in love. Her priorities completely change. She entirely forgets about her father! There's an interesting off-scene moment between Rosalind and Duke Senior at the end of Act 4. Rosalind casually mentions that she met her father the day before while dressed as a boy:

> I met the Duke yesterday, and had much question with him: he asked me of what parentage I was; I told him, of as good as he; so he laughed and let me go. But what talk we of fathers, when there is such a man as Orlando?

She jokes about being of the same high birth as the duke, then moves the conversation straight back to Orlando!

She's not particularly attractive at that point. Her behaviour is so crass. It's not until the end of the play, the day of the wedding, that she calms down from this crazy, loved-up state, embraces her dad again and gives him the love that has always been there.

Shakespeare wrote the part for a boy-actor, which would have made it easy for the original Rosalind to assume the role of Ganymede – but what's it like for a female actor to play a boy?

I once had to play Jesus in Dennis Potter's *Son of Man*, and I spent the first two weeks of rehearsals working out how to be a man; but then about a fortnight in, it occurred to me that Jesus wasn't preoccupied with that: he was a man, and therefore I just had to be a man and get on with it. Obviously Rosalind isn't a man – she's just acting like a man – but the guise works so well for her because her own personality has a lot of masculine qualities anyway. So for me, it's about exploring this aspect further, not having to obey any of the female etiquette, just being a guy.

In production, I think Rosalind has an obligation to become as much of a boy as possible in everybody's minds, including her own. This is partly for the sake of Orlando, who totally mistakes her for a boy (as does Corin and various others who aren't in on the game); if she is really rather womanly and just happens to be wearing blokes' clothes, then Orlando looks very stupid. Moreover, Rosalind's immersion in the Ganymede role governs the heart of the play. Here is a woman who chooses a disguise for her own protection, enters imaginatively into that role and finds it so liberating, so exciting being that person, that she actually forgets she is Rosalind.

I heard lots of interesting things about the way men operate from the other guys in the company! Of course, everybody is an individual, but if you're content with broad generalizations, the differences between men and women are striking. For example, I was forbidden to walk backwards in rehearsals, because it's too apologetic and humble and looks like you are making excuses; as a boy, it's imperative to show a natural assertiveness and not even ask the other person what they think, but just go for it straight, and say, 'Yeah, this is what I think'. There is a physicality that goes with that, and when you stop being nervous of it and get into the groove of it, it's really fun and quite seductive.

I had voice sessions with Jan Haydn-Rowles [voice coach] and I thought it was going to be her saying, 'Drop your shoulders, lower your voice', but she proved to be more like a psychologist! And of course, she's right to approach it that way, because the voice is the expression of the soul. It's how she gets people to do accents that are entirely foreign to their own, because they are more to do with psychology and culture and the way that you think.

The wonderful thing about working with Jan is that it's not a case of thinking about what I should or shouldn't be doing next in terms of my voice. Instead, it's to think about the way boys think (which is exactly what Rosalind adopts anyway). That's the best disguise: if you stop thinking like a woman, you actually stop behaving like one. And if you stop behaving like a woman, then, in some respects, you stop being a woman. If you've got a few helpful things like short hair and trousers, then you're quite far down the track to convincing other people that you are a boy.

So Jan pointed out a couple of the boys in the cast as very good examples of straightforward guys who say what they think and don't apologize for it. Interestingly, male thinking is often quite factual. Jan and I had a fascinating chat all about football, and why it ticks all the boxes for male behaviour: there's a team, with positions that can be compared; there is a league table where everything gets lined up and points allocated; and it's a competition where you wait to find out who is going to win. It's such a cliché that when men get together they talk about sport, but there are reasons for it! So I thought about that – after all, sport (first wrestling and then hunting) is very important in this play.

I had my hair cut short, and it was very helpful to look in the mirror and realize, 'Oh yeah, I don't have a ponytail to worry about any more!' It's much less fuss having short hair. What particularly helps is seeing other people's reactions and how they respond according to the way you are. My husband said to me at home recently, 'I can't wait for you to wear a skirt again', but of course I felt I couldn't while I was rehearsing for Rosalind – the element of the role I really had to conquer was being a boy. So I deliberately chose jeans and T-shirts for rehearsals; as a result, I frequently turned up looking like Jack [Laskey], my Orlando. The wardrobe choices for men aren't vast, as I have discovered! If you happen to put on jeans and a grey T-shirt, you're bound to match somebody else.

All of that helps, because it's about entering into the character and committing to being believable as a man. So you benefit from looking more boyish, because then it rebounds back to you via other people's reactions, and this corroborates your sense of the character.

When I was in the forest, my costume was leather: leather jacket, leather breeches, long leather boots – leather top to toe! It's very different to the layers of silk and petticoats and bodices and corsets and all of that that goes on at the beginning with Rosalind's dress. Because my hair was cut short, I wore a long wig at the beginning which I then whipped off backstage after Act 1, as if Rosalind had cut her hair. It would be so nice to cut your hair every night – that would be so satisfying! – but obviously that can't happen, so at the beginning, I had short hair underneath my wig.

Were there any key scenes that you really felt you unlocked in the rehearsal process?

The whole relationship with Celia needed a lot of unlocking, because the play starts with Celia asking Rosalind to be merrier, to which Rosalind replies: 'Unless you could teach me to forget a banished father, you must not learn me how to remember any extraordinary pleasure.' Initially, we were playing with Rosalind being in a bad temper, but then we realized that that could be a problem. The audience has to learn the relationship between these two very quickly, and if you open with them fighting, then the fact that these two girls adore each other isn't very clear. Obviously, you do have fights with the people you love very much, but if that's the first thing you show the audience, it's a bit dangerous. These two have grown up together and are woven together, so we knew that we had to play it more like it was a chat, so that even while she is missing her dad terribly, Rosalind is so grateful for Celia's comfort and love. Celia knows that Rosalind is not herself and asks what is wrong, which allows Rosalind to admit that she is feeling upset. You've got to be

8. Naomi Frederick as Rosalind, cross-dressed and in leather, with Laura Rogers as an exceptionally lively Celia, and the wooden pillars of Shakespeare's Globe standing for the Forest of Arden.

careful with what you present, so that was an interesting moment, discovering which might be the better way to start.

There were also developments in the scene where Rosalind encounters Silvius and Phoebe. I had been playing it that Rosalind watches Phoebe decimating Silvius, and because of her own frustration that she can't be with Orlando, Rosalind then lays into Phoebe: 'How dare you speak like that when you're a woman!' Later, an element of that remained, but I also developed the idea that Rosalind realizes that quite simply she can get away with giving Phoebe a hard time because she is still disguised as Ganymede. So there is a huge element of enjoyment in the telling off, rather than it just being an angry scolding. These interpretative shifts are significant in terms of how we tell the story; and via these shifts we gradually unlock the characters, a process which may never be fully done.

And during the run itself?

Nothing prepares you for 1500 people all sat there (or should I say standing there?). The space felt immediately smaller, really quite cosy, whereas the first time I walked into the empty Globe I remember thinking, 'This is vast! I couldn't even begin to fill it!' But actually it's not vast. The space only feels big when it's empty. The audience is packed quite tightly in; when it's full the walls just seem to close in, it is quite amazing.

I played to the audience an awful lot on the first night, which I did much less subsequently. There is no way of preparing for your first performance in that space – the Globe is unique in that the audience is present and close and vocal in a way that they aren't in other theatres. There is a different theatre dynamic and a different audience relationship. I made the mistake of wanting to play too much to the audience at first, just because I felt them there, when actually the point is that you should play less to them, because they are right there. Every character has a different relationship with the audience, and I could never have guessed that, but I have been gradually discovering that and exploring it.

The more we performed the show the more things grew and you think, 'Oh, now I know what that line means', or someone else says something and you think 'Oh, that's why I say that a couple of lines later!' The writing is so detailed that you can't really pick it all up in rehearsals. It is a pleasure that the play reveals itself to you as you go along. So you just keep doing the show and every now and then you say, 'Wow – I've never understood that before!' Every now and then you have the impression of stepping up a level, but I believe that happens naturally by keeping on playing.

SHAKESPEARE'S CAREER IN THE THEATRE

BEGINNINGS

William Shakespeare was an extraordinarily intelligent man who was born and died in an ordinary market town in the English Midlands. He lived an uneventful life in an eventful age. Born in April 1564, he was the eldest son of John Shakespeare, a glove-maker who was prominent on the town council until he fell into financial difficulties. Young William was educated at the local grammar in Stratford-upon-Avon, Warwickshire, where he gained a thorough grounding in the Latin language, the art of rhetoric and classical poetry. He married Ann Hathaway and had three children (Susanna, then the twins Hamnet and Judith) before his twenty-first birthday: an exceptionally young age for the period. We do not know how he supported his family in the mid-1580s.

Like many clever country boys, he moved to the city in order to make his way in the world. Like many creative people, he found a career in the entertainment business. Public playhouses and professional full-time acting companies reliant on the market for their income were born in Shakespeare's childhood. When he arrived in London as a man, sometime in the late 1580s, a new phenomenon was in the making: the actor who is so successful that he becomes a 'star'. The word did not exist in its modern sense, but the pattern is recognizable: audiences went to the theatre not so much to see a particular show as to witness the comedian Richard Tarlton or the dramatic actor Edward Alleyn.

Shakespeare was an actor before he was a writer. It appears not to have been long before he realized that he was never going to grow into a great comedian like Tarlton or a great tragedian like Alleyn. Instead, he found a role within his company as the man who patched up old plays, breathing new life, new dramatic twists, into tired repertory pieces. He paid close attention to the work of the university-educated dramatists who were writing history plays and tragedies for the public stage in a style more ambitious, sweeping and poetically grand than anything which had been seen before. But he may also have noted that what his friend and rival Ben Jonson would call 'Marlowe's mighty line' sometimes faltered in the mode of comedy. Going to university, as Christopher Marlowe did, was all well and good for honing the arts of rhetorical elaboration and classical allusion, but it could lead to a loss of the common touch. To stay close to a large segment of the potential audience for public theatre, it was necessary to write for clowns as well as kings and to intersperse the flights of poetry with the humour of the tavern, the privy and the brothel: Shakespeare was the first to establish himself early in his career as an equal master of tragedy, comedy and history. He realized that theatre could be the medium to make the national past available to a wider audience than the elite who could afford to read large history books: his signature early works include not only the classical tragedy *Titus Andronicus* but also the sequence of English historical plays on the Wars of the Roses.

He also invented a new role for himself, that of in-house company dramatist. Where his peers and predecessors had to sell their plays to the theatre managers on a poorly-paid piecework basis, Shakespeare took a percentage of the box-office income. The Lord Chamberlain's Men constituted themselves in 1594 as a joint stock company, with the profits being distributed among the core actors who had invested as sharers. Shakespeare acted himself – he appears in the cast lists of some of Ben Jonson's plays as well as the list of actors' names at the beginning of his own collected works – but his principal duty was to write two or three plays a year for the company. By holding shares, he was effectively earning himself a royalty on his work, something no author had ever done before in England. When the Lord Chamberlain's Men collected their fee for performance at court in the Christmas season of 1594, three of them went along to the Treasurer of the Chamber: not just Richard Burbage the tragedian and Will Kempe the clown, but also Shakespeare the scriptwriter. That was something new.

The next four years were the golden period in Shakespeare's career, though overshadowed by the death of his only son Hamnet, aged eleven, in 1596. In his early thirties and in full command of both his poetic and his theatrical medium, he perfected his art of comedy, while also developing his tragic and historical writing in new ways. In 1598, Francis Meres, a Cambridge University graduate with his finger on the pulse of the London literary world, praised Shakespeare for his excellence across the genres:

> As Plautus and Seneca are accounted the best for comedy and tragedy among the Latins, so Shakespeare among the English is the most excellent in both kinds for the stage; for comedy, witness his *Gentlemen of Verona*, his *Errors*, his *Love Labours Lost*, his *Love Labours Won*, his *Midsummer Night Dream* and his *Merchant of Venice*: for tragedy his *Richard the 2*, *Richard the 3*, *Henry the 4*, *King John, Titus Andronicus* and his *Romeo and Juliet*.

For Meres, as for the many writers who praised the 'honey-flowing vein' of *Venus and Adonis* and *Lucrece*, narrative poems written when the theatres were closed due to plague in 1593–94, Shakespeare was marked above all by his linguistic skill, by the gift of turning elegant poetic phrases.

PLAYHOUSES

Elizabethan playhouses were 'thrust' or 'one-room' theatres. To understand Shakespeare's original theatrical life, we have to forget about the indoor theatre of later times, with its proscenium arch and curtain that would be opened at the beginning and closed at the end of each act. In the proscenium arch theatre, stage and auditorium are effectively two separate rooms: the audience looks from one world into another as if through the imaginary 'fourth wall' framed by the proscenium. The picture-frame stage, together with the elaborate scenic effects and backdrops beyond it, created the illusion of a self-contained world – especially once nineteenth-century developments in the control of artificial lighting meant that the auditorium could be darkened and the spectators made to focus on the lighted stage. Shakespeare, by contrast, wrote for a bare platform stage with a standing audience gathered around it in a courtyard in full daylight. The audience were always conscious of themselves and their fellow-spectators, and they shared the same 'room' as the actors. A sense of immediate presence and the creation of rapport with the audience were all-important. The actor could not afford to imagine he was in a closed world, with silent witnesses dutifully observing him from the darkness.

Shakespeare's theatrical career began at the Rose Theatre in Southwark. The stage was wide and shallow, trapezoid in shape, like a lozenge. This design had a great deal of potential for the theatrical equivalent of cinematic split-screen effects, whereby one group of characters would enter at the door at one end of the tiring-house wall at the back of the stage and another group through the door at the other end, thus creating two rival tableaux. Many of the battle-heavy and faction-filled plays that premiered at the Rose have scenes of just this sort.

At the rear of the Rose stage, there were three capacious exits, each over ten feet wide. Unfortunately, the very limited excavation of a fragmentary portion of the original Globe site, in 1989, revealed nothing about the stage. The first Globe was built in 1599 with similar proportions to those of another theatre, the Fortune, albeit that the former was polygonal and looked circular, whereas the latter was rectangular. The building contract for the Fortune survives and allows us to infer that the stage of the Globe was probably substantially wider than it was deep (perhaps forty-three feet wide and twenty-seven feet deep). It may well have been tapered at the front, like that of the Rose.

The capacity of the Globe was said to have been enormous, perhaps in excess of three thousand. It has been conjectured that about eight hundred people may have stood in the yard, with two thousand or more in the three layers of covered galleries. The other 'public' playhouses were also of large capacity, whereas the indoor Blackfriars theatre that Shakespeare's company began using in 1608 – the former refectory of a monastery – had overall internal dimensions of a mere forty-six by sixty feet. It would have made for a much more intimate theatrical experience and had a much smaller capacity, probably of about six hundred people. Since they paid at least sixpence a head, the Blackfriars attracted a more select or 'private' audience. The atmosphere would have been closer to that of an indoor performance before the court in the Whitehall Palace or at Richmond. That Shakespeare always wrote for indoor production at court as well as outdoor performance in the public theatre should make us cautious about inferring, as some scholars have, that the opportunity provided by the intimacy of the Blackfriars led to a significant change towards a 'chamber' style in his last plays – which, besides, were performed at both the Globe and the Blackfriars. After the occupation of the Blackfriars a five-act structure seems to have become more important to Shakespeare. That was because of artificial lighting: there were musical interludes between the acts, while the candles were trimmed and replaced. Again, though, something similar must have been necessary for indoor court performances throughout his career.

Front of house there were the 'gatherers' who collected the money from audience members: a penny to stand in the open-air yard, another penny for a place in the covered galleries, sixpence for the prominent 'lord's rooms' to the side of the stage. In the indoor 'private' theatres, gallants from the audience who fancied making themselves part of the spectacle sat on stools on the edge of the stage itself. Scholars debate as to how widespread this practice was in the public theatres such as the Globe. Once the audience were in place and the money counted, the gatherers were available to be extras on stage. That is one reason why battles and crowd scenes often come later rather than early in Shakespeare's plays. There was no formal prohibition upon performance by women, and there certainly were women among the gatherers, so it is not beyond the bounds of possibility that female crowd members were played by females.

The play began at two o'clock in the afternoon and the theatre had to be cleared by five. After the main show, there would be a jig – which consisted not only of dancing, but also of knockabout comedy (it is the origin of the farcical 'afterpiece' in the eighteenth-century theatre). So the time available for a Shakespeare play was about two and a half hours, somewhere between the 'two hours' traffic' mentioned in the prologue to *Romeo and Juliet* and the 'three hours' spectacle' referred to in the preface to the 1647 Folio of Beaumont and Fletcher's plays. The prologue to a play by Thomas Middleton refers to a thousand lines as 'one hour's words', so the likelihood is that about two and a half thousand, or a maximum of three thousand lines made up the performed text. This is indeed the length of most of Shakespeare's comedies, whereas many of his tragedies and histories are much longer, raising the possibility that he wrote full scripts, possibly with eventual publication in mind, in the full knowledge that the stage version would be heavily cut. The short Quarto texts published in his lifetime – they used to be called 'Bad' Quartos – provide fascinating evidence as to the kind of cutting that probably took place. So, for instance, the First Quarto of *Hamlet* neatly merges two occasions when Hamlet is overheard, the 'Fishmonger' and the 'nunnery' scenes.

The social composition of the audience was mixed. The poet Sir John Davies wrote of 'A thousand townsmen, gentlemen and whores, / Porters and servingmen' who would 'together throng' at the public playhouses. Though moralists associated female play-going with adultery and the sex trade, many perfectly respectable citizens' wives were regular attendees. Some, no doubt, resembled the modern groupie: a story attested in two different sources has one citizen's wife making a post-show assignation with Richard Burbage and ending up in bed with Shakespeare – supposedly eliciting from the latter the quip that William the Conqueror was before Richard III. Defenders of theatre liked to say that by witnessing the comeuppance of villains on the stage, audience members would repent of their own wrongdoings, but the reality is that most people went to the theatre then, as they do now, for entertainment more than moral edification. Besides, it would be foolish to suppose that audiences behaved in a homogeneous way: a pamphlet of the 1630s tells of how two men went to see *Pericles* and one of them laughed while the other wept. Bishop John Hall complained that people went to church for the same reasons that they went to the theatre: 'for company, for custom, for recreation . . . to feed his eyes or his ears . . . or perhaps for sleep'.

Men-about-town and clever young lawyers went to be seen as much as to see. In the modern popular imagination, shaped not least by *Shakespeare in Love* and the opening sequence of Laurence Olivier's

Henry V film, the penny-paying groundlings stand in the yard hurling abuse or encouragement and hazelnuts or orange peel at the actors, while the sophisticates in the covered galleries appreciate Shakespeare's soaring poetry. The reality was probably the other way round. A 'groundling' was a kind of fish, so the nickname suggests the penny audience standing below the level of the stage and gazing in silent open-mouthed wonder at the spectacle unfolding above them. The more difficult audience members, who kept up a running commentary of clever remarks on the performance and who occasionally got into quarrels with players, were the gallants. Like Hollywood movies in modern times, Elizabethan and Jacobean plays exercised a powerful influence on the fashion and behaviour of the young. John Marston mocks the lawyers who would open their lips, perhaps to court a girl, and out would 'flow / Naught but pure Juliet and Romeo'.

THE ENSEMBLE AT WORK

In the absence of typewriters and photocopying machines, reading aloud would have been the means by which the company got to know a new play. The tradition of the playwright reading his complete script to the assembled company endured for generations. A copy would then have been taken to the Master of the Revels for licensing. The theatre book-holder or prompter would then have copied the parts for distribution to the actors. A partbook consisted of the character's lines, with each speech preceded by the last three or four words of the speech before, the so-called 'cue'. These would have been taken away and studied or 'conned'. During this period of learning the parts, an actor might have had some one-to-one instruction, perhaps from the dramatist, perhaps from a senior actor who had played the same part before, and, in the case of an apprentice, from his master. A high percentage of Desdemona's lines occur in dialogue with Othello, of Lady Macbeth's with Macbeth, Cleopatra's with Antony and Volumnia's with Coriolanus. The roles would almost certainly have been taken by the apprentice of the lead actor, usually Burbage, who delivers the majority of the cues. Given that apprentices lodged with their masters, there would have been

9. Hypothetical reconstruction of the interior of an Elizabethan playhouse during a performance.

ample opportunity for personal instruction, which may be what made it possible for young men to play such demanding parts.

After the parts were learned, there may have been no more than a single rehearsal before the first performance. With six different plays to be put on every week, there was no time for more. Actors, then, would go into a show with a very limited sense of the whole. The notion of a collective rehearsal process that is itself a process of discovery for the actors is wholly modern and would have been incomprehensible to Shakespeare and his original ensemble. Given the number of parts an actor had to hold in his memory, the forgetting of lines was probably more frequent than in the modern theatre. The book-holder was on hand to prompt.

Backstage personnel included the property man, the tire-man who oversaw the costumes, call-boys, attendants and the musicians, who might play at various times from the main stage, the rooms above and within the tiring-house. Scriptwriters sometimes made a nuisance of themselves backstage. There was often tension between the acting companies and the freelance playwrights from whom they purchased scripts: it was a smart move on the part of Shakespeare and the Lord Chamberlain's Men to bring the writing process in-house.

Scenery was limited, though sometimes set-pieces were brought on (a bank of flowers, a bed, the mouth of hell). The trapdoor from below, the gallery stage above and the curtained discovery-space at the back allowed for an array of special effects: the rising of ghosts and apparitions, the descent of gods, dialogue between a character at a window and another at ground level, the revelation of a statue or a pair of lovers playing at chess. Ingenious use could be made of props, as with the ass's head in *A Midsummer Night's Dream*. In a theatre that does not clutter the stage with the material paraphernalia of everyday life, those objects that are deployed may take on powerful symbolic weight, as when Shylock bears his weighing scales in one hand and knife in the other, thus becoming a parody of the figure of Justice who traditionally bears a sword and a balance. Among the more significant items in the property cupboard of Shakespeare's company, there would have been a throne (the 'chair of state'), joint stools, books, bottles, coins, purses, letters (which are brought on stage, read or referred to on about eighty occasions in the complete works), maps, gloves, a set of stocks (in which Kent is put in *King Lear*), rings, rapiers, daggers, broadswords, staves, pistols, masks and vizards, heads and skulls, torches and tapers and lanterns which served to signal night scenes on the daylit stage, a buck's head, an ass's head, animal costumes. Live animals also put in appearances, most notably the dog Crab in *The Two Gentlemen of Verona* and possibly a young polar bear in *The Winter's Tale*.

The costumes were the most important visual dimension of the play. Playwrights were paid between £2 and £6 per script, whereas Alleyn was not averse to paying £20 for 'a black velvet cloak with sleeves embroidered all with silver and gold'. No matter the period of the play, actors always wore contemporary costume. The excitement for the audience came not from any impression of historical accuracy, but from the richness of the attire and perhaps the transgressive thrill of the knowledge that here were commoners like themselves strutting in the costumes of courtiers in effective defiance of the strict sumptuary laws whereby in real life people had to wear the clothes that befitted their social station.

To an even greater degree than props, costumes could carry symbolic importance. Racial characteristics could be suggested: a breastplate and helmet for a Roman soldier, a turban for a Turk, long robes for exotic characters such as Moors, a gabardine for a Jew. The figure of Time, as in *The Winter's Tale*, would be equipped with hourglass, scythe and wings; Rumour, who speaks the prologue of *2 Henry IV*, wore a costume adorned with a thousand tongues. The wardrobe in the tiring-house of the Globe would have contained much of the same stock as that of rival manager Philip Henslowe at the Rose: green gowns for outlaws and foresters, black for melancholy men such as Jaques and people in mourning such as the Countess in *All's Well that Ends Well* (at the beginning of *Hamlet*, the prince is still in mourning black when everyone else is in festive garb for the wedding of the new king), a gown and hood for a friar (or a feigned friar like the duke in *Measure for Measure*), blue coats and tawny to distinguish the followers of rival factions, a leather apron and ruler for a carpenter (as in the opening scene of *Julius Caesar* – and in *A Midsummer Night's Dream*, where this is the only sign that Peter Quince is a carpenter), a cockle hat with staff and a pair of sandals for a pilgrim or palmer (the disguise assumed by Helen in *All's Well*), bodices and kirtles with farthingales beneath for the boys who are to be dressed as girls. A gender switch such as that of Rosalind or Jessica seems to have taken between fifty and eighty lines of dialogue – Viola does not resume her 'maiden weeds', but remains in her boy's costume to the end of *Twelfth Night* because a change would have slowed down the action at just the moment it was speeding to a climax. Henslowe's inventory also included 'a robe for to go invisible': Oberon, Puck and Ariel must have had something similar.

As the costumes appealed to the eyes, so there was music for the ears. Comedies included many songs. Desdemona's willow song, perhaps a late addition to the text, is a rare and thus exceptionally poignant example from tragedy. Trumpets and tuckets sounded for ceremonial entrances, drums denoted an army on the march. Background music could create atmosphere, as at the beginning of *Twelfth Night*, during the lovers' dialogue near the end of

The Merchant of Venice, when the statue seemingly comes to life in *The Winter's Tale*, and for the revival of Pericles and of Lear (in the Quarto text, but not the Folio). The haunting sound of the hautboy suggested a realm beyond the human, as when the god Hercules is imagined deserting Mark Antony. Dances symbolized the harmony of the end of a comedy – though in Shakespeare's world of mingled joy and sorrow, someone is usually left out of the circle.

The most important resource was, of course, the actors themselves. They needed many skills: in the words of one contemporary commentator, 'dancing, activity, music, song, elocution, ability of body, memory, skill of weapon, pregnancy of wit'. Their bodies were as significant as their voices. Hamlet tells the player to 'suit the action to the word, the word to the action': moments of strong emotion, known as 'passions', relied on a repertoire of dramatic gestures as well as a modulation of the voice. When Titus Andronicus has had his hand chopped off, he asks 'How can I grace my talk, / Wanting a hand to give it action?' A pen portrait of 'The Character of an Excellent Actor' by the dramatist John Webster is almost certainly based on his impression of Shakespeare's leading man, Richard Burbage: 'By a full and significant action of body, he charms our attention: sit in a full theatre, and you will think you see so many lines drawn from the circumference of so many ears, whiles the actor is the centre . . . .'

Though Burbage was admired above all others, praise was also heaped upon the apprentice players whose alto voices fitted them for the parts of women. A spectator at Oxford in 1610 records how the audience were reduced to tears by the pathos of Desdemona's death. The puritans who fumed about the biblical prohibition upon cross-dressing and the encouragement to sodomy constituted by the sight of an adult male kissing a teenage boy on stage were a small minority. Little is known, however, about the characteristics of the leading apprentices in Shakespeare's company. It may perhaps be inferred that one was a lot taller than the other, since Shakespeare often wrote for a pair of female friends, one tall and fair, the other short and dark (Helena and Hermia, Rosalind and Celia, Beatrice and Hero).

We know little about Shakespeare's own acting roles – an early allusion indicates that he often took royal parts, and a venerable tradition gives him old Adam in *As You Like It* and the ghost of old King Hamlet. Save for Burbage's lead roles and the generic part of the clown, all such castings are mere speculation. We do not even know for sure whether the original Falstaff was Will Kempe or another actor who specialized in comic roles, Thomas Pope.

Kempe left the company in early 1599. Tradition has it that he fell out with Shakespeare over the matter of excessive improvisation. He was replaced by Robert Armin, who was less of a clown and more of a cerebral wit: this explains the difference between such parts as Lancelet Gobbo and Dogberry, which were written for Kempe, and the more verbally sophisticated Feste and Lear's Fool, which were written for Armin.

One thing that is clear from surviving 'plots' or story-boards of plays from the period is that a degree of doubling was necessary. *2 Henry VI* has over sixty speaking parts, but more than half of the characters only appear in a single scene and most scenes have only six to eight speakers. At a stretch, the play could be performed by thirteen actors. When Thomas Platter saw *Julius Caesar* at the Globe in 1599, he noted that there were about fifteen. Why doesn't Paris go to the Capulet ball in *Romeo and Juliet*? Perhaps because he was doubled with Mercutio, who does. In *The Winter's Tale*, Mamillius might have come back as Perdita and Antigonus been doubled by Camillo, making the partnership with Paulina at the end a very neat touch. Titania and Oberon are often played by the same pair as Hippolyta and Theseus, suggesting a symbolic matching of the rulers of the worlds of night and day, but it is questionable whether there would have been time for the necessary costume changes. As so often, one is left in a realm of tantalizing speculation.

THE KING'S MAN

On Queen Elizabeth's death in 1603, the new king, James I, who had held the Scottish throne as James VI since he had been an infant, immediately took the Lord Chamberlain's Men under his direct patronage. Henceforth they would be the King's Men, and for the rest of Shakespeare's career they were favoured with far more court performances than any of their rivals. There even seem to have been rumours early in the reign that Shakespeare and Burbage were being considered for knighthoods, an unprecedented honour for mere actors – and one that in the event was not accorded to a member of the profession for nearly three hundred years, when the title was bestowed upon Henry Irving, the leading Shakespearean actor of Queen Victoria's reign.

Shakespeare's productivity rate slowed in the Jacobean years, not because of age or some personal trauma, but because there were frequent outbreaks of plague, causing the theatres to be closed for long periods. The King's Men were forced to spend many months on the road. Between November 1603 and 1608, they were to be found at various towns in the south and Midlands, though Shakespeare probably did not tour with them by this time. He had bought a large house back home in Stratford and was accumulating other property. He may indeed have stopped acting soon after the new king took the throne. With the London theatres closed so much of the time and a large repertoire on the stocks, Shakespeare seems to have focused his energies on writing a few long and complex tragedies that could have been played on demand at court: *Othello*, *King Lear*, *Antony and Cleopatra*, *Coriolanus* and *Cymbeline* are among his longest and poetically grandest plays. *Macbeth* only survives in a shorter text, which shows signs of adaptation after Shakespeare's death. The bitterly satirical *Timon of Athens*, apparently a collaboration with Thomas Middleton that may have failed on the stage, also belongs to this period. In comedy, too, he wrote longer and morally darker works than in the Elizabethan period, pushing at the very bounds of the form in *Measure for Measure* and *All's Well that Ends Well*.

From 1608 onwards, when the King's Men began occupying the indoor Blackfriars playhouse (as a winter house, meaning that they only used the outdoor Globe in summer?), Shakespeare turned to a more romantic style. His company had a great success with a revived and altered version of an old pastoral play called *Mucedorus*. It even featured a bear. The younger dramatist John Fletcher, meanwhile, sometimes working in collaboration with Francis Beaumont, was pioneering a new style of tragicomedy, a mix of romance and royalism laced with intrigue and pastoral excursions. Shakespeare experimented with this idiom in *Cymbeline* and it was presumably with his blessing that Fletcher eventually took over as the King's Men's company dramatist. The two writers apparently collaborated on three plays in the years 1612–14: a lost romance called *Cardenio* (based on the love-madness of a character in Cervantes' *Don Quixote*), *Henry VIII* (originally staged with the title 'All is True'), and *The Two Noble Kinsmen*, a dramatization of Chaucer's 'Knight's Tale'. These were written after Shakespeare's two final solo-authored plays, *The Winter's Tale*, a self-consciously old-fashioned work dramatizing the pastoral romance of his old enemy Robert Greene, and *The Tempest*, which at one and the same time drew together multiple theatrical traditions, diverse reading and contemporary interest in the fate of a ship that had been wrecked on the way to the New World.

The collaborations with Fletcher suggest that Shakespeare's career ended with a slow fade rather than the sudden retirement supposed by the nineteenth-century Romantic critics who read Prospero's epilogue to *The Tempest* as Shakespeare's personal farewell to his art. In the last few years of his life Shakespeare certainly spent more of his time in Stratford-upon-Avon, where he became further involved in property dealing and litigation. But his London life also continued. In 1613 he made his first major London property purchase: a freehold house in the Blackfriars district, close to his company's indoor theatre. *The Two Noble Kinsmen* may have been written as late as 1614, and Shakespeare was in London on business a little over a year before he died of an unknown cause at home in Stratford-upon-Avon in 1616, probably on his fifty-second birthday.

About half the sum of his works were published in his lifetime, in texts of variable quality. A few years after his death, his fellow-actors began putting together an authorized edition of his complete *Comedies, Histories and Tragedies*. It appeared in 1623, in large 'Folio' format. This collection of thirty-six plays gave Shakespeare his immortality. In the words of his fellow-dramatist Ben Jonson, who contributed two poems of praise at the start of the Folio, the body of his work made him 'a monument without a tomb':

> And art alive still while thy book doth live
> And we have wits to read and praise to give . . .
> He was not of an age, but for all time!

SHAKESPEARE'S WORKS:
A Chronology

1589–91	*? Arden of Faversham* (possible part authorship)
1589–92	*The Taming of the Shrew*
1589–92	*? Edward the Third* (possible part authorship)
1591	*The Second Part of Henry the Sixth*, originally called *The First Part of the Contention betwixt the Two Famous Houses of York and Lancaster* (element of co-authorship possible)
1591	*The Third Part of Henry the Sixth*, originally called *The True Tragedy of Richard Duke of York* (element of co-authorship probable)
1591–92	*The Two Gentlemen of Verona*
1591–92 perhaps revised 1594	*The Lamentable Tragedy of Titus Andronicus* (probably co-written with, or revising an earlier version by, George Peele)
1592	*The First Part of Henry the Sixth*, probably with Thomas Nashe and others
1592/94	*King Richard the Third*
1593	*Venus and Adonis* (poem)
1593–94	*The Rape of Lucrece* (poem)
1593–1608	*Sonnets* (154 poems, published 1609 with *A Lover's Complaint*, a poem of disputed authorship)
1592–94/ 1600–03	*Sir Thomas More* (a single scene for a play originally by Anthony Munday, with other revisions by Henry Chettle, Thomas Dekker and Thomas Heywood)
1594	*The Comedy of Errors*
1595	*Love's Labour's Lost*

1595–97	*Love's Labour's Won* (a lost play, unless the original title for another comedy)
1595–96	*A Midsummer Night's Dream*
1595–96	*The Tragedy of Romeo and Juliet*
1595–96	*King Richard the Second*
1595–97	*The Life and Death of King John* (possibly earlier)
1596–97	*The Merchant of Venice*
1596–97	*The First Part of Henry the Fourth*
1597–98	*The Second Part of Henry the Fourth*
1598	*Much Ado about Nothing*
1598–99	*The Passionate Pilgrim* (20 poems, some not by Shakespeare)
1599	*The Life of Henry the Fifth*
1599	'To the Queen' (epilogue for a court performance)
1599	*As You Like It*
1599	*The Tragedy of Julius Caesar*
1600–01	*The Tragedy of Hamlet, Prince of Denmark* (perhaps revising an earlier version)
1600–01	*The Merry Wives of Windsor* (perhaps revising version of 1597–99)
1601	'Let the Bird of Loudest Lay' (poem, known since 1807 as 'The Phoenix and Turtle' (turtle-dove))
1601	*Twelfth Night, or What You Will*
1601–02	*The Tragedy of Troilus and Cressida*
1604	*The Tragedy of Othello, the Moor of Venice*
1604	*Measure for Measure*
1605	*All's Well that Ends Well*
1605	*The Life of Timon of Athens*, with Thomas Middleton
1605–06	*The Tragedy of King Lear*
1605–08	? contribution to *The Four Plays in One* (lost, except for *A Yorkshire Tragedy*, mostly by Thomas Middleton)
1606	*The Tragedy of Macbeth* (surviving text has additional scenes by Thomas Middleton)
1606–07	*The Tragedy of Antony and Cleopatra*
1608	*The Tragedy of Coriolanus*

1608	*Pericles, Prince of Tyre*, with George Wilkins
1610	*The Tragedy of Cymbeline*
1611	*The Winter's Tale*
1611	*The Tempest*
1612–13	*Cardenio*, with John Fletcher (survives only in later adaptation called *Double Falsehood* by Lewis Theobald)
1613	*Henry VIII (All is True)*, with John Fletcher
1613–14	*The Two Noble Kinsmen*, with John Fletcher

FURTHER READING AND VIEWING

CRITICAL APPROACHES

Barber, C. L., *Shakespeare's Festive Comedies* (1959). One of the best critical books on Shakespeare ever written.

Bloom, Harold, ed., *William Shakespeare's As You Like It*, Modern Critical Interpretations (1988). Diverse collection of recent influential essays.

Brown, John Russell, ed., *Shakespeare: Much Ado about Nothing and As You Like It*, Casebook Series (1979). Valuable collection of early essays and production reviews.

Colie, Rosalie, *Shakespeare's Living Art* (1974). Elegant and sophisticated account of the play's language.

Frye, Northrop, *A Natural Perspective: The Development of Shakespearean Comedy and Romance* (1965). A slim work of supreme power.

Gay, Penny, *As She Likes It: Shakespeare's Unruly Women* (1994). Now classic account of plays' gender politics; chapter 2 on *As You Like It* discusses productions from 1952 to 1990, pp. 48–85.

Gay, Penny, *William Shakespeare: As You Like It*, Writers and their Work Series (1999). Fascinating introduction which attempts to recreate the original Elizabethan response to the play – full of interesting detail.

Halio, Jay, ed., *Twentieth-Century Interpretations of As You Like It* (1968). Useful introductory collection of essays.

Maslen, R. W., *Shakespeare and Comedy* (2005). Sets the Elizabethan comedies in the context of both theatrical traditions and anti-stage polemic.

Neely, Carol Thomas, 'Lovesickness, Gender, and Subjectivity: *Twelfth Night* and *As You Like It*', in *A Feminist Companion to*

Shakespeare, ed. Dympna Callaghan (2000). Theoretically informed account of desire and plays' gender-bending.

Tomarken, Edward, ed., *As You Like It From 1600 to the Present: Critical Essays* (1997). Wide selection of material from early essays to discussions of recent productions; includes Samuel Johnson's notes on the play.

THE PLAY IN PERFORMANCE

Jackson, Russell, 'Remembering Bergner's Rosalind: *As You Like It* on Film in 1936', in *Shakespeare, Memory and Performance*, ed. Peter Holland (2006), pp. 237–55. Account of the distinguished Austrian actress's career and her acclaimed Rosalind.

Jackson, Russell, and Robert Smallwood, eds, *Players of Shakespeare 2* (1988). Includes Fiona Shaw and Juliet Stevenson on playing Celia and Rosalind, and Alan Rickman on Jaques.

Jackson, Russell, and Robert Smallwood, eds, *Players of Shakespeare 3* (1993). Sophie Thompson on Rosalind (and Celia).

Mann, David, *Shakespeare's Women: Performance and Conception* (2008). Focuses on female roles in Elizabethan plays, examining them in terms of the dramatic conventions of cross-dressing rather than an exploration of gender politics; numerous passing references to *As You Like It*.

Marshall, Cynthia, ed., *As You Like It*, Shakespeare in Production Series (2004). Introduction has a comprehensive stage history of the play and footnotes to text with stage directions from important productions.

Parsons, Keith, and Pamela Mason, *Shakespeare in Performance* (1995). Useful introduction, lavishly illustrated.

Rutter, Carol, *Clamorous Voices* (1988). Actresses discuss roles they've played – in the last chapter Juliet Stevenson and Fiona Shaw talk about playing Rosalind and Celia respectively in Adrian Noble's 1985 RSC production.

Smallwood, Robert, ed., *Players of Shakespeare 4* (1998). Includes David Tennant on the trials of playing Touchstone, pp. 30–44.

Smallwood, Robert, *As You Like It*, Shakespeare and Stratford Series (2003). Comprehensive account of RSC productions up to 2001.

AVAILABLE ON DVD

As You Like It, directed by Paul Czinner (1936, DVD 1999). Charming, eccentric, with Elisabeth Bergner's unconventional Rosalind and the young Laurence Olivier as Orlando; script was adapted by J. M. Barrie and the film's editor was David Lean.

As You Like It, directed by Alexei Karayev, one of the Welsh/Russian co-productions, The Animated Tales of Shakespeare series (1992, DVD 2004). One of twelve plays adapted by Leon Garfield for this award-winning series. Oil painting on film cells is a device that creates a magical Forest of Arden, with Rosalind voiced by Sylvestra le Touzel

As You Like It, directed by Basil Coleman for BBC Shakespeare (1978, DVD 2008). Worthy if very pedestrian BBC version shot (perhaps unwisely) on location at Glamis Castle, with a distinguished cast including Helen Mirren as Rosalind, Richard Pasco as Jaques, James Bolam as Touchstone and Tony Church as Duke Senior.

As You Like It, directed by Christine Edzard (DVD 1992). Unconventional modern-dress version in the gritty setting of London's Docklands. Many critics felt the disjunction from the play's pastoral language too great, despite interesting individual performances.

As You Like It, directed by Kenneth Branagh (DVD 2008). Set in Japan in the late nineteenth century, it opens with Duke Frederick's violent usurpation of his brother (both roles played by Brian Blessed) with a glance to Kurosawa's *Throne of Blood*. The rest of the film is an all-singing, all-dancing romp. Bryce Dallas Howard as Rosalind was nominated for a Golden Globe award, but the film did not win general critical favour.

REFERENCES

1 T. W. Baldwin, *The Organization and Personnel of the Shakespearean Company* (1927), p. 240.
2 E. K. Chambers, *William Shakespeare: A Study of Facts and Problems* (1930), Vol. 2, p. 278.
3 Cynthia Marshall, ed., *As You Like It: Shakespeare in Production* (2004), p. 7.
4 Marshall, *As You Like It*, p. 8, suggests a contemporary political reference to George I's proclamation regarding hunting rights and the Black Act of 1723.
5 Anthony Vaughan, *Born to Please: Hannah Pritchard, Actress, 1711–1768* (1979), p. 19.
6 John Hill, *The Actor: or, A Treatise on the Art of Playing* (1755, reprinted 1972), pp. 61, 274.
7 Marshall, *As You Like It*, p. 12.
8 Hill, *The Actor*, pp. 104–5.
9 Marshall, *As You Like It*, p. 12.
10 For a full account of her life see Claire Tomalin, *Mrs Jordan's Profession: The Actress and the Prince* (1994).
11 Leigh Hunt, *The Autobiography of Leigh Hunt: With Reminiscences of Friends and Contemporaries* (1850) Vol. I, pp. 148–9.
12 Marshall, *As You Like It*, pp. 14–15.
13 Charles H. Shattuck, *Mr Macready Produces As You Like It; A Prompt-Book Study* (1962).
14 Marshall, *As You Like It*, pp. 25–6.
15 William Winter, 'As You Like It', in his *Shakespeare on the Stage*, second series (1915), pp. 215–341.
16 *Athenaeum*, 8 February 1851, quoted in Marshall, *As You Like It*, p. 29.
17 *Observer*, 2 March 1845, quoted in Marshall, *As You Like It*, p. 30; Tiresias in Greek mythology was the blind prophet of Thebes transformed into a woman for seven years.
18 Jeanette Gilder, *The Critic*, New York, Vol. CXLI, No. 51, 16 December 1882, p. 348.
19 *Pall Mall Gazette*, 24 January 1885, quoted in Marshall, *As You Like It*, p. 34.
20 Marshall, *As You Like It*, p. 34.
21 *Theatre*, 2 March 1885, quoted in Marshall, *As You Like It*, p. 35.
22 Mary Anderson, *A Few Memories: With Portraits* (London: 1896), p. 199.
23 Jeanette Gilder, *The Critic*, New York, Vol. XII, No. 313, 28 December 1889, p. 329.
24 Gilder, *The Critic*, 28 December 1889, p. 329.
25 George Bernard Shaw, *Shaw on Shakespeare: An Anthology of Bernard Shaw's Writings on the Plays and Production of Shakespeare*, ed. Edwin Wilson (1961, reprinted 1971), pp. 23–35.
26 Marshall, *As You Like It*, p. 49.
27 Marshall, *As You Like It*, p. 51.

28 Oscar Asche, *Oscar Asche* (1929), p. 120.
29 Marshall, *As You Like It*, p. 55.
30 Marshall, *As You Like It*, p. 53.
31 Marshall, *As You Like It*, p. 53.
32 *The Times* (London), 23 April 1919.
33 *Manchester Guardian*, 23 April 1919.
34 Related in Sally Beauman, 'The New Chairman', in *The Royal Shakespeare Company: A History of Ten Decades* (1982), pp. 47–67.
35 J. C. Trewin, *Shakespeare on the Stage, 1900–1964: A Survey of Productions* (1964), pp. 127–98.
36 Brooks Atkinson, *New York Times*, 27 January 1950.
37 *The Times* (London), 30 April 1952.
38 Muriel St Clare Byrne, *Shakespeare Quarterly*, Vol. VIII, Autumn 1957, pp. 461–92.
39 H. Granville-Barker, *Plays and Players*, Vol. 4, No. 8, May 1957, p. 13.
40 Marshall, *As You Like It*, p. 64.
41 Marshall, *As You Like It*, p. 67.
42 Marshall, *As You Like It*, p. 68.
43 Marshall, *As You Like It*, p. 68.
44 Marshall, *As You Like It*, p. 68.
45 Marshall, *As You Like It*, p. 69.
46 Marshall, *As You Like It*, p. 69.
47 Marshall, *As You Like It*, p. 81.
48 Irving Wardle, *The Times* (London), 4 October 1967.
49 Dana Adams Schmidt, *New York Times*, 6 October 1967.
50 Wardle, *The Times* (London), 4 October 1967.
51 Martin Gottfried, 'British Theater: "As You Like It"', in his *Opening Nights: Theater Criticism of the Sixties*, (1969), pp. 284–7.
52 Wardle, *The Times*, 4 October 1967.
53 Colin Chambers (RSC Literary Manager at the time) quoted in Marshall, *As You Like It*, p. 33.
54 Glenn Loney, 'Shakespeare, the Canadian', *Christian Century*, Vol. XCIV, No. 31, 5 October 1977, pp. 882–4.
55 Roger Warren, *Shakespeare Survey*, Vol. 33, 1980, pp. 169–80.
56 Marshall, *As You Like It*, p. 60.
57 Marshall, *As You Like It*, p. 69.
58 *Independent*, 4 January 1995.
59 *City Limits*, 12 December 1991.
60 Jonathan Bate and Russell Jackson, eds, *Shakespeare: An Illustrated Stage History* (1996), p. 6.
61 Robert Brustein, *New Republic*, Vol. 221, No. 14, 4 October 1999, pp. 35–6.
62 Lois Potter, *Shakespeare Quarterly*, Vol. 50, No. 1, Spring 1999, pp. 76–7.
63 Potter, *Shakespeare Quarterly*.
64 Marshall, *As You Like It*, p. 65.
65 Marshall, *As You Like It*, p. 86.
66 Amelia Marriette, 'Urban Dystopias: Reapproaching Christine Edzard's *As You Like It*', in *Shakespeare, Film, Fin de Siècle*, ed. Mark Thornton Burnett and Ramona Wray (2000), pp. 73–88.
67 Marshall, *As You Like It*, p. 86.
68 Marshall, *As You Like It*, p. 86.
69 Richard David, 'Reality and Artifice', in *Shakespeare in the Theatre* (1978).
70 Bamber Gascoigne, *Spectator*, Vol. 207, No. 6943, 14 July 1961.

71 J. W. Lambert, *Sunday Times*, 9 July 1961.
72 Marshall, *As You Like It*.
73 Penny Gay, *As She Likes It: Shakespeare's Unruly Women*, 1994.
74 Roger Warren, *Shakespeare Quarterly*, vol.37, no. 1, Spring 1986.
75 Benedict Nightingale, *New Statesman*, vol. 99, no. 2560, 11.4.80.
76 Irving Wardle, *The Times* (London), 5 April 1980.
77 John Bowe, 'Orlando', in *Players of Shakespeare*, ed. Philip Brockbank (1985).
78 Nicholas de Jongh, *Guardian*, 19 December 1985.
79 De Jongh, *Guardian*, 19 December 1985.
80 Marshall, *As You Like It*.
81 Gregory Doran on his idea for the setting of *As You Like It*, 2000, interviewed by Nigel Cliff, *The Times* (London), 22 March 2000.
82 Donald Baker, *Cahiers Elisabethains*, No. 18, October 1980.
83 John Elsom, *Listener*, Vol. 98, No. 2526, 15 September 1977.
84 B. A. Young, *Financial Times*, 9 November 1977.
85 *Sunday Times*, 11 November 1977.
86 Robert Speaight, *Shakespeare Quarterly*, Vol. XXIV, No. 4, Autumn 1973.
87 Jeremy Kingston, *Punch*, 20 June 1973.
88 B. A. Young, *Financial Times*, 13 June 1973.
89 Marshall, *As You Like It*, quoting from the *Financial Times*' review, 13 June 1973.
90 Katharine Duncan-Jones, 'The Play in Performance', in *William Shakespeare: As You Like It*, ed. H. J. Oliver (2005).
91 Bernard Levin in a review of 'As You Like It', in *Royal Shakespeare Theatre Company 1960–1963*, ed. John Goodwin (1964).
92 Gascoigne, *Spectator*, 14 July 1961.
93 Penny Gay, *As She Likes It: Shakespeare's Unruly Women* (1994).
94 Noel Witts, *Plays and Players*, Vol. 25, No. 2, November 1977.
95 Nicholas de Jongh, *Evening Standard*, 23 April 1992.
96 Fiona Shaw and Juliet Stevenson, 'Celia and Rosalind in As You Like It', in *Players of Shakespeare 2*, ed. Russell Jackson and Robert Smallwood (1988).
97 Benedict Nightingale, *New Statesman*.
98 Michael Billington, *Guardian*, 19 August 2005.
99 Suzie Mackenzie, *Time Out*, 2 January 1986.
100 Warren, *Shakespeare Quarterly*.
101 Michael Billington, *Guardian*, 13 June 1973.
102 Michael Billington, *Guardian*, 30 April 1996.
103 Paul Taylor, *Independent*, 22 August 2005.
104 Peter Holland, *English Shakespeares* (1997), quoting from the *Times Literary Supplement*, 8 May 1992.
105 Benedict Nightingale, *The Times* (London), 12 April 1990.
106 David, 'Reality and Artifice'.
107 Irving Wardle, *The Times* (London), 5 April 1980.
108 Stanley Wells, *Shakespeare: The Poet and his Plays* (1997).
109 Young, *Financial Times*, 9 November 1977.
110 David Tennant, 'Touchstone', in *Players of Shakespeare 4*, ed. Robert Smallwood (1998).
111 Christopher Edwards, *Spectator*, Vol. 254, No. 8184, 18 May 1985.
112 Susan Irvine, *Sunday Telegraph*, 21 August 2005.
113 Charles Spencer, *Daily Telegraph*, 19 August 2005.
114 Billington, *Guardian*, 19 August 2005.
115 David, 'Reality and Artifice'.

116 David, 'Reality and Artifice'.
117 J. W. Lambert, *Sunday Times*, 17 June 1973.
118 *The Times* (London), 5 July 1961.
119 Wardle, *The Times*, 5 April 1980.
120 Duncan-Jones, 'The Play in Performance'.
121 Peter Holland, *Shakespeare Survey*, Vol. 44, 1991.
122 Robert Smallwood, *Shakespeare Quarterly*, Vol. 41, No. 4, Winter 1990.
123 John Peter, *Sunday Times*, 26 April 1992.
124 John Mullan, *Times Literary Supplement*, 17 May 1996.
125 Billington, *Guardian*, 30 April 1996.
126 Gay, *As She Likes It*.

ACKNOWLEDGEMENTS
AND PICTURE CREDITS

Preparation of 'As You Like It in Performance' was assisted by a generous grant from the CAPITAL Centre (Creativity and Performance in Teaching and Learning) of the University of Warwick for research in the RSC archive at the Shakespeare Birthplace Trust. The Arts and Humanities Research Council (AHRC) funded a term's research leave that enabled Jonathan Bate to work on 'The Director's Cut'.

The interview with Naomi Frederick is adapted from her rehearsal blog, on playing Rosalind at Shakespeare's Globe in the summer of 2009, with her generous permission and that of the Shakespeare Globe Trust.

Picture research by Michelle Morton. Grateful acknowledgement is made to the Shakespeare Birthplace Trust for assistance with reproduction fees and picture research (special thanks to Helen Hargest).

Images of RSC productions are supplied by the Shakespeare Centre Library and Archive, Stratford-upon-Avon. This Library, maintained by the Shakespeare Birthplace Trust, holds the most important collection of Shakespeare material in the UK, including the Royal Shakespeare Company's official archive. It is open to the public free of charge.

For more information see www.shakespeare.org.uk.

1. Ada Rehan as Rosalind (1889) Reproduced by permission of the Royal Shakespeare Company
2. Directed by Glen Byam Shaw (1957) Angus McBean © Royal Shakespeare Company

3. Directed by Terry Hands (1980) Joe Cocks Studio Collection ©
Shakespeare Birthplace Trust
4. Directed by Michael Elliot (1961) Angus McBean © Royal
Shakespeare Company
5. Directed by Steven Pimlott (1996) Malcolm Davies ©
Shakespeare Birthplace Trust
6. Directed by Dominic Cooke (2005) Keith Pattison © Royal
Shakespeare Company
7. Directed by Michael Boyd (2009) Ellie Kurttz © Royal
Shakespeare Company
8. Directed by Thea Sharrock (2009) © Donald Cooper/
photostage.co.uk
9. Reconstructed Elizabethan Playhouse © Charcoalblue

FROM THE ROYAL SHAKESPEARE COMPANY AND MACMILLAN

PB: 9780230243804   PB: 9780230243828   PB: 9780230243866   PB: 9780230243842

MORE HIGHLIGHTS IN THE RSC SHAKESPEARE SERIES

PB: 9780230576223   PB: 9780230232105   PB: 9780230232136   PB: 9780230232150   PB: 9780230232082

PB: 9780230576148   PB: 9780230576209   PB: 9780230576162   PB: 9780230576186   PB: 9780230576247

PB: 9780230217850 PB: 9780230217874 PB: 9780230217898 PB: 9780230217911 PB: 9780230221116 PB: 9780230200951

AVAILABLE IN ALL GOOD BOOKSHOPS OR TO ORDER ONLINE VISIT:
www.rscshakespeare.co.uk

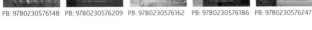